The Financial Implications of China's Belt and Road Initiative

Piotr Łasak · René W. H. van der Linden

The Financial Implications of China's Belt and Road Initiative

A Route to More Sustainable Economic Growth

palgrave
macmillan

Piotr Łasak
Faculty of Management and Social Communication
Jagiellonian University
Kraków, Poland

René W. H. van der Linden
Faculty of Business, Finance & Marketing
The Hague University of Applied Sciences
The Hague, The Netherlands

ISBN 978-3-030-30117-0 ISBN 978-3-030-30118-7 (eBook)
https://doi.org/10.1007/978-3-030-30118-7

This Palgrave Pivot imprint is published by the registered company Springer Nature Switzerland AG
The registered company address is: Gewerbestrasse 11, 6330 Cham, Switzerland

Preface

This pivot is the outcome of two papers presented at the annual 'European Association of University Teachers in Banking & Finance Conference,' also known as Wolpertinger Conference, held in Santander, Spain, in August 30–September 2, 2017. The co-authors met each other for the first time in Santander, and one year later at the Wolpertinger Conference 2018 held in Modena, Italy, they mutually agreed to write a chapter on this topic in a Palgrave Macmillan Studies in Banking and Financial Institutions. Because of their excellent mutual cooperation and shared interest in this subject, they have decided to subsequently make a more extensive version of this chapter, which eventually has resulted in the publication of this pivot.

Kraków, Poland
The Hague, The Netherlands
July 2019

Piotr Łasak
René W. H. van der Linden

Acknowledgements

Both co-authors are aware that in the eventual creation of this booklet, the collaboration of many other people was necessary, to whom we are sincerely grateful. With the risk of forgetting some of these people, we would like to mention the following people in particular. First of all, this project was made possible through constructive consultations with Tula Weis, senior editor Finance and Scholarly & Professional Palgrave Macmillan. From the early start during our stay in Modena, she saw a possibility to have this current topic published, but also in the following period she has always encouraged us from her office in New York to let this project go ahead. At a later stage in the implementation of this project, we are also grateful to Ashwini Elango, project coordinator Palgrave Macmillan as part of Springer Nature, for her cooperative collaboration from her office in India to meet the deadlines taking into account possible unexpected circumstances that may delay this project. In addition, we also thank the organizers of the many Wolpertinger conferences that René has attended since 1995 and Piotr since 2017. Several publications about China's financial-economic reforms that René has been able to present at Wolpertinger and publish in Palgrave have become an important input for this booklet. This applies in particular to the publication of Chapter 12 in the book *Frontier Topics in Banking*, published in May 2019, for which we also thank the co-editors Elisabetta Gualandri, Valeria Venturelli, and Alex Sclip. Finally, we are also grateful to our employers for recognizing the significance of our research on this theme with the spin-off to education and the financial support and time allocated to visit the Wolpertinger conferences.

Contents

About the Authors

Piotr Łasak, Ph.D. graduated from the University of Economics in Krakow (M.A. in Economics, 2003) and the Jagiellonian University (Ph.D. in Finances, 2008). He is currently a professor in the Institute of Economics, Finance and Management at the Jagiellonian University. His research interests focus on topics related to international financial markets development. Among the most important topics are financial markets regulation and supervision, mechanisms of financial and currency crises, and shadow banking systems development (especially in China). He is an author of several dozen articles related to these abovementioned topics.

René W. H. van der Linden, M.Sc. graduated from the economic faculty at the University of Amsterdam (in 1987) and is currently a senior lecturer economics and finance in the International Business program at The Hague University of Applied Sciences in the Netherlands. His research interests with a practical application on education focus on topics in the field of international financial markets, transition economies and emerging markets, banking and finance, international trade economics, and doing business in Asia and the EU. He has published several papers on the Chinese economy and financial system and is co-author of the textbook *European Business Environment.*

List of Figures

List of Tables

CHAPTER 1

Introduction

Abstract In the introduction section, the Global Financial Crisis (GFC) of 2008–2009 is described as an important reason for the inevitable economic downturn in China. This possible scenario created a momentum for a grand infrastructure program called 'One Belt, One Road' (OBOR), intended to look like a new global economic order. This 'Belt and Road Initiative' (BRI) aims to 'break the bottleneck of Asian connectivity' and could be seen as a way of 'helping oneselves by helping others.' Though with the stimulus package implemented in 2010 the Chinese economy seemed to be back on track again with double-digit annual GDP growth rates, the flip side of this injection was a legacy of debt with many 'ghost' cities, bubbles in the housing and stock markets, a rise in 'bad' assets and the creation of massive excess capacity in many industrial sectors from steel to cement. Combined with the slowing economy and the sluggish international demands, it is anticipated that the overcapacity will squeeze corporate profits, increase debt levels, and make the country's financial system more vulnerable. The biggest weakness of the system is that it lacks the ability to allocate credit according to market-conform risk assessment principles and leads to excessive debt growth. Finally as a way to reach a more sustainable growth path, this habit of debt-financed growth due to the so-called financial dependency triangle has been addressed with the implementation of a policy of 'deleveraging'. One of the most crucial objectives as part of this 'new normal' economy is to induce an economic shift

P. Łasak and R. W. H. van der Linden, *The Financial Implications of China's Belt and Road Initiative*,
https://doi.org/10.1007/978-3-030-30118-7_1

that will steer the country away from a reliance on exports and investments toward growth driven by domestic consumption and innovation. The restructuring of the Chinese economy entails two essential adjustments to the financial system: first, the need to improve the efficiency of banks and financial markets and expand their services to dynamic sectors of the economy and beyond the state sector; and second, the need to avoid instability in the increasingly complex financial sector stemming from either the NPL/credit overhang problem in the banking sector, and/or a crash in the asset market, and a negative spillover from an over-expanding shadow banking sector. In this environment, it becomes increasingly important to strengthen systemic risk oversight and to further improve regulation and supervision. From this perspective, a vital part of implementing the BRI would be to enhance financial integration between countries. Although there is no agreed-upon definition for what qualifies as an OBOR project, but so far it is clear that the funding mainly comes from China's huge, but shrinking, financial resources. Since the RMB, despite its internationalization, is still not a fully functioning global currency, the BRI largely requires dollar-denominated financial resources to fulfill its objectives. This 'dollar-constraint' obviously reduces the leeway for OBOR projects to be financed by China, at least in hard currency. Against this background, different financing options and implications are considered for the BRI plan within a policy trilemma context.

Keywords 'One Belt, One Road' · Asian connectivity · Stimulus package · Double-digit annual GDP growth rates · 'Ghost cities' · 'Bad' assets · Debt-financed growth · 'Financial dependency triangle' · 'Deleveraging' · 'New normal' economy · NPL/credit overhang problem · Shadow banking sector · Systemic risk oversight · 'Dollar-constraint' · Policy trilemma context

The Global Financial Crisis (GFC) of 2007–2008 disrupted international capital flows, but China was able to limit the adverse effects of this credit crunch. The country boosted domestic demand through a massive stimulus package at the end of 2008 aimed largely in funding the infrastructure, and loosening monetary policies to increase bank lending. The Chinese government cleverly used its state-owned enterprises (SOEs)

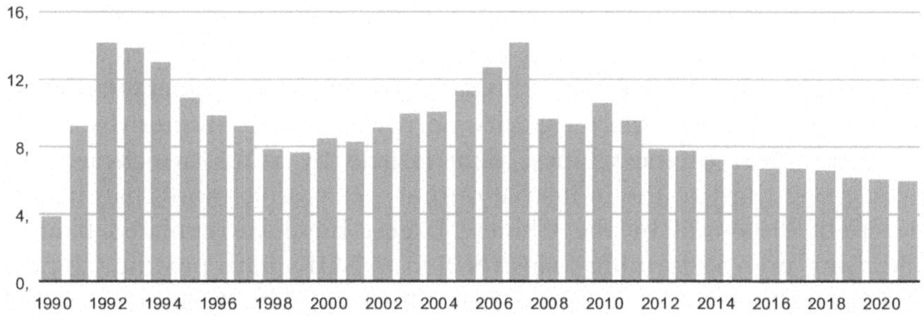

Fig. 1.1 China's slowing economy—real GDP growth at market prices in percentages (forecast for the period 2019–2021) (*Source* Adapted from IMF and World Bank)

which formed the backbone of China's economy during the central planning era and is used as an instrument to implement its aggressive stimulus package. In early 2010, China's economy seemed to be back on track again with double-digit annual GDP growth rates. However, it temporarily boosted GDP and export growth, but it left a legacy of debt with many ghost cities and 'bad' assets that could not support the first growth injection from early 2010 until present. Despite the fact that China's GDP growth usually exceeds target, the rate of GDP has slowed since then, declining from 10.6% in 2010 to around 6.6% in 2018 (Morrison 2018) and a forecasted 6.1% at the end of 2019. A major fall of GDP growth also occurred during the 1990s, but the turnaround came with the turn of the millennium and led to unprecedented growth with double-digit GDP figures until the start of the GFC (see Fig. 1.1). A big difference with the current decade compared to the previous decades of enormous economic growth is that the authorities now focus much more on lower growth of higher quality. Moreover, in this decade the lower growth, it accounts for one-third of global growth, has much more influence on the economies of rest of the world. China's inevitable economic slowdown in this decade also means that it will be harder to tackle its debt problem effectively, even with the undisputed ability of the Communist Party of China (CPC) to support the economy (BBC Business 2019).

Though the stimulus program implemented in China in general was effective, one of its lasting side effects was the creation of massive excess capacity in many industrial sectors from steel to cement. Combined with the slowing economy and the sluggish international demands, it is anticipated that the overcapacity will squeeze corporate profits, increase debt levels, and make the country's financial system more vulnerable. Many SOEs in sectors with spare capacity borrowed heavily during the financial crisis. Most of the Chinese debt is held by SOEs, which account for just one-third of the industrial output, yet receive more than half of the credit dispensed by the Chinese largest Big Five regulated banks.[1] The rising non-performing loans (NPLs) to SOEs have put the Chinese banking system under a great deal of stress. The biggest weakness of the system is that it lacks the ability to allocate credit according to market-conform risk assessment principles. The regulated banks feel safe lending to SOEs, no matter how indebted they are, because the government implicitly guarantees their debt. As a result, the SOEs have developed a habit of debt-financed growth.[2] This credit overhang may not have been a problem when China's economy was growing, but it represents a serious economic risk in times of economic slowdown. In order to restrain borrowing by local governments and SOEs, the government declared curbing SOE leverage as 'the priority of priorities' and warned local officials to be held accountable for building up regional debt. The implementation of the policy of 'deleveraging' can be considered as one of its major tasks for the coming years (Cai 2017).

China's economic slowdown, stock crashes, and currency realignments are highlighting the downturn of the world's second largest economy and the main driver of global growth. The attention of global markets was focused on China's exchange rate in August 2015 when the People's Bank of China (PBC) announced a nearly 2.0% devaluation of the Renminbi[3] (RMB) against the US dollar (USD). Since then, China

[1] Traditionally China has a bank-based financial system whereby most businesses are funded by traditional bank loans mainly coming from the 'Big Five' regulated banks, namely the Agricultural Bank of China (ABC), Bank of China (BoC), China Construction Bank (CCB), Industrial and Commercial Bank of China (ICBC), and the Bank of Communications (BOCOM). Started from 2007, China Banking and Regulatory Commission (CBRC) added BOCOM to this segment as a state-owned commercial bank, while this bank was segmented as joint-state commercial bank prior to 2007.

[2] A phenomenon from the former planned economy referred to as 'financial dependency triangle' between the state council, state-owned banks, and SOEs, whereby the state banks were instructed mainly to lend to SOEs (van der Linden 2008).

[3] The Renminbi (RMB) or sometimes called 'redback' is the name of the currency meaning 'the people's currency', whereas the Chinese Yuan (CNY) is the basic unit of account issued and administered by the central bank or People's Bank of China (PBC).

has devalued the RMB multiple times while making a transition from its 12th to its 13th Five Year plan (FYP) in which the Chinese authorities have laid out a clear and concise list of objectives as to how they want to develop their 'new normal' economy and to avoid a 'middle-income trap' in the near future. The main characteristics of this 'new normal' growth model consist of a slower growth level with a higher quality and more emphasis on efficiency and social security with a strong role of the government; the ability to adjust in accordance with the current market circumstances; opening-up of the financial markets and services sector as the current economy's primary driver of growth to offset contractions in China's traditional powerhouses of heavy industry and manufacturing. The aim is to keep a strict balance in restructuring China's economy, i.e., making sure growth in one sector offsets slowdowns in another in order to guarantee enough employment. One of the most crucial objectives as part of this plan is to induce an economic shift that will steer the country away from a reliance on exports and investments toward growth driven by domestic consumption and innovation. This is part of China's narrative to decrease its reliance on its global partners, a lesson learned from the GFC when China became dangerously dependent on debt-fueled investments in infrastructure, housing, and heavy industries with a significant overcapacity as a result. The restructuring of the Chinese economy entails two essential adjustments to the financial system; first, the need to improve the efficiency of banks and financial markets and expand their services to dynamic sectors of the economy and beyond the state sector; and second, the need to avoid instability in the increasingly complex financial sector stemming from either the NPL/credit overhang problem in the banking sector, and/or a crash in the asset market, and a negative spillover from an over-expanding shadow banking sector. In this environment, it becomes increasingly important to strengthen systemic risk oversight and to further improve regulation and supervision.

President Xi Jinping largely motivated by China's pressing economic concerns and China's attempt to gain political leverage over its neighbors, launched in 2013 the 'One Belt, One Road' (OBOR) or 'Belt and Road' Initiative (BRI)[4] as an infrastructure project which connects

[4]Xi initially introduced the term '*One* Belt, *One* Road' initiative in 2013, but after some criticism about the naming and it became apparent that this transport network encompasses several land and sea routes, the term BRI or B&R in official government translations was increasingly used. In this booklet, the terms OBOR and BRI are used interchangeably. The BRI includes

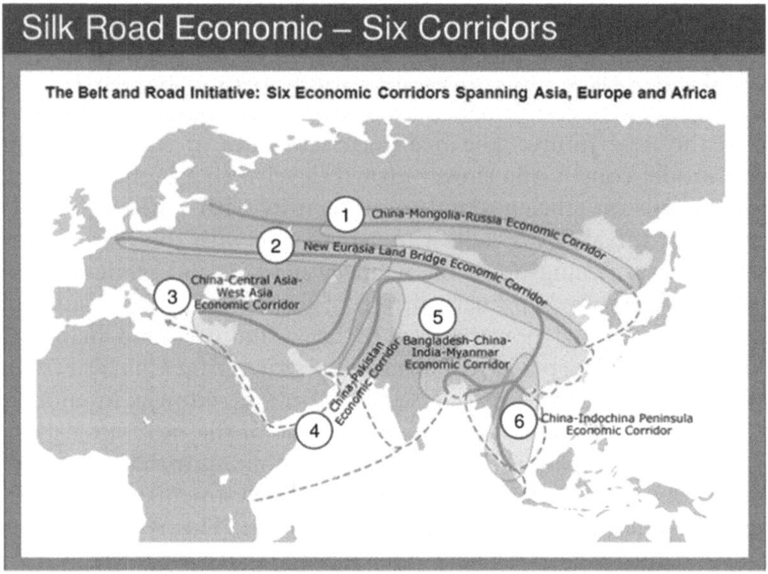

Fig. 1.2 The six economic corridors of the Belt and Road Initiative (*Source* http://china-trade-research.hktdc.com)

Asia with Europe and Africa along six corridors (see Fig. 1.2). With a network of pipelines, ports, railways, highways, and road infrastructure, the BRI aims to 'break the bottleneck of Asian connectivity.' In addition to physical infrastructure, China plans to build fifty special economic zones (SEZs), modeled after the Shenzhen SEZ, which China launched in 1980 during its economic reforms under leader Deng Xiaoping (Chatzky and McBride 2019). The entire OBOR project includes a land-based 'Belt' from China to Europe, evoking 'Old' Silk Road trade paths and a 'Road' referring to ancient maritime routes and the scale is ambitiously large.

The geopolitical context of the BRI is different from the US-led Marshall plan in post-Second World War era and the BRI is much more ambitious in terms of the number of countries involved and in terms of the scale of financing that could be available (Citi GPS 2018).

more than 125 countries and 29 international organizations having signed 173 cooperation agreements under the initiative framework as of March 27, 2019 (*China Daily* 2019).

However, to a certain extent the aims of the BRI are quite similar to the strategic aims of the Marshall plan, namely boosting export, currency internationalization, countering a rival, fostering strategic divisions, and obtaining diplomatic support. Globally, the BRI positions China as the leader of a new form of 'globalization with Chinese characteristics' as a response on US President Trump's new protectionism. It is likely that economic steps of the OBOR implementation come first as has usually been the case with the rise of China as a major economic power. As long as political stability is guaranteed, then possible political and institutional adjustments can be expected if necessary. So it is expected that at least in the short-run the BRI does not emphasize ideological factors as heavily as was the case in the Marshall plan which was fully funded by the US government (Shen and Chan 2018).

A vital part of implementing the BRI would be to enhance financial integration between countries. There are plans to build a currency stability system, investment and financing system, and credit information system in Asia. There will also be other financial initiatives in the pipeline for the deepening of multilateral financial cooperation. Despite resistance from Western countries due to their overlapping purposes with their international financial institutions, among others, three important financial institutions have been established to fund the OBOR infrastructure projects, namely the Silk Road Infrastructure Fund, the Asian Infrastructure Investment Bank (AIIB), and the New Development Bank (NDB), the former Development Bank of BRICS (BDO 2015). Also, recapitalizations in USDs of the China Development Bank and China Export–Import Bank play an important role in OBOR projects. Although there is no agreed-upon definition for what qualifies as an OBOR project, but so far it is clear that the funding mainly comes from China's huge, but shrinking, financial resources. Such a logical deduction was probably well taken in times when China was flooded with capital inflows and foreign exchange reserves had nearly reached USD 4 trillion in June 2014. However, China's economy has slowed down, its shadow banking system has become more significant, and the regular banks' balance sheets are saddled with doubtful loans, which keep on being refinanced and do not leave much room for the massive lending needed to finance the BRI. This is particularly important as Chinese banks have been the largest lenders so far and although Multilateral Development Organizations (MDOs) geared toward this objective certainly do not have the necessary financial means. Even the AIIB has so far only approved investments of USD 1.7 billion in 2016, USD 2.5 billion in 2017, and USD 3.3 billion in 2018 on OBOR projects and China's reserves lost nearly USD 1 trillion due to massive capital outflows. Since the RMB is not a fully functioning global currency, the BRI largely requires dollar-denominated financial resources to fulfill its objectives. Although USD 3.09 trillion of reserves (as of September 2019) still look ample with a rising trend in 2019 despite persistent trade tensions with the USA, the Chinese authorities seem to have set that level as a floor under which reserves should not fall so that financial stability is restored. This 'dollar-constraint' obviously reduces the leeway for OBOR projects to be financed by China, at least in hard currency (García-Herrero 2017). Against this background, Sect. 4.2 will review different financing options for Xi's grand plan and the financial implications within a policy trilemma context.

After the GFC China seemed to have circumvented the impossible trinity or policy trilemma. This theory states that it is impossible for a country to have control of all three of the following main aims at the same time: free capital mobility, a stable exchange rate management, and monetary autonomy. A country that attempts to get all three policy aims at once will be broken by the international markets as they force a run on the currency. Although China has never completely abolished all capital controls, there have always been several ways to channel money into the country. At the same time, the RMB has started to float more against the USD. China was also able to increase or lower interest rates without too much impact on the exchange rate. Thus, the policy makers made the argument that China negotiated between the three choices and in essence circumvented the logic of the impossible trinity. With the rise of shadow banking and the desire for more RMB internationalization since the late 2000s, the increasing financial liberalization is at odds with the striving for more financial stability. The question then arises to what extent the authorities can circumvent or bend not only a policy trilemma but also fine-tune a quadrilemma as described in Sect. 2.4 (Aizenman 2011). Also, the impact of the OBOR project in the policy trilemma or quadrilemma will be examined.

Despite the fact that the BRI was supposed to be a plan to tackle the problems of funding, debt, and overcapacity, it might not work after all. With an experience of six years in the execution of all kinds of projects in different Euro-Asian and African countries, several drawbacks of the

OBOR plan have now become more visible and will be dealt with in this 'pivot' booklet. The following research questions will be addressed:

- What is the effectiveness of the BRI to help China bounce back from its economic slowdown?
- To what extent the BRI is a 'win-win' cooperation between China and the recipient countries?
- What are the financial implications of the BRI within a policy trilemma context?
- What are alternative ways to continue financing the BRI on the route to a more sustainable economic growth path?
- What will be the impact of the BRI on China's financial markets and its regulatory framework?

The aim of this conceptual and descriptive booklet is to provide a systematic discussion of the contribution of the BRI in tackling China's economic slowdown and its financial implications. From a historical perspective of four decennia of reforms and socioeconomic development, this booklet explains China's route to a more sustainable economic growth path with the BRI as a catalyst. The novelty of this booklet is the investigation of both the rationale of the OBOR project and its pitfalls with a focus on different options on how to finance this project within a policy trilemma context. On the one hand, the Mundell–Fleming model of the impossible trinity theory is applied to the current financial-economic situation in China. Moreover, this paper describes the impact of the BRI on this theory including possible policy options to cope with China's policy trilemma or even quadrilemma in a 'new normal' economic settlement. An important contribution of the booklet lays in an analysis of financial stability issues concerning liberalization policies in China. A lot of the secondary sources are anecdotal and come from press releases, magazines, journals, and occasional studies and reports by banks, MDOs, research and consultancy agencies. Also, updated versions of previous publications of the co-authors are a source of input for this booklet.

This 'pivot' booklet is structured as follows. China's four decades of economic development and gradual reforms from plan to market including the inevitable economic slowdown in this decade and all its problem areas will be explained in Chapter 2. China's new style of globalization as a route to a more sustainable growth path including its trade, investment, monetary, and exchange rate policy position in the world and China's specific situation within the impossible trinity theory are all addressed in Chapter 3. The rationale for the BRI including its aims, financial means and options, its tool in a new development stage, its drawbacks, and benefits are further elaborated on in Chapter 4. China's financial deepening and its 'Belt and Road' funding dilemma will be dealt with in Chapter 5. With the background knowledge and understanding of the first four chapters, the implications of China's BRI including possible policy options and an adjusted regulatory framework will be discussed in particular in the last chapter. Finally, the paper highlights some concluding remarks and recommendations in Chapter 6.

References

Aizenman, J. (2011, March 1). *The Impossible Trinity: From the Policy Trilemma to the Policy Quadrilemma*. Santa Cruz: University of California.

BBC Business. (2019, January 21). *China Economy: Annual Growth Slowest Since 1990.*

BDO. (2015, November). *One Belt One Road*. Singapore: BDO Advisory Pte Ltd. Retrieved from www.bdo.com.sg.

Cai, P. (2017, March). *Understanding China's Belt and Road Initiative*. Sydney: Lowy Institute for International Policy.

Chatzky, A., & McBride, J. (2019, May 21). *China's Massive Belt and Road Initiative*. Council on Foreign Relations (cfr.org).

China Daily. (2019, April 22). *Belt and Road Projects: Past, Present and Future.*

Citi GPS. (2018, December). *China's Belt & Road at Five*. A Progress Report, Global Perspectives & Solutions.

García-Herrero, A. (2017, August). *China Cannot Finance the Belt and Road Alone*. HKUST IEMS No. 17.

Morrison, W. M. (2018, February 5). *China's Economic Rise: History, Trends, Challenges, and Implications for the United States*. Congressional Research Service 7-5700. www.crs.gov. RL33534.

Shen, S., & Chan, W. (2018, March 27). A Comparative Study of the Belt and Road Initiative and the Marshall Plan. *Palgrave Communications, 4*(1), 32.

van der Linden, R. W. H. (2008). Frontiers of Banks in a Global Economy, Chapter 8. In P. Molyneux & E. Vallelado (Eds.), *Palgrave Macmillan Studies in Banking and Financial Institutions*. London: Palgrave Macmillan.

CHAPTER 2

China's Four Decades of Reforms and Development

Abstract This chapter gives an overview of the major socio-economic transformations that occurred in China for more than four decades. They include transitions from a centrally planned to market economy, from a closed to an open economy, and from a manufacturing and export-driven to a more consumption- and innovation-led growth path. It also describes the main features of the socialist market economy with 'Chinese characteristics' including the gradual 'step-by-step' approach in the economic reforms in the different production sectors of the economy. In particular, the financial reforms that were given a major boost in the early 1990s and still require the necessary deepening of the current transition to a more sustainable economy are discussed. This chapter also elaborates on the adverse consequences of the rapid growth model and China's incomplete transition to a market economy. The traditional development model caused a huge depletion of natural resources, serious environmental pollution, which hindered the sustained economic development. Special emphasis is given to some current problem areas in the housing and stock market; the huge local government and increasing corporate debt; and the capital flight and excess capacity described in their relation with the current inevitable economic slowdown which could be seen as a breeding ground for new initiatives where the BRI can be seen as an important example and is central to this pivot.

P. Łasak and R. W. H. van der Linden, *The Financial Implications of China's Belt and Road Initiative*,
https://doi.org/10.1007/978-3-030-30118-7_2

Keywords Centrally planned economy · Socialist market economy with 'Chinese characteristics' · Incomplete transition · Excess capacity · Economic slowdown

2.1 The Main Socio-economic Transformations from a Planned to Socialist Market Economy

In the past, after the Second World War, China was a closed centrally planned communist state. In this command economy with a socialist or communist economic system, where land and capital are collectively owned, all monetary means belong to the state who plans the allocation of resources; money, capital, and foreign exchange markets do not exist and interest and exchange rates are not determined by the market; central and commercial banking is combined ('mono-banking system'); and the domestic currency (RMB or yuan[1]) is not convertible into foreign currencies. During the Mao-era (1949–1976), the central planning combined with the removal of all property rights resulted in low productivity, a poor infrastructure, and famine. Since a command economy is also characterized by a barter trade system, whereby money is not used as a medium of exchange, China barely owned any currency reserves at the end of the 1970s.

The financial system in a market economy is fundamentally different from that in a command economy, in terms of both structure and the main goals of the system. In a command economy, the financial sector's main role is to support the implementation of the central planning's targets. It also takes deposits from individuals and makes loans, but the loans are not used for investments, but are used more to guarantee enough working capital. Investment decisions in China were made by central, provincial, and local planners and much of the financing came

[1] The Renminbi (RMB) or sometimes called 'redback' is the name of the currency meaning 'the people's currency,' whereas the Chinese Yuan (CNY) is the basic unit of account issued and administered by the PBC. While the banking sector uses the RMB for its settlements and the authorities for its internationalization objective, the values are denominated in CNYs. For many years, the RMB was pegged to the USD, but the RMB has now switched to a managed floating exchange rate with reference to a basket of foreign currencies. Depending on the macroeconomic circumstances, the authorities sometimes allow the value of the currency to float a little more and at other times to remain somewhat more stable.

directly from the government budget. In a market economy, the financial system mobilizes the savings after which this funding is used to lend to profitable investments. It is essential that the financial system is properly aligned with the real economy in order to minimize recessions and other macroeconomic imbalances. However, within different market economies there is an ongoing debate about how the financial system should be designed and managed. A common distinction is made between more bank-based financial systems such as in Germany and Poland and more market-oriented financial systems as in the USA or UK. The failure of the financial system in conjunction with the economic situation contributed to both the origins of the Asian financial crisis of 1997–1998 and the GFC which caused the severe world recession of 2007–2009. In the early 1980s, China created a market-oriented financial system by abolishing the 'mono-bank system' and replacing it with four state-owned commercial banks (SOBs) and a central bank, the PBC. This financial system, of which elements still exist today, is characterized by a so-called financial dependency triangle between the state council, SOBs, and SOEs. Similar as in the old 'mono-banking system,' when SOEs needed money, the state council instructed the SOBs to grant them loans whether or not they were creditworthy. Savers could either hoard cash at home or put their money in one of these commercial banks and receive a modest rate of interest. Interest rates were fixed by government approval for both savers and borrowers and done in a way to ensure the banks made a profit (Perkins 2018). Although many attempts have been made in recent decades to break through this 'financial dependency triangle,' ultimately this has never been executed entirely successful. This causes one of the biggest weaknesses of the Chinese banking system, namely that it lacks the ability to ration and allocate credit according to market principles, such as risk assessment and as a result created a 'bad debt' or NPL problem.

After the death of Mao and his Prime Minister Zhou Enlai in 1976, a new breed of Chinese authorities came to power with an increasingly pragmatic approach to combine the aspects of capitalism alongside government control of the economy. This socialist market economy with 'Chinese characteristics'[2] consists of a gradual transition from plan to

[2]This is the official term used to refer to the economic system of the People's Republic of China (PRC) after the reforms of Deng Xiaoping. According to Deng, socialism and capitalism need to be mutually exclusive. His pragmatic approach states that 'it doesn't

market without a 'shock therapy' as was the case with the radical more political rather than economic market-oriented reforms that took place at the 'big bang' transition from the Soviet Union to Russia in 1991. Basically, Deng introduced the market economy outside the power of the central planning.[3] Existing allocation mechanisms were retained; new ones were adopted at the margin on an incremental and experimental basis. Deng's gradual and pragmatic process of economic reforms can be referred to his advises of 'crossing the river by touching the stones' and 'hide your capabilities and bide your time' and motivated him to push forward the gradual implementation. It sought to identify which policies produced favorable economic outcomes (and which did not) so that they could be implemented in other parts of the country. Another feature of this socialist market economy was the dual-track system in which the command and market economy coexisted; transition was to be achieved through a gradual strengthening of the market and a step-by-step weakening of the plan. This approach created more opportunities for the development of the private sector, creativity, and entrepreneurship. Nonetheless, under the incremental reform strategy, whereby the private sector and the state sector coexisted in parallel, the dual-track pricing strategy for many products and services allowed those in power to reap huge personal gains and ultimately led to large-scale official profiteering and corruption which is currently perceived as one of the biggest plagues of the CPC. Deng's push to implement economic reforms was largely motivated by a belief that the resulting economic growth would ensure that the CPC stayed in power (Morrison 2018).

Since the end of 1978, China initiated the change from central planning to the introduction of market mechanism simultaneously with opening-up to international trade and investment. Both the domestic economic development and the participation in globalization have gone forward hand in hand. Deng initiated a new 'open door' policy to open the door to foreign businesses that wanted to set up in China

matter if a cat is black or white; as long as it catches mice, it's a good cat.' In essence, the 'black and white cat' stands for 'planned and market economy' and 'the one who is able to do a job properly will be hired for the job' (Fan 2016).

[3]Already in 1975, Deng and Prime Minister Zhou Enlai introduced the so-called Four Modernizations of agriculture, industry, defense, science and technology. From 1979 onwards, these modernizations were further introduced by Deng without satisfying the call for a fifth modernization of more political reforms or democratization.

which altered China's development strategy of self-sufficiency to one of active participation in the world market. In 1979, the central government decided to establish SEZs in Shenzhen, Zhuhai, and Shantou in Guangdong province and Xiamen in Fujian province. This signaled the start of China's opening to the outside world. Since 1978, there were both some economic and political motives for this 'open door' policy. The economic motives were focused on the promotion of market forces, foreign trade and foreign investments in order to attract foreign exchange reserves and high-tech technologies. The political motives consisted of the fact that the 'open door' policy has also been used by the People's Republic of China (PRC) as one justification for its demands that nations do not provide diplomatic recognition to the Republic of China (Taiwan). SEZs were set up in Deng's belief that in order to modernize China's industry and boost its economy, it needed to welcome foreign direct investment (FDI). Chinese economic policy then shifted to encouraging and supporting foreign trade and investment, and laws on intellectual property rights (IPRs) to stimulate innovation. It is the turning point in China's economic fortune that truly started China on the path to becoming 'The World's Factory.' The main objectives of the SEZs consisted of the transfer of hi-tech industries into these regions; becoming the showroom for high-tech, modern management and an efficient labor force; the creation of employment and export-oriented production in order to attract foreign exchange reserves for import of more advanced technologies; and the promotion of economic and regional development. The arrival of SEZs had both its pros and cons. Some of the advantages of SEZs are the limited or absence of interference of the local authorities; huge funds to invest in infrastructural projects; and special business preferences for foreign investors. On the other hand, as one of the first experiments of China's economic reforms, it soon became apparent that the SEZs turned out to be ideological controversial. Within the CPC, the conservatives and radicals strongly differ in their approach regarding the implementation of the reforms.[4] These two visions about political-economic reforms have always played a role in the transition from plan to market. Therefore, the authorities sometimes tightened the reins more, such as at the end of the 1980s, and in other times allowing the reins to loosen more toward more decentralization since the late

[4]A proverb of the conservatives is 'crossing the river step by step, while groping for the stones,' while the radicals state 'you cannot jump a chasm in two steps.'

1990s (Leonard 2008). However, with the arrival of Xi Jinping in 2013, these different views on the method and extent of economic reforms have been brought more to the background. Initially, another problem of the SEZs was that they hardly benefited from any high-tech capital inflow from Western advanced economies, while the vast majority of the capital inflow came from the region (Hong Kong, Taiwan, and South Korea) and consisted of low-tech consumer goods. However, much later in 1990s and early 2000s when China expanded its 'open door' policy into 'open coastal cities' in 1984 and a host of cities along the Yangtze River and interior border cities in the early 1990s, this pattern has changed drastically. Gradually, the domestic steps to open to the international economy were extended to global institutions with China's application to resume the status of a contracting party to the General Agreement on Tariffs and Trade (GATT) in 1986 and its accession to the World Trade Organization (WTO) in 2001 (Wu and Ma 2016).

China's entry to the WTO is accompanied by advantages and disadvantages. It was a milestone in China's integration into economic globalization, marking a new historic stage of reform and opening-up. Since its accession to the WTO, China has been a strong advocate for free trade and is now even the promoter of China's new style of globalization at a time when the current Trump administration has begun a new wave of protectionism. Foreign firms are no longer required to hand over technology in exchange for entry to China's market; China's WTO membership has increased the export growth and led to cheaper import of more luxury products; local banks have been more encouraged to offer more differentiated services to various degrees of foreign investments and last but not least the application of the use of WTO codes on IPRs and investments will be more guaranteed. It is obvious that China's WTO entry also has its drawbacks. For example, the reduction of tariffs on agricultural products has threatened the livelihoods of hundreds of millions of farmers. Also, there is a risk of more bankruptcies of SMEs and hence more unemployment and social unrest due to more international competition. Although WTO access will in principle lead to less trade control, in practice it has led to many antidumping cases, partly because many foreign firms feel they must compete not with Chinese firms, but with the Chinese state. However, after almost twenty years of membership China has comprehensively fulfilled its commitments to the WTO, substantially opened its market to the world, and delivered mutually beneficial and 'win-win' outcomes on a wider scale.

There is an ongoing debate around the world about how faithfully China has implemented WTO rules and practices, and there are certainly some Chinese practices that involve subsidies to exports or restrictions on imports that are inconsistent with WTO rules. Nevertheless, it can be stated that China has fulfilled the following WTO accession commitments: provision of non-discriminatory treatment to all WTO members; elimination of 'dual pricing' practices[5] as well as differences in treatment accorded to goods produced for sale in China in comparison with those produced for export; substantial reduction of tariff- and non-tariff barriers; price controls will not be used for purposes of affording protection to domestic industries or services providers; revision of existing domestic laws and enacting new legislation fully in compliance with the WTO agreement; and extensively reducing restrictions for foreign investments to enter the services market and fulfilling commitments on IPR protection. In principle, China will not maintain or introduce any export subsidies on agricultural products. However, the latter point has often led to trade disputes with other WTO member states since Chinese prices are considered to be too distorted due to significant government subsidies and intervention, for instance with key export products like solar panels, wines, and mobile telecommunication networks. According to WTO law, the EU may impose an anti-subsidy duty to remove the benefit of a foreign subsidy, or an anti-dumping duty when the imported product is sold at a lower price in the EU than the price in the exporting country, i.e., where there is international price discrimination (The State Council 2018; Perkins 2018).

Not only the 'open door' policy and WTO accession can be considered as two essential foundations of the current BRI since 2013, this certainly also applies to China's 'Going West' campaign or 'great western development' regional policy and its 'Going Global' or 'Going Out' policy initiated at the turn of the century. The BRI coincides with China's 'Going West' policy encouraged by former president Jiang Zemin to close the development gaps between coastal and inland China. The economic growth in Central Asian region will surely have positive effects for Chinese western provinces, whose development is a priority for the Chinese government in order to compensate their lag behind the eastern coastal area. In particular, the Chinese government aims at stabilizing

[5] Since the mid-1980s, a 'dual track' system of plan and market was set up with the aim to strengthen the SOEs with market forces.

the Xinjiang autonomous province, one of the most problematic areas due to the presence of the Uighur minority areas, having a strong separatist tendency with Islamist influence, which caused in the past social unrest. Xinjiang is a region rich in natural resources (it originates 22% of oil and 40% of the coal mined in China) and therefore represents an area of great importance for the economy of the country. Beijing government's strategy to reduce the risks related to the separatist aspirations of the Uighur minority has been to promote the development of this province, building infrastructures and promoting the establishment of new businesses. A drawback of China's 'great western development' is the fact that there is little emphasis on the Go West campaign on measures to alleviate poverty, while the government is obsessed with gigantic, and correspondingly expensive, infrastructure projects. One acute side effect of heavy state subsidies in these western provinces has been a high concentration of SOEs and low penetration of private-owned enterprises (POEs) (*The Economist* 2000).

The 'Go Out' policy (also referred to as the 'Going Global' Strategy) was an effort initiated in 1999 by the Chinese government to promote Chinese investments abroad. This policy has the following causes. First, China has amassed huge amounts of foreign reserves, thus putting upward pressure on the foreign exchange rate of the RMB; there has been much demand from the international community for China to float its currency. In order to deflate that demand, China seeks to employ its foreign reserves by acquiring assets overseas. Second, further acceleration of the WTO commitments has led to the situation that global competitors are now competing for business in the Chinese market, and so China is seeking to equip the domestic firms and their management with international experience so that they can take the competition to the home markets of the foreign nations and so that they can compete better at China's own domestic market. Finally, the 'Go Out' policy has led to programs launched by the Chinese government with the following goals in mind: to increase Chinese FDI; to pursue product diversification; to improve the level and quality of the projects; to expand financial channels with respect to the national market; and to promote brand recognition of Chinese companies in EU and US markets (Cai 2017).

China's rapid economic growth over the past four decades transformed it from a developing to an emerging economy and thus from a low to a much higher standard of living, which also has led to a greater income inequality. During the same period, China has also changed from a rural to a more urban society. The unprecedented growth rates were (partly) due to the large-scale capital investment financed by large domestic savings and foreign investment and the rapid productivity growth. These two factors appear to have gone together hand in hand. Economic reforms led to higher efficiency in the economy, which boosted output and increased resources for additional investment in the economy. Also, the 'one-child' and current 'two-child' policy, implemented in 1979 and 2016, respectively, is beginning to have a significant impact on the current Chinese economy. First, China is beginning to lose a labor advantage, i.e., access to a nearly endless supply of low-cost labor. As the labor force shrinks, Chinese wages could begin to rise faster than productivity and profits growth, which could make Chinese firms less competitive, and result in a shift of labor-intensive manufacturing overseas. Second, this policy has also resulted in a rapidly aging society in China. With a declining working population and a rising elderly population, the Chinese government will face challenges trying to boost worker productivity (such as enhancing innovation and high-end technology development) and to expand spending on health care and elderly services. China's current '*hukou*' or household (population) registration card system also poses challenges to the government in terms of the control of internal migration, the management of social protection, and the preservation of social stability. The discrimination in favor of city dwellers, partly caused by '*hukou*,' has contributed to the increasing inequalities in recent decades. However, there is hope to delay this development by loosening the '*hukou*' in the future, given the economic growth in Central and West China, the higher wages of migrant workers and the reduced income disparities between migrants and natives in cities. This trend change can continue to take place depending on the '*hukou*' reforms that will enable all citizens to seize existing opportunities. The inability of migrants to gain adequate access to social protection is currently one of China's biggest obstacles in restructuring its economy to increase consumption-driven growth (Pradier 2018).

The current state of the Chinese economy is described by some economists as a 'middle-income trap' whereby growth in this upper-middle-income country tends to stagnate when GDP per capita rises above a certain level, as higher wages push up production costs. This phenomenon became more common in China since 2010, when double-digit growth rates begin to fall to a lower level as soon as the individual prosperity of a growing middle class starts to rise. This means that a developing low-income economy is able to transform to a middle-income economy, but because it is unable to sustain high levels of productivity gains (in part because it could not address structural inefficiencies in the economy), it is unable to transform to a high-income economy (Morrison 2018, pp. 7; 29; 44–45). To a certain extent, China's 'middle-income trap' could be perceived as a result of China's rebalancing strategy to shift from higher-growth manufacturing to slower-growing services industries and in that sense is more a 'gap' than a 'trap.' In order to avoid or reduce the 'middle-income trap,' China's productivity growth needs to increase building up a more advanced technological and innovative production capacity. Also, investments in a highly qualified education system and a stronger focus on export upgrading can contribute to reduce the 'middle-income trap' (Shek 2019).

As part of the 13th FYP, the Chinese authorities are determined to restructure the economy in order to prevent the 'middle-income trap.' In that context, the BRI can be seen as a new initiative to facilitate the transition from middle- to high-income and from an emerging to an advanced economy by using Chinese capital and know how to drive infrastructure development overseas. The BRI offers new more upgraded import and export possibilities, creating new production value chains that can bring the development of the Chinese economy to a higher level.

2.2 The Ongoing Process of Gradual Financial-Economic Reforms

Since 1978, the reforms were introduced step by step in the various production sectors of the economy in a gradual and experimental way. First in agriculture, then in the mid-1980s in the manufacturing industry, and from the early 1990s the financial services were also reformed. The agricultural reforms consisted mainly of the household or contract responsibility system (HRS), a private farming in a market economy whereby each farm household was assigned a piece of land and was held responsible for delivering a given quantity of a specified product so the commune could satisfy its procurement requirement. After fulfilling the delivery quota, the farm household was free to keep the remaining output for its own consumption or for sale in the market. This reform immediately improved incentives for agricultural production by granting farmers autonomy over operations and rights to profits from more efficient use of their land and labor, which gave them motivation to raise productivity. Due to the HRS, technological changes, market reforms, and agricultural investments mainly in areas of water control, roads, and communications, a more diversified agricultural growth and rising off-farm employment has dramatically reduced rural poverty. However, the food production has risen at the expense of the environment which has created tremendous challenges to achieving sustainable rural development with the BRI as a supporter and stimulator. Rising wages have increased the cost of food production and lowered China's agricultural competitiveness in global markets, while concerns about national food security are high. Despite steady growth in rural incomes, the rural–urban income gap remains large (see Sect. 2.3).

From the mid-1980s, reforms were more focused on the manufacturing sector including some autonomy regarding the use of retained profits; production planning; sales of output; experimentation with new products and capital investment; payment according to productivity; increasing the role of markets; encouragement of collectively owned enterprises; and streamlining the administrative system at the local level for SOEs under local control, i.e., the SOE reform. Unlike the former socialist countries in Europe, SOE reform in China, in contrast to the reforms in agriculture, was hardly accompanied by privatization but mainly consisted of corporatization.[6] While the overhaul of the SOE sector from the mid-1990s occurred with a large-scale sell-off of loss-making SOEs, only partial privatization was pursued, as the government kept the majority stakes in large SOEs. Although the reforms were designed to tackle the obvious inefficiencies inherent in SOEs, they needed to be done slowly in order to preserve China's political and social stability and reduce the risks of falling tax revenues. Partly due to the aforementioned 'financial dependency triangle,' the SOE reforms as the core of urban reforms turned out to be more difficult to implement than that for agricultural production and had several aspects. One aspect is related to making SOEs viable market players, and began with the expansion of enterprises' autonomy, building up to corporatization. Granting autonomy to enterprises began with pilot programs in some cities since 1979. It was quickly extended to more regions and then to the whole country in the early 1980s. A second aspect involved redefining the

[6]As part of the SOE reforms, China's 'corporatisation without privatisation' measures are designed and implemented around a central target of establishing a competitive market, leaving the ownership structure basically unchanged.

relationship between SOEs and government. Early reforms in this area featured the state sharing profits with enterprises through a host of measures aimed at introducing market discipline and accountability. The third aspect was the introduction and then the encouragement of POEs. SOEs generally operate less efficiently than POEs because the government provides them 'soft budget constraints', and therefore, SOEs were subject to various 'moral hazard' problems. However, since the property rights were reformed to allow a wider range of POEs, the competition between enterprises with different kinds of (mixed) ownership helped to increase the efficiency of SOEs as well (Cai et al. 2018). Due to SOE reforms, the productivity of SOEs has been steadily increasing in the past two decades, although at a slower rate than that of the POEs. Also, the relative importance of SOEs has been declining, and the effect of the state sector's performance on the growth of the entire economy is less important than before. However, SOEs remain a significant burden for the government and the economy, even though it remains a huge dilemma to completely reform them. The 'soft budget constraints' are a drain on government budgets and economic resources, but reducing the size of SOEs creates an unemployment problem and the risk of social instability. Several factors affect the economic efficiency of SOEs. There is a shortage of competent and well-trained managers and staff to operate a modern enterprise, along with a tendency to make management decisions based on personal relations and for personal gain at the expense of the enterprise. The system does not provide managers with appropriate incentives to work for the benefit of the enterprise; they are on a much lower pay scale than managers in similar collective enterprises. In the absence of a suitable governance system, many workers still subscribe to the concept of the 'iron rice bowl' which referred to the now-abolished system of guaranteed lifetime job security. China's transition from a centrally planned to a market economy has abolished the old government guarantees as much as possible. Millions of workers have been laid off as SOEs have been restructured or shut down. This has sparked angry protests from their workers, who complain they have been left without the welfare benefits they were once promised. This dilemma becomes even greater for the government, as it has increasingly become apparent that the equipment and technology of some SOEs need to be updated. One important condition favorable to the SOE reforms is the high degree of competition from collective and foreign enterprises in both domestic and foreign markets. The main challenge for continued reform of SOEs in the late 1990s is to restructure them to shareholding companies and make them public limited companies (Chow 2018).

Since 2016, a new round of mixed-ownership reforms will put the SOEs in key roles of the BRI via 'win-win' projects in new sources of energy, telecommunications, and information technology, automation, transport equipment power, space technologies, and defense. Most of the recent SOE reform programs had a much wider coverage and emphasized the importance of corporate governance, risk management, performance appraisal, and strategic planning. As part of the BRI, the 'bringing in and going global' strategy will be encouraged more for SOEs to remain competitive in order to guarantee strong and sustainable growth (Nan and Shuiyu 2019). An example of an economic influence via the BRI on the privatization of foreign investments is the agreement between the Greek government and China's state-controlled ocean shipping company (COSCO) in 2016 to acquire 51% of the Piraeus port with the rights to operate the port until 2052 and the possibility to reinvest in the port infrastructure in order to be eligible for a further 16% stake. Although this investment has led to much local protests and EU resistance, from the Greek government's point of view this is seen as a way to alleviate the many years of austerity measures resulting from the euro sovereign debt crisis whereby Greece's budget deficit reached 15.4% of their GDP in 2009 and their 10-year bond rates surpassed 35% from 2010 to 2012. In the past decade, Chinese companies have acquired stakes in 13 ports in Europe, including in Greece, Spain and, most recently, Belgium, which handle in total about 10% of Europe's shipping container capacity. The takeover of the terminal in Zeebrugge, the second-largest port in Belgium, marks the first bridgehead of Chinese state-owned port operators in northwestern Europe. It clearly manifests China's ambitious plans to physically connect Europe via the maritime part of the BRI (Johnson 2018).

The Chinese government has also called on SOEs to play a critical role in achieving the goals of the 'Made in China 2025' policy[7] set up in

[7] In a way, the 'Made in China 2025' plan to use state direction to dominate high-tech industries has alarmed the rest of the world, USA in particular, and ignored the advice of Deng Xiaoping to 'hide your capabilities and bide your time.' Although the 'Made in China 2025' plan has not produced any results yet, with Xi Jinping's slogan' 'socialism with Chinese characteristics' a parallel is often drawn with the Maoist era in China (Shazada 2019).

2015 which aims to shift China's economy into higher value-added manufacturing sectors, such as robotics, aerospace, and energy-saving vehicles (Song 2018). This industrial upgrading strategy or promotion plan reveals China's future goal of belonging to a highly developed country by encouraging China's technology, technical standards, equipment and engineering know how. It has also become China's first two-FYP, including the 13th FYP (2016–2020) and the 14th FYP (2021–2025). It is also intended that 'Made in China 2025' is supported in part by the BRI through a deepening of international cooperation in the industry (Chen 2018).

During the 1990s, the Chinese banking system was facing a huge NPL problem which mainly resulted from the 'financial dependency triangle.' According to the commonly accepted definition, NPL is defined as a loan that is in default or close to being default. The Chinese authorities formally introduced a loan classification to the country's financial market regulation in 1995. Originally, the NPLs were divided into three categories, namely part-due loans, doubtful loans, and bad debts. In 2002, the country changed the classification and implemented the universal international standard with four categories of NPLs, i.e., special attention, sub-standard, doubtful, and loss (Tan 2014, p. 14). The Chinese approach, however, in some situations is still more liberal than the general approach. It means that a bank policy might determine the loans classification and the collaterals and guarantees may reduce the recognized risk of the borrowers. Additionally, banks are able to implement their own policies and procedures on recognition and assessment of collateral. It leads to a situation that although Chinese banks are obligatory to use the international loan classification system, banks have a lot of leeways or alternative options in deciding when a loan turns bad (Chen and Wu 2015). The situation in a particular bank might be worse than the official NPLs classification shows, and it is uncertain whether the banks' financial statements in fact meet the international standards or is different from the standards.

Technically, Chinese banks were almost bankrupt before the banking sector reforms started, but during the gradual reforms a downward trend in the 'bad debts' has been driven by the transfer of impaired assets (i.e., NPLs) to state-owned asset management companies[8] (AMCs) and

[8]An AMC is an investment company that buys outstanding debts and then manages and resells these debts in order to recover (some of) the funds. For each of the major state-owned commercial banks, there is one AMC which are funded by the MoF and a loan by the PBC. AMCs exchange bonds with the respective banks for NPLs.

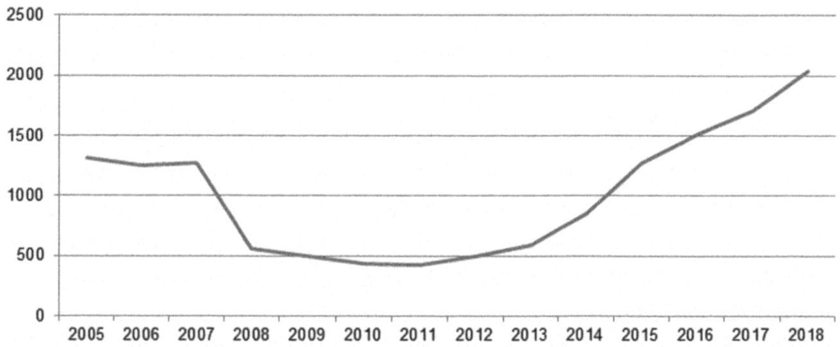

Fig. 2.1 Non-performing loans in China in the period of 2005–2018 (RMB bn) (*Source* Own elaboration based on CEIC database [accessed: 10.03.2019])

the banks were made solvent by simply paying these companies the full value of the loans (van der Linden 2010). In effect, the central bank printed the money and gave it to the banks. Since the launch of four national-level AMCs in 1999, the Chinese government has taken steps to gradually deregulate the sector with the objective to attract more players (including foreign acquirers of NPLs). By the late 1990s, the banking system had begun a process of changing the behavior of those running the banks to make them behave more like commercial banks in a high-income market economy. Gradually, the banks began to make loans to POEs and mortgages to consumers. They began to pursue profits and to establish systems for properly appraising the creditworthiness of their borrowers. New credit instruments such as personal credit cards were introduced, along with a wide variety of modern banking practices from abroad. Many new smaller banks were founded, and government policy banks were established in 1994 to take over the government-directed spending functions of the four SOBs in order to remove politics from bank lending (Mehran et al. 1996, pp. 13–14). Modernizing the banking system in China has been an ongoing process, not a one-step radical reform. This has reduced the NPL ratio drastically in the period of 2008–2012. Since 2016, the practice of buying banks' NPLs at a discount and recovering them for a profit has grown rapidly even though it is becoming increasingly difficult in a slowing economy to dispose of NPLs, and as a result, the NPL ratio has gradually risen again (see Fig. 2.1). As the Chinese government continues to open up the financial sector, it provides challenges for domestic AMCs to further explore opportunities overseas and to emerge as global companies with international standards and quality. This is in line with two ongoing trends in which the BRI can play a useful role, namely global investors' rising interest in China, the world's second-largest economy, as well as domestic investors' demand for a more diversified asset portfolio. Although the Chinese banking system takes over many practices from other market-oriented banking systems, the dominant banks (the 'Big-5' except the Bank of Communications) are still state-owned and so far there is no plan to privatize them.

The domestic Chinese stock market is very large; its A-share market is the second largest in the world in terms of market capitalization after the USA. However, it is characterized by a high degree of inefficiency and volatility, and it primarily serves the SOEs. The Shanghai and Shenzhen stock exchanges were formally started in 1990, but during the first decade they were mainly vehicles for selling shares of SOEs to private interests. Over time, the stock exchanges have listed more and more firms, including private ones. The China Securities Regulatory Commission (CSRC) regulates the stock market. Its regulations, like those of the China Banking Regulatory Commission (CBRC), are similar to those of high-income market economies. Despite the strong rise of China's shadow banking system from the start of the credit crunch in 2007, its current traditional banking system is still highly regulated because of ongoing direct state ownership of the largest institutions. Given that China avoided the major recessions caused by the Asian and the GFC, it has experienced only a few periods where there were some balance of payments concerns and inflation has been negligible for the past two decades. It is therefore reasonable to state that China's financial regulatory environment is functioning adequately. However, in the transition to a more sustainable growth model it is likely that China's supervision and regulation of its financial system needs to be adjusted (see Sect. 5.5).

The fast-growing bond market is currently the world's third largest, but is dominated by the banking sector as the main source of financing for private companies. Through advanced financial reforms, the opening of capital markets has led to more easy capital inflow and outflow. However, many of the controls over these capital flows were used to restrict openness in 2015 and early 2016 when capital outflows led foreign exchange reserves to fall by more than USD 700 billion in less than a year, before leveling off later in 2016. That experience suggests that, at

China's current stage of development, complete market-oriented reforms should probably not include full opening of its capital markets. It may be in the interests of financial institutions in high-income countries for China to fully open its capital markets, but it is not in China's interests to have to deal with more volatile huge short-term capital inflows and outflows or 'hot money.' China needs time to reach a more sustainable balance in its international capital markets before lifting capital controls entirely.

When assessing the state of financial reforms in China, it is important to take into account the fact that not all financial innovations in recent years in high-income countries have had a positive impact on those economies, as 2007–2009 made clear. The excessive use of risky and innovative off-balance sheet products by many financial institutions in advanced economies before the GFC have been a good lesson for China to be more cautious about it. Financial reform is a complex topic, but there is no doubt that China has made major progress in creating a modern financial system suitable for a market economy. Some of the older financial institutions such as the regulated banks are now quite sophisticated, while new institutions such as insurance companies and the stock exchanges are far away from the level where they should be. Progressing to an efficient financial system will take time, but, in most respects, the direction is clear and substantial progress has been made. One change that would make the financial systems of China more like those in most high-income countries, however, is not going to occur. The Chinese government and the CPC are not going to substantially reduce their role in controlling and directing that system. The development that is taking place in many advanced economies, but will highly likely not take place in China, is the removal of direct government control over the financial sector and leaving supervision to more indirect controls of monetary and fiscal policy (Perkins 2018).

2.3 The Incomplete Transition to a Market Economy

The status of China's economy has been very often taken into consideration during the last years. Many economists are searching for an answer to the question whether the country has become a pure 'market economy.' To answer this question, two points of view can be highlighted: first, a general assessment of the economy's development, and second, the formal market economy status (MES) as understood by the international institutions such as the WTO. Both approaches do not lead to an obvious answer. The first approach does not give a clear answer because the Chinese economy is incomparable to other economies. During the past half-century, China has the most outstanding economic growth rates comparing to other emerging markets, but China applied its own way of development and this process is still unfinished. The country successfully increased its GDP, lifted hundreds of millions of its citizens out of poverty, and managed to be a global leader in some technologically advanced branches of industry, especially electronics, and IT. Currently, the country aspires to become the largest economy in the world (Ning 2018). On the other hand, there are many obstacles that China must overcome before the country is awarded a MES. The incomplete transition to a market economy is associated with the lacking of infrastructure in some parts of the country (or at least the great variety of access to infrastructure in different parts of the country) and a lack of human capital. Despite the acceptation by the government to stimulate the free market forces to help to grow the economy, the government still plays a primary role in the country's economic development (Morrison 2018, pp. 28–29).

The second point of view on the Chinese economy is its MES. This mainly plays a role in China's accession to the WTO on December 11, 2001 preceded to a 15-year transition period with the ultimate goal of achieving real status as a 'market economy.' The USA, Japan, Canada, and some EU countries still refuse to treat China as a market economy because of outstanding anti-dumping cases, even though they agreed to commit to MES recognition when China entered into WTO. According to these WTO member states, Chinese goods, especially commodities such as steel and aluminum, were not fully determined by the market and are still heavily underpriced because of subsidies and state-backed oversupply, giving Chinese exporters an unfair competitive advantage. China responds that its economy meets the generally accepted definition of a market economy in most anti-dumping cases. In addition to a large number of trade liberalization efforts, China has revised many laws and regulations at the central government level, and many more at local level, to bring the Chinese legal system in line with WTO standards. Chinese authorities also argue that the USA and other major trading nations agreed when China entered the WTO that the non-MES provision would expire on December 11, 2016. This date has passed, but the USA continues to label China a non-MES (Gao 2017). After four decades of reforms, China has understandably not become a pure market economy knowing that those reforms have come a long way from central planning. Especially during the current US–China trade conflict, this is an unfavorable situation because it is easier to introduce trade barriers with a similar MES for all WTO member states (Griswold 2019). This situation deserves a solution within the WTO as it is currently very difficult to distinguish pure market economies in a time of a new protectionist wave under the Trump administration.

Although the Chinese economy is characterized by rapid growth during the last four decades, this extensive approach to economic development has been accompanied by many adverse consequences. Some of the most important consequences of the incomplete transition process are the following:

- huge inequality of income distribution;
- relatively low GDP per capita;
- corruption and social unrest;
- continuous rural migration ('urban-rural' gap);
- environmental and congestion problems;
- demographic problems and population aging;
- shortage of availability of energy and raw materials;
- government support for SOEs and inefficiency of the financial system.

Taking into account the economic perspective, the most important short-term problems are connected with the excessive state intervention, shortage of energy and resources, labor market inefficiencies, and financial market underdevelopment. In the long run, crucial will be demographic constraints and other social problems, like social unrest, inequalities of income, and the urban–rural gap. Another group of threats are ecological problems. One of the most visible aspects of the incomplete transition of the Chinese economy toward a market economy is the inefficient financial market in the country. The banking sector reforms can be divided into several phases, namely the stage of specialization (1978–1993), commercialization (1994–2002), ownership restructuring since 2003, and public listings since 2005 (van der Linden 2010). Since GFC, Chinese banking is also putting more emphasis on prudent risk management for maintaining financial stability. However, already from the start of the financial reforms the financial sector was treated more as an important tool used by the authorities for their political aims than as an important intermediary between the different parties acting in the economy. Such approach leads to a situation that commercial banks have discriminatory lending policies, especially for SMEs. Due to the 'financial dependency triangle,' SOEs are able to get cheap credit; however, very often they are not able to repay the loans. As a result, the regular banking system was and still is rather inefficient and is making massive losses which led to the growth of NPLs (see Sect. 2.2) (Tan 2014, p. 9). On the other hand, the small- and medium-sized POEs are required to pay higher rates and often are not able to get loans from the SOBs.

The abovementioned circumstances led to the development of an unregulated part of the financial market alongside the regular banking system. The term shadow banking refers to a range of informal financial vehicles such as the Wealth Management Products (WMPs) with the principal purpose to attract savings funds that are seeking higher returns than could be achieved at the low state-fixed interest rates on deposits paid by the banking system. China's shadow banking system has developed especially in the last decade as a result of the immature Chinese capital markets and a shortage of funds provided by regulated traditional banks. Since the GFC, shadow banking became a very important alternative funding for the real economy in China, and in contrast to the shadow banking in the Western economies, the Chinese system established a strong interconnectedness between traditional 'commercial' regulated banks and the unregulated 'financial' institutions (e.g., trust companies, leasing companies, pawnshops, or microfinance companies) (van der Linden 2015). The commercial banks themselves initiated many of these products, but they were recorded separately from the banks' formal balance sheets and were unregulated by the CBRC. The central bank dealt with this in part by abolishing the state-set ceiling on deposit rates in 2015. In 2017, however, market interest rates in China as well as around the world remained very low, so WMPs remained attractive. Gradually, this led to a rather interwoven financial sector in China without a clear distinction between the regulated traditional and unregulated shadow banking system (Sheng et al. 2015; Sheng and Soon 2016, pp. 98–99). It is likely that both parts of the banking system will play an important role in the Chinese economy in the coming years. Since virtually all of the money is lent and borrowed by domestic individuals and institutions and the government has always been both able and willing to bail out NPLs, it is unlikely that China's shadow banking, given its large and growing size, could lead to another major financial crisis (Perkins 2018). The danger from continuing bailouts, if they become necessary, is less a financial crisis and more the possibility of increasingly risky and poor decision making by lenders leading to slower long-term growth. Handling of NPLs has become a top priority over the past decade as they posed a threat to financial and social stability. The first regulatory activity was undertaken in 2010 when CBRC introduced regulations related to direct bank-trust cooperation and channel investments. Then were implemented further regulations related to bank's WMPs (2011 and 2013), trust companies (2014), and some interbank activities (2014). All of them imposed some prudential measures or prohibited risky transactions (Bowman et al. 2018). The next wave of regulations was implemented since 2016. President Xi Jinping has made the reduction of corporate indebtedness (see Sect. 2.4) a key element of his policy over the last two years (Weinland 2019). The PBC prepared a new set of regulations and other measures aimed at reducing the risks in the financial sector in the country. The policy makers are aware that any regulatory closing must be progressive, because rapid tightening is likely to hurt the economy. Policy makers must manage the frequency and intensity of regulations and apply some monetary policy toolkit to deleverage the economy without stymieing its growth. It means that the new regulations are interrelated with expansionary monetary policy aimed at averting any severe cash shortages and provide the necessary efficiency (*China Daily* 2017).

Another concern associated with the incomplete transition of China to a market economy is related to the labor market. Some of the problems occur in market economies as well, but in the context of the Chinese economy they assume a particular relevance. The labor market problem might be divided into two groups: wages problems and unemployment problems. The wages in China have been rising rapidly in recent years what triggered the erosion of labor cost advantage. As China's economy expanded, the wages in the country begin to grow. This creates a big problem for the future, because for decades cheap labor is considered as the main factor behind the economy's growth. The process of rising wages may erode China's low-cost manufacturing advantage very soon. As compared with developed markets, labor costs in China are still low, but compared with other emerging markets they are rising more strongly (see Fig. 2.2). It leads to a situation that China's manufacturing sector is

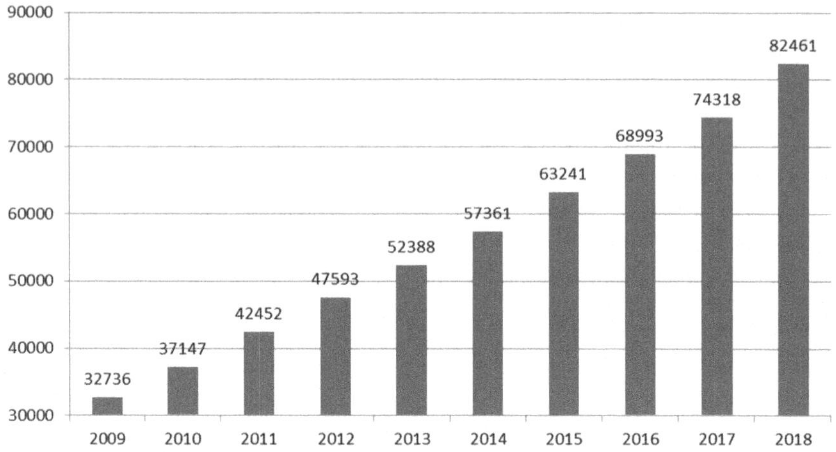

Fig. 2.2 China average yearly wages 2009–2019 (RMB) (*Source* Own elaboration based on Tradingeconomics.com [accessed: 26.05.2019])

under pressure with factories shifting labor-intensive production to low-cost countries (*The Economist* 2015).

Another feature of the Chinese economy is the rising unemployment which is difficult to estimate since China's unemployment rate only measures the rate of unemployment of those with an urban registration in accordance with the urban '*hukou*' framework (see Sect. 2.1). In the past, China's unemployment problem mainly consists of structural unemployment due to a rapidly changing pattern of the structure of the economy. This problem could be tackled through supply-side policies (e.g., training and improving the state of technology) as part of the 13th FYP. However, since the inevitable economic slowdown China is also facing cyclical or demand-deficient unemployment which could be solved by (expansionary) demand-side policies such as lower taxes, higher government spending, or lower interest rates but conflicts with the social security taxation system. There are several reasons for the new situation of rising unemployment. Among the most important are the withdrawal of foreign capital, internal tax policy, and technological changes. Massive withdrawal of foreign capital as a result of international competition between China and other countries has undermined the labor market and has become one of the most important causes of the problems in the labor market. Additionally, the economy's growth rate has been falling year-on-year and during the last few years achieved the slowest growth rate since the GFC. As the economic growth is slowing, the employment is declining. The problem is relevant in particular to the growing number of college graduates (Xing et al. 2018). Although China's official unemployment rate has been remarkably stable at roughly 4% for decades, which is rather surprising considering the more fluctuating growth rates of the economy over the same period, it is likely that unemployment is one of the prices that China may need to pay for future prosperity (Fidrmuc and Huang 2013, p. 21). An important contributor to the growth of unemployment (especially in the near future) plays the implementation of robotic production in manufacturing. In China, competition for jobs between robots and people is becoming stronger and this is leading to a reduction in employment for many companies. Another feature is the social security taxation system. The policy introduced on January 1, 2018 has led to an increase of corporate tax rate from 31 to 44% (the second highest in the world). While the burden on enterprises increases, especially the businesses of SMEs are forced to reduce their workforce (Quinglian 2018).

The problem of corruption is without doubt one of the biggest problems faced by economies, irrespective of their level of development. Although the relationship between economic growth and corruption in China is difficult to assess, it may be assumed that the scale of the problems caused by corruption is relevant, and the level of corruption in the country is far greater than that of most high-income economies. During the transition from a centrally controlled to a market-driven economy, the system was vulnerable to corruption. It has an impact on the economy in both ways, directly and indirectly. The first dimension embraces such mechanisms as tax evasion, money laundering, and other illicit activities. The second one leads to distorting market mechanisms, increasing the cost of business and daunting competition. High level of corruption leads to the lack of confidence among investors (especially foreign ones) and creates unpredictable conditions for business. It renders the economy inefficient to some extent and causes distortions and inefficiency for the market mechanisms. There are also some positive results of corruption in China. The regulations for business are too strict, and corruption is a way for firms to sidestep the requirements imposed by the government (D'Amico 2015). Additionally, corruption committed by firms enhances the growth of their sales income. This refers, however, to countries with a less developed financial market.

Some evidence suggests that corruption and financial development are substitutes to promote business growth (Wang and You 2012, p. 33). The substitution should occur automatically while market mechanisms play a stronger role. The market economy and the primary market force for allocating resources might lead to the constraint of corruption. The mechanism has also an opposite impact—breaking the corruptive relationships between the key players in the Chinese economy and separating the roles and responsibilities of the major parties (the Party, the government, enterprises, and banks) may be favorable and lead to the stronger market forces. It means that the elimination of corruption is necessary in order for China's economic growth to be sustainable in the future. This explains why fighting corruption as the CPC biggest plague is the main priority since Xi Jinping took office in 2013 in order to implement the BRI as successfully as possible.

Another important problem for the Chinese economic growth is the limited energy resources. The development of the Chinese economy during the last four decades was based on high energy consumption. Despite the simultaneous rapid growth in energy production during the last decades, energy supply and demand still lag behind the economic growth. Since the beginning of 1990s, China has become a net importer of oil. It is predicted that during the next years the oil and other energy sources will be further declining. To some extent, oil consumption might be replaced by gas and coal, but it is a solution for short and middle term. In the long run, the supply–demand gap for energy resources could be growing, and it can endanger the Chinese energy security and economic growth. Additionally, such a change undermines some parts of the market already based on this kind of energy source, e.g., leads to shortages of gas for households, etc. (Hornby and Zhang 2017). Without finding an alternative source of energy, the further Chinese economic growth will be undermined. Regarding the possibility, there are some important problems for enhancing the supply, e.g.,

- insufficient capital investment in the power industry;
- low energy efficiency;
- artificially low electricity tariffs.

All of these causes undermined market forces and simultaneously restricted the energy supply (Lam 2005). Except for the energy supply, there are some other problems with the energy consumption in China.

Among them can be enumerated: environment pollution and greenhouse gas emission, and energy supply in rural areas.

The environmental problems during the last decade become another challenge in the whole world, but for the Chinese economy it has a special dimension. The severe pollution and environmental problems are the consequences of an extensive use of energy in the country. The Chinese extensive economic model leads to huge problems with air and soil pollution and continuous problem with smog (Weidou 2007). All of them triggered the ecological degradation in the country and poses the question about the proper energy policy for the future. As a consequence of the environment degradation, the ecological policy became crucial political factor and the government initiated and implemented national large-scale policies. The ecologically oriented incentives were introduced since the 11th FYP (2006–2010). The energy was pointed as one of the most important causes of the pollution, and the measures were oriented on the limitation of the pollution (Jin et al. 2016). This is, however, another example of the state intervention into market mechanism.

In addition to the pollution, the model of the development of the Chinese economy has led to a shortage of raw materials in the country including minerals, water, timber, and energy sources. The need to find the resources necessary for the further economic development leads to high activity of the Chinese companies not only in its own neighborhood but also much further afield. The country spreads its influence and investments across Africa, South America, Arab countries, Asia, and other parts of the world (Vörös 2010). For stabilizing its import of new raw materials, China is determined to apply extensive national interventions. However, such an approach conflicts with the aim of more market forces and places the country at a greater distance from the MES.

China's economic boom has widened the wealth gap over the years despite the rapid growth of GDP per capita. The official statistics are very optimistic, but in reality they are not properly reflecting the situation of the society. It is often highlighted that China made a huge progress during the last four decades in the GDP per capita growth. In 1978, only 0.5% of the global population lived in countries with lower GDP per capita than China, while 73.5% lived in countries with a higher ratio. According to the IMF statistics in 2012 (a bit outdated, what about 2018?), only 30.2% of the world's population lived in countries with a higher GDP per capita than China, while 50.2% lived in countries with a lower one (Ross 2013). Such data show that in the analyzed

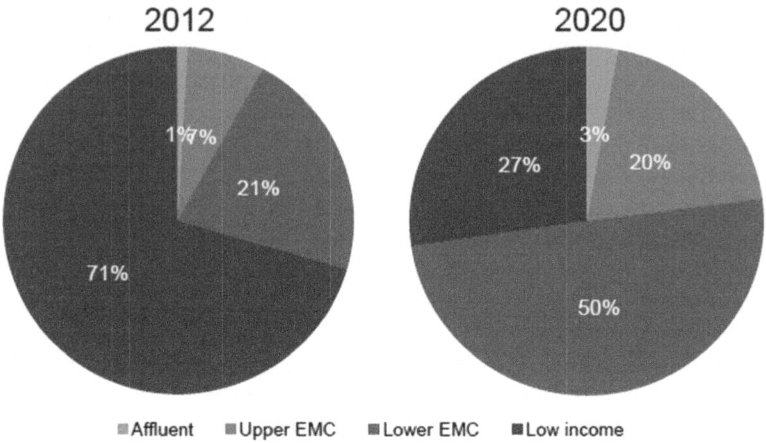

Fig. 2.3 China's emerging middle class (EMC) in 2012 and 2020 (*Source China Daily Asia*, July 21, 2019)

period, the Chinese GDP per capita raised almost 49-fold, lifting 800 million people out of poverty. It is estimated that China's emerging urban middle class totaled 125 million in 2012, and the number is expected to reach 356 million by 2020 (Fig. 2.3). In urban centers in China, poverty has been almost totally eliminated. The major problem is that the income per capita in the country is still below the world average, and there are huge income inequalities (Eckert 2016). Aaron K. Lee emphasizes, on the basis of calculations made by the Boston Consulting Group, that in 2008 less than 1% of China's richest households possed 70% of the total private wealth in the country, what seriously undermines the development of the Chinese economy (Lee 2015, p. 71). Such situation restricts the development opportunities and seriously undermines the development of the Chinese economy. The income inequality leads to a huge gap between productivity growth and the real wage rate growth, what impacts on the middle-class-income growth. Low GDP per capita reflects the fact that the retail consumer prices are very high for the majority of the society. The vast majority of wage earners in China are earning income slightly above subsistence incomes. In consequence, it impacts the retail demand. It must be highlighted that the huge responsibility for such situation remains with the SOEs. They have monopolistic positions and are main providers of basic goods and services such as energy, telecommunication, and commodities what firmly impacts on the consumer goods prices and as a result ultimately undermines the MES (Lee 2015, pp. 71–73).

To some extent, the very high level of income inequality in China might be justified by and seen as an inevitable consequence of the transition from a planned to a market economy. The unprecedented growth rates of recent decades have also been accompanied by massive urbanization with the result that the migrant's incomes raised dramatically and millions of people were lifted out of poverty. Although the total standard of living for both the urban and rural population has increased, the urbanization has also led to greater income inequality within urban areas, but especially between urban and rural areas (Shi 2016). While urban households have experienced significant income progress, a large part of the rural population lives in poverty and is still heavily dependent on the rather self-sufficient agricultural sector. Despite the economic progress, a large proportion of the urban population still has limited or no access to basic services such as health care, social security, and education. The rising income inequality gap not only relates to the distribution of consumption patterns, but also has a major impact on economic development as a whole through the limitations of investment in education for the poor and thus discouraging them from accumulating capital. In the long term, increasing income inequality will become an increasingly inhibitory factor for a sustainable society and therefore the development of social capital. Additionally, the income inequality gap might lead to social conflicts and may harm the economic growth (Ren and Chao 2018).

The export-driven growth model, on which the Chinese economic development is largely based, has also many drawbacks. The potential on which the ongoing Chinese development was based is beginning to fade due to the fact that other countries of the world are not interested anymore in buying all the cheap and low-quality goods which were massively produced in China. Nowadays, the country is forced to develop more technologically advanced goods, meanwhile suffering from other shortcomings, e.g., the high corporate debt (see Sect. 2.4) and trade conflict with the USA (see Sect. 3.1). The model of export-oriented economic development is negatively affected not only by the external factors (e.g., declining foreign demand) but also by the internal ones. The net surplus in international trade is strictly correlated with China's relative high national savings rate in comparison with other Western and Asian

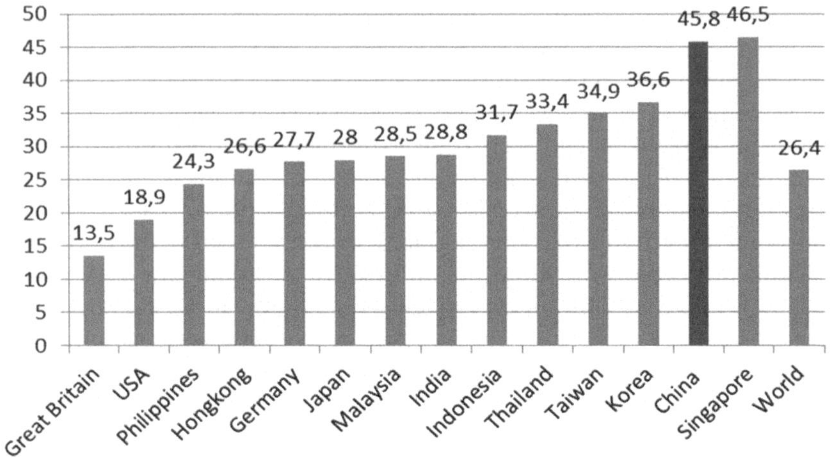

Fig. 2.4 China's national savings rate in percent of GDP in comparison with other major Western and Asian countries (*Source* Own elaboration based on Taylor [2019])

countries except Singapore (see Fig. 2.4). The savings in turn are responsible for excessive domestic investment, which leads to excess supply over demand together with low level of consumption. There is also a risk of a business cycle shock and its negative impact on the indebted businesses.

Since the introduction of an 'open door' policy, Chinese exports have been heavily dependent on imports and foreign needs, so that domestic economic growth has become increasingly linked to developments in the global economy. However, the traditional development model caused a huge depletion of natural resources, serious environmental pollution, which hindered the sustained economic development (Morrison 2018, p. 29).

The level of migration in China during the last twenty years has more than tripled. It is a result of the fact that since the beginning of twenty-first century the Chinese government has gradually eased migration restrictions including the following actions:

- loosening the household registration card system ('*hukou*');
- abolition of some fees charged from rural migrants;
- introduction of some social security provisions for rural migrants;
- increase access to public services.

Unfortunately, the migrations from rural to urban areas are the next challenge for the Chinese economic development. Human population movement process leads to the 'urban-rural' gap development and is interconnected with many problems, such as difficult working conditions and low wages, low social security coverage, poor housing conditions, and many difficulties in access to public services (e.g., education for children, health care, etc.) (Shi 2008, pp. 8–19; *Urban China* 2014, pp. 100–110).

The migration process is related to the problem of congestion in Chinese urban areas. A free flow of people to the big cities causes a concentration of a large number of people in relatively small areas with all kinds of transport problems and traffic jams as a result. Moreover, this congestion leads to problems with excessive carbon emissions that require a new development of communication infrastructure, which in the meantime can lead to more growth inequality in different cities.

China's 'one-child' policy was introduced in 1979 with the aim to control the size of population and this policy continued until October 2015, when a 'two-child' policy was introduced to address the aging problem in China. The 'one-child' policy has led to a demographic problem in Chinese society with two dimensions, namely an aging society and a declining labor force in the future. From the economic dimension, this situation will have a huge impact on the Chinese labor costs and the rise of the working age. In the long run, the economy may suffer from a shortages of unskilled workers and other significant problems such as lower housing prices, stagnation in domestic demand, and imbalance in public budgets (undermined by the expenses for social protection system to support the elderly) (Du and Yang 2015, pp. 25–44; Luo 2015). The demographic development is also an important determinant of decreasing savings because the reinforced social services will raise consumption at the expense of savings, and as a consequence, the income is becoming to be shifted away from corporates to households. All of the enumerated factors are leading to a conclusion that it is essential for China to find a new growth model because the country can no longer make an increasing use of its large low-cost labor force and huge savings surpluses anymore (Lee et al. 2013).

Another drawback of the transition from plan to market concerns the industrial overcapacity and over-investment on the Chinese market mainly due to the focus on fixed investments embracing plants and equipment building infrastructure during the last decades.

It regards especially such sectors as iron and steel, glass, chemicals, cement, paper, aluminum, solar panel, and power generation equipment, with overcapacity exceeding 30%, which is considered as a threshold value where deficits can occur in companies that have borrowed and subsequently seen their profits fall. The overproduction is partly caused by the vicious competition between local governments whereby they stimulate new production facilities by offering all kinds of financial subsidies. Moreover, local governments help companies to get cheap loans from SOBs. In this way, industrial overcapacity has become a ticking time bomb that threatens the Chinese economy because it has led companies to incur debts to repay loans. In order to move up in the value chain in manufacturing, the country must reshape its production plants and reduce the overcapacity. Avoiding the overcapacity problem is an essential part of the BRI. To combat this, strict rules must be drawn up for local governments that apply regular tax facilities. All government subsidies to private companies must also become more transparent. Since over-protection of failing companies has contributed to the maintenance of bad management and low efficiency, the authorities will have to encourage more bankruptcies, despite the opposition of local governments. In addition, the government must speed up the reforms of the financial markets. In the current financial system dominated by SOBs, companies focus more on quantity than quality growth leading to overcapacity. The excess capacity problem also regards the impact of the production plants on the environment. The heavy industry plants are associated with air, water, and soil pollutions, and the first place of China as the largest greenhouse gases emitter (Cheng 2015; Wildeau 2017).

2.4 The Major Problem Areas of the Controlled Market Economy

For decades, the Chinese government views a growing economy as vital to maintain social stability. Since 1979, the unprecedented double-digit GDP growth meant that the living standards double about every seven years. The fixed investment and export-driven growth strategy led to a very high level of national savings, investments, infrastructure development, and foreign exchange reserves. However, since 2009 the controlled Chinese economy is experiencing a turning point when there is a significant recession in many other parts of the world. The Chinese government spent a lot of money on infrastructure at a time where maybe less government-led fixed investment was needed. The stimulus package kept the economy running at a higher level, but actually the debt rose to the point where it was too high relative to the rates of return available on these investment projects. China's controlled economy consists of too many production sectors with too much stimulation of investments by too many firms that are not or hardly profitable. Many of the POEs are kept afloat by cheap credit from China's SOBs which is not based on proper risk assessment, while the SOEs are mostly not creditworthy and still benefit from political privileges based on the 'financial dependency triangle.' With the transition from a middle- to a high-income advanced economy, the aforementioned drawbacks of the incomplete transition to a market economy will have to be tackled. The main problem areas of the current Chinese economy, especially increased since the GFC, have become an increasing burden in the transition to a new more sustainable growth model. The major interrelated economic problem areas consist of a real estate and stock market bubble partly as a result of too extensive credit growth which could undermine future growth by sharply boosting debt levels with an excess level of municipal debt. This has caused overcapacity in many industries (especially extending credit to firms that are unprofitable to keep them operating) and contributing to real estate bubbles (partly spread throughout the rest of the world and kept afloat through China's massive shadow banking system, see Sect. 5.2). This will reduce productivity by proving preferential treatment to SOEs and other government-supported entities. Especially, the rising corporate debt with unaffordable property prices creates the risk of a bubble that might burst. The Chinese government has maintained restrictions on capital inflows and outflows for many years, in part to stabilize the RMB against the dollar and other currencies in order to boost exports. It is argued that the Chinese government's restrictions on capital flows have greatly distorted financial markets in China, preventing the most efficient use of capital, such as over-investment in some sectors (such as real estate) and under-investment in others (such as services) (Morrison 2018, p. 32). Another potential problem is capital flight. There is a risk that capital within China, both foreign capital, but especially domestic capital, seeks to leave the country out of fear of the current economic problems and further economic slowdown. If the capital flight accelerates, as seen before during the Asian crisis of 1997–1998, this will actually make the current problem areas much worse (Cowen 2017). The biggest economic challenge for the Chinese authorities to find a new sustainable growth path with the help of the BRI in the coming period is determined by addressing the aforementioned problem areas. As the interdependence between the real estate and debt problem and its consequences for further deepening of the financial reforms stand out here, this will be described in more detail in the rest of this section.

The Chinese real estate market has experienced enormous changes over the last decades through the introduction of a system of land use rights followed by the privatization of the housing market which encourages a tremendous urbanization process. This development was not only combined with a great construction activity but also a significant increase in property prices and a mortgage credit boom. A rapid growth of income and rising urbanization, high price-to-income and price-to-rent ratios for property and the high number of unoccupied residential and commercial units throughout China contributed substantively to this credit boom. At the same time, the housing reform in the late 1990s, whereby the government announced that all vacant residential housing units built after 1998 were to be sold instead of allocated, helped to unleash the huge demand for modern commodity housing. While commercial and industrial properties have gone through comparatively stable price increases over the years, the prices for housing, especially in the developed coastal regions, have risen significantly. As a result, it has become more unaffordable to own a house in the major cities of China. However, among other things, the government tries to limit a potential overheating of the housing market through a mandatory 20% down payment on houses and a limit on the number of houses that one person can buy.

Besides a rapid income growth, a rising urbanization trend, abundant liquidity, low cost of home ownership, and low mortgage debt of households, there are several other fundamental factors which drive the property prices. The main cause of this real estate sector mania is that this is the most lucrative and safest investment option available compared to the alternatives. Firstly, the domestic stock market has been highly volatile since 2007 and has performed poorly recently partly due to the current US–China trade war. Secondly, the RMB is still not a fully convertible currency; therefore, capital controls still prevent domestic investors from investing abroad despite China's 'going out' strategy to encourage its enterprises to invest overseas. Thirdly, although the unfavorable bank saving deposits is not the main reason of resulting surging property prices, since the last decade a bank saving deposit is mostly not beneficial, and in some periods even below consumer price inflation rates. Since real estate is considered the most profitable alternative investment,

China's economy has a surplus of physical capital, infrastructure, and property evident in many new parks, highways and subways, sleek and empty airports, thousands of colossal new central, and provincial government buildings and ghost towns (*The Economist* 2011). Because China's economy is still heavily dependent on the real estate market, it remains to be seen to what extent the authorities are able to stabilize the housing market. This dilemma will become even more striking after the country's plan to build more affordable homes for targeted residents and its aim to put more emphasis on consumption than on export and fixed investment as the traditional main drivers of China's growth model.

A property bubble is characterized by increasing housing prices fueled by speculation. Housing bubbles usually start with an increase in demand, in the face of limited supply which takes a relatively long period of time to replenish and increase. Speculators enter the market, assuming that profits can be made through short-term buying and selling which further drives demand. At some point, demand decreases, or stagnates at the same time supply increases, resulting in a sharp drop in prices and the bubble bursts. In Hyman Minsky's model, more demand fueled by credit leads to more bank lending to ever more dubious borrowers, often creating new financial instruments to do the job. At the top of the market, banks are not able to meet its obligations. Losses on loans begin to mount, and the drop in the value of loans falls relative to liabilities, driving down capital which forces banks to cut back on lending. It's interesting to know if China's bank lending nears its so-called Minsky moment whereby the bubble is about to burst and banks are forced to pay off debts (*'deleveraging'*). Since 2016, the government has implemented a tightening of housing measures across China, particularly toward 'speculative' housing purchases, to moderate property price inflation. It has simultaneously implemented targeted, incremental measures to improve longer-term housing supply. Even so, construction activity has weakened and prices have continued to rise rapidly. However, if the authorities succeed in simultaneously maintaining relatively tight demand-side policies, while delivering on the government's social housing objectives, this would fulfill President Xi's aspiration that housing should be 'for living in and not for speculation.'

Several policy measures to reduce the property boom have not been very effective due to an ambiguous approach of the housing market reforms from state to market control and back again.

This is partly due to China's lack of property rights in land, all of which is owned by the government and leased out to POEs and SOEs

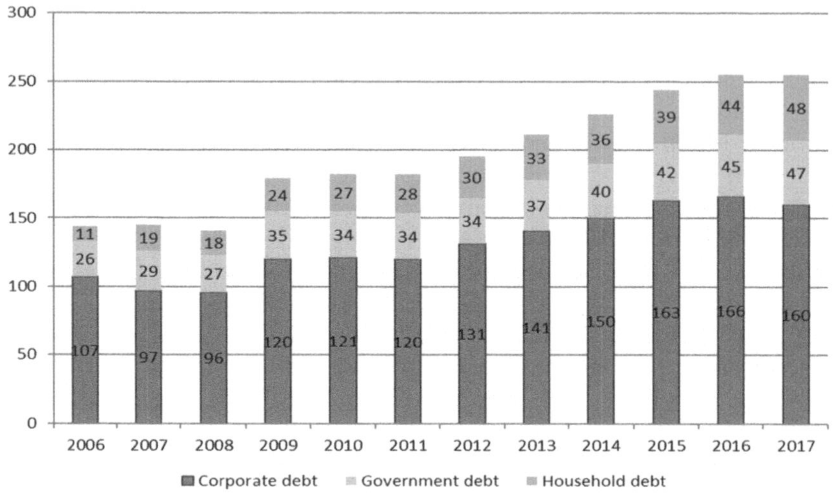

Fig. 2.5 Debt-to-GDP in China in the period of 2006–2017 (*Source* ChinaPower.csis.org [accessed: 27.02.2019])

through the land use rights. In turn, the sale of these rights constitutes a vital revenue stream for local authorities, providing powerful incentives for them to help spur the real estate boom. This contributes to another explanation to the ghost towns all across China. Many local governments will find themselves in economic peril as revenue dries up since around two-third of the purchase costs of property goes directly to the government. This explains the bias toward the construction aspect of urbanization whereby local governments have the tendency to urbanize suburban areas. Due to a narrow interdependency between property developers who buy land from the local government and generally enjoy a very high-profit margin, the firms and households (buyers of property), the SOBs who give loans to developers and home buyers and the fund-raising local governments (sellers of state land), the overall real economy gets disturbed (van der Linden 2013). In theory, local governments were supposed to run a balanced budget without borrowing money. In practice, however, they were encouraged by the central government to borrow money to spend on all kinds of infrastructure investments, which not only caused industrial overcapacity (see Sect. 2.3), but also a steady rise in mainly local government debt (see Fig. 2.5).

The central government had to rescue many local governments from bankruptcy by turning a large part of that debt into government bonds. One of the principal problems of the local government debt was that the central government had too little knowledge of how fast that debt was rising (Perkins 2018). Since many local governments are not able to pay back their loans, it is the central government that feels forced to bail out the local government debts (Cowen 2017).

One of the biggest challenges to be solved for the future sustainable growth path will be to control and reduction the rising debt problem. China's economic recovery after the GFC was supported by a rapid credit growth which could be considered as a natural consequence of strong underlying growth and a reflection of deeper financial reforms. Since 2011, more credit has been allocated to the services than the manufacturing sector but the credit is less efficiently used due to a continued allocation to less productive SOEs in mainly northeast provinces with a heavy exposure to mining sectors. Although the POEs in the services sector create more value added, overall the credit intensity has risen since more credit is needed to create value added in the manufacturing sector. The development of this 'credit binge' partly explains China's inevitable economic downturn. The recent rise in credit growth, partly reflected in China's total social financing,[9] is mainly due to the risk of a further escalation of the current trade conflict with the USA (*The Economist* 2019). In the short term, China's high savings ratio, current account surplus, and small external debt can help mitigate the immediate risks of necessary disruptive adjustments. However, in the long term, further financial deepening, a more efficient credit allocation and a 'deleveraging' policy is needed to break the negative spiral effect between slowing growth, excessive credit provision, and worsening debt service capacity (Chen and Kang 2018).

While credit growth has moderated to come in line with economic growth, the rapid increase and composition of China's total debt-to-GDP is certainly worrying. According to Bloomberg, China's debt buildup has been more than quadrupled since 2004 with a total debt-to-GDP (including corporate, household, government, and

[9] China's total social financing (TSF) is a broad official measure of credit and liquidity in the economy that consists mainly of bank loans and bond issuance, but it also includes off-balance sheet forms of financing such as initial public offerings, shadow banking credit such as trust loans, and bankers' acceptance bills.

banking sector) surpassed the 266% at the end of 2017 (see Fig. 2.5). Although the advent of the obscure high-yielding shadow banking and real estate-driven debt has boosted the Chinese economy through the GFC, it has also saddled it with a heavy repayment burden reflected in a high level of debt servicing ratio which made its banking system more vulnerable (Shih 2017). Therefore, several trends have become potential ticking time bombs and cannot sustain such a high pace of leveraging before another crisis will occur. First, half of all loans are linked to China's overheated real estate market; second, unregulated shadow banking accounts for nearly half of new lending (55% to GDP in 2017); and third, the debt of many local governments is probably unsustainable. Also, the credit overhang has caused overcapacity in many unprofitable government-supported industries. Much of the credit flowed to property developers creating an excess of unsold homes often displayed as ghost towns. As a result, many local governments are now finding it hard to cope with debts and tax receipts especially when land sales suffer from the slowing economy. In particular, the rising corporate debt with unaffordable property prices creates the risk of a bubble that might burst. Since around two-thirds of the corporate debt is owed by SOEs who are quite often indirectly involved in the construction industry, the turbulence in the real estate market will have a huge impact on the banking sector. This explains why the Chinese government is looking for a transition of a policy shift away from an economy fueled by non-financial sector debt, such as corporate debt and government stimulus, toward a more sustainable consumer-driven economy (Morrison 2018).

2.5 The Inevitable Economic Slowdown as Momentum for New Initiatives

After four decades of unprecedented growth since China started it economic reforms and more than six years since it launched its BRI, its current economy is exposed to several dangers which can undermine further development. Besides, the slow progress of the deepening of China's financial reforms, other possible threats for China's future economic development are the following: an inevitable economic downturn and related credit binge and debt problem; the international trade conflicts and a possible new role for the WTO with the BRI in the background, the unbalanced inward and outward investments patterns; and the aging and overcapacity problem already described in Sect. 2.3. In 2018, the Chinese stock market fell by no less than 25% and the RMB has been falling since 2017. Although the current trade dispute with the USA is not the cause of these problems, it does not help to fight against China's economic downturn. China's hardest challenge as planned in its latest 13th FYP is to enter into the next stage of a high-income advanced economy whereby the GDP share of the services sector overtakes the agricultural and manufacturing production sector with sustainable lower growth rates with more focus on quality than quantity. Due to China's 'middle-income trap,' it is difficult to gain high levels of productivity with structural inefficiencies in its economy. Currently, China is the world's second-largest economy and the bigger an economy gets, the harder it is to keep growing at a fast pace, so a single-digit growth path has become an inevitable reality. China's economy has long been built on its manufacturing sector. Being the factory of the world is easy when you have a huge and growing population, but becomes harder when your 'one-child' and currently 'two-child' policy slows growth, ages your population, and creates a generation unwilling to accept the low-paid jobs of their ancestors. China's government is trying to move from a manufacturing and export-driven economy to a service and consumption-driven one, so exports are declining after decades of double-digit annual growth (Morrison 2018).

China's economic slowdown, stock crashes, and currency realignments are highlighting the downturn of the world's second-largest economy and the main driver of global growth. Apart from the differences in approach between the conservatives and radicals within the CPC (see Sect. 2.1), since the Asia crisis and later the GFC, there has been an increasing debate about the extent to which the foregoing model of Chinese development is approaching to a breakdown. Among the main arguments in such a scenario is that China's model of development is excessively unbalanced (e.g., as a relation to a personal consumption to the size of the economy) (Huang 2017, p. 8).

It is likely that in the coming decade the international financial markets, especially the foreign exchange market, will exert more influence on China's real economy. The Chinese authorities try to stimulate its economy and adjust the exchange rate to its own goals, sometimes against the external pressure on the change of RMB exchange rate in opposite direction. The recent attention of global markets was focused on China's exchange rate in August 2015 when the PBC announced a nearly 2.0%

devaluation of the RMB against the USD. Since then, China has devalued the RMB several times during the transition from the 12th to the 13th FYP, in which the Chinese authorities have established a clear and concise list of objectives on how they want to develop their 'new normal' economy and avoid a 'middle-income trap' in the near future.

The main characteristics of this 'new normal' growth model consist of a slower growth level with a higher quality and more emphasis on efficiency and social security with a strong role of the government; the ability to adjust in accordance with the current market circumstances; and opening-up of the financial markets and services sector as the current economy's primary driver of growth to offset contractions in China's traditional powerhouses of heavy industry and manufacturing. The aim is to keep a strict balance in restructuring China's economy, i.e., making sure growth in one sector offsets slowdowns in another in order to guarantee enough employment. One of the most crucial objectives as part of this plan is to induce an economic shift that will steer the country away from a reliance on exports and investments toward growth driven by domestic consumption and innovation. This is part of China's narrative to decrease its reliance on its global partners, a lesson learned from the GFC when China became dangerously dependent on debt-fueled investments in infrastructure, housing, and heavy industries with a significant overcapacity as a result.

The 'new normal' model of China's economy development should be more adjusted to the needs of contemporary world and the processes occurring on global markets. The crucial expectation is that the country will no longer be committed only to the single-minded GDP increase at all costs. The contemporary growth of the Chinese economy should be accompanied by appropriate structural adjustment and have a broader context than China applied in the past. The economy should be reoriented and transformed from the supply-side source of economic growth to a mixture of demand- and supply-side source of growth (domestic and external) and high-technology development. Among the most important changes might be enumerated:

- new technological transformation;
- change of businesses, processes and habits (orientation on private, very diversified business);
- more important role of services, especially financial services;
- more focus on environmental issues and a 'green' economy.

The need for a new technological transformation is the best way to combat the 'middle-income trap.' The goal of creation a group of high-value export industries that can help to combat the current problems with export might be such a solution. It stems from the fact that the current growth of Chinese economy can be sustainable mainly by technology-based sectors of industry. There are numerous scientific works highlighting the importance of a large share of high-technology exports in total manufacturing export for reducing the likelihood of growth slowdown. The current problem for the economy stems from the fact that China's main proportion of high-tech exports originates from foreign-owned enterprises, and the Chinese value-added to high-tech industries in the country are relatively low. From this reason, the technology development seems to be one of the most important determinants of growth, leading to the more mature stage of development (Glawe and Wagner 2019, p. 17). As part of the 'open door' policy, economic development has in the past been strongly focused on attracting foreign technologies, but especially this decade, China is increasingly transforming from a high-tech importer to a high-tech domestic producer. For instance, China's robot-makers want to dominate their domestic market, aiming to supply 50% of local demand by 2020, rising to 70% by 2025. On the other hand, it is not an easy step to become a technology supplier (see Fig. 2.6). Firstly, China is no longer the lower-cost labor market; secondly, the country is not the strongest player in the high-tech industry. In order to enhance its industrial capability, the country must foster its transition through some steps: 'made-in-China,' 'designed-in-China,' and 'innovated-in-China.' Additionally, there are some basic principles, which must be taken into account in the Chinese strategy (Li 2018, p. 69):

- enhance industrial capability through innovation-driven manufacturing;
- emphasize quality over quantity;
- achieve green development;
- nurture human talents.

All of these principles are crucial for fostering the development of hi-tech industry. The achievement of these objectives requires, however, an adequate work environment oriented on creativity and innovativeness.

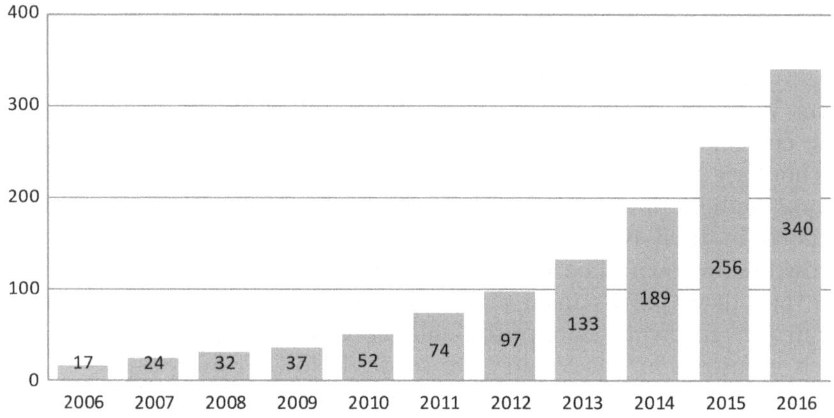

Fig. 2.6 Estimated operational stock of industrial robots at year-end in China (thousand of units) (*Source* Adapted from IFR International Federation of Robotics 2017)

Current technological developments including information technology (IT), digitization of services, the use of big data, robotics and artificial intelligence (AI) will have a crucial impact on future Chinese business strategies. The new business approach should be oriented on direct interaction with customers and accelerate data sharing throughout the supply chain, promoting customized manufacturing (Wei et al. 2017). Another trend in the future development model for China is the promotion of the private sector. In the past, it was common for a new development phase to allow the inefficient public sector to pave the way for the more efficient private sector, while it will be obvious that in the coming decade the private sector will play crucial role and there is no need to treat the public enterprises as the initiators of further changes.

In the current process of transition of the Chinese economy, services are playing increasingly more important role. The quality of offered products needs producer's change from product to service-oriented model (relationship-based model). Firms must adjust to consumer's expectations, which nature is more intangible. Such a change requires a radical transformation and setting up of new strategies, designing new offers and processes, restructuring organization and supply chain, and introducing new technology (Tan et al. 2019, p. 16). The core issue for such approach is to meet customer's expectations. It requires good understanding of the market and the customer's needs, as well as the creation of channels of information exchange between the business and consumer needs. Producers should be oriented on the process of product-service integration.

Although the Chinese financial services have grown very dynamically during the last decade, the financial institutions mainly offer basic services as banking, insurances, payments, consumer finance, and stock investments. Over the years, the Chinese financial system has increasingly developed into one of the world's examples of financial inclusion. Despite the success in rapid transformation of the banking industry and development of the capital market, the new challenges are coming up. It is increasingly important to make the system more sustainable and closely aligned to the local expectations, which creates the need of:

- further development of financial infrastructure (especially in remote and rural areas);
- striking the right balance between the innovations and managing the risk arising from the innovations (development of well-tailored regulations);
- reducing the role of government as financial inclusion provider (strengthening the role of market forces in the process).

All of the enumerated challenges highlight the need to shift toward more market-based orientation in shaping the Chinese financial market (Chien and Randall 2018). An important challenge for the Chinese financial sector will be the opening-up for foreign investors. It means higher sophistication of the services. The market should become part of the international financial system and be prepared for foreign competition.

The rapid economic development of China is responsible for a number of negative environmental consequences. Among the most important are water and air pollution; cropland losses; and desertification and biodiversity losses. All of them pose a great threat to the sustainable development of the country. On the other hand, all of them are a side effect of the ongoing national policies, promoting high levels of economic growth. The new model of economic growth must consider and implement mechanisms leading to a reduction of the negative environmental problems. It means that China faces a dilemma to reconcile its economy, energy system, and environmental security. It is very difficult for the country to find easy solutions to the complicated problem with accommodating the inconsistent goals, at least in the short run. In the coming decade as part of the 13th and most likely also the coming 14th FYP, China will have to find a good balance between sufficient economic growth for social stability and sufficient environmentally friendly sustainable economic growth to cope with its 'middle-income trap.' The authorities need to identify balanced policies that offer the best trade-off between these components (Tang et al. 2015).

In the context of the unbalanced economy, it seems that the Chinese current slowdown nature is not a cyclical, but it is a result of a structural changes in the economy. It means that the slowdown is inevitable and irreversible. The country's original growth drivers have been already exhausted. Now China must search for some other determinants of its development than it applied in the past, to overcome the current drawbacks. The most important factor encouraging the further economic growth is the BRI. It is considered the new engine of economic growth and an incentive to stabilize the aforementioned Chinese macroeconomic imbalances. The main intention of the initiative is to enhance cooperation between participating countries with the aim to foster their growth. The cooperation has many potential dimensions such as political dialogue, infrastructure development, trade, and interpersonal relations between people (see Sect. 4.1). It is likely that the cooperation will stimulate economic growth and bring other benefits for all the countries involved in the project (Kostecka-Tomaszewska 2018, p. 174). Very important added value of the initiative is that it has a broad dimension and is able to combine together the internal and external (international) factors, impacting on the economy. The international approach of the project is treated as an 'upgraded' version of China's Go Global strategy. The main role of BRI is to become an important vehicle shaped to develop the reforms intended to deepen further the Chinese global footprint (Yu 2018).

References

Bowman, J., Hack, M., & Waring, M. (2018, March). *Non-bank Financing in China*. Reserve Bank of Australia Bulletin.

Cai, F., Garnaut, R., & Song, L. (2018). *China's 40 Years of Reform and Development: How Reform Captured China's Demographic Dividend*. Canberra: Australian National University Press.

Cai, P. (2017, March). *Understanding China's Belt and Road Initiative*. Sydney: Lowy Institute for International Policy.

Chen, C. C. H. (2018). *ASEAN Financial Integration and the Belt and Road Initiative: Legal Challenges and Opportunities for China in Southeast Asia*. In Z. Yun (Ed.), *International Governance and the Rule of Law in China Under the Belt and Road Initiative*. Cambridge: Cambridge University Press.

Chen, S., & Kang, J. S. (2018, January). *Credit Booms—Is China Different?* (IMF Working Paper, WP/18/2).

Chen, S., & Wu, N. (2015, October 7). *China Banking Sector*. DBS Group Research.

Cheng, S. W. (2015, September 28). Overcapacity a Time Bomb for China's Economy. *South China Morning Post*.

Chien, J., & Randall, D. (2018). *Key Lessons for Policymakers form China's Financial Inclusion Experience*. The World Bank.

China Daily. (2017, April 26). *China Moves to Deleverage Without Destabilizing Growth*.

Chow, G. (2018). China's Economic Transformation. In F. Cai et al. (Eds.), *China's 40 Years of Reform and Development: 1978–2018*. Acton: ANU Press.

Cowen, T. (2017). *The Rise and Fall of the Chinese Economy*. YouTube.

D'Amico, N. (2015, March). *Corruption and Economic Growth in China: An Empirical Analysis*.

Du, Y., & Yang, C. (2015). Demographic Transition and Labour Market Changes: Implications for Economic Development in China. In I. Claus & L. Oxley (Eds.), *China's Economy: A Collection of Surveys*. Chichester, West Sussex: Wiley Blackwell.

Eckert, J. (2016, June 23). *8 Things You Need to Know About China's Economy*. World Economic Forum.

Fan, D. (2016, October 18). Reflecting on Deng Xiaoping's 'Cat Theory' of Economic Reform. *The Epoch Times*.

Fidrmuc, J., & Huang, S. (2013). *Unemployment, Growth and Speed of Transition in China* (CESifo Working Paper Series No. 4410).

Gao, C. (2017, December 2). China, US Fight Over China's Market Economy Status. *The Diplomat*.

Glawe, L., & Wagner, H. (2019). China in the Middle-Income Trap? *China Economic Review*. https://doi.org/10.1016/j.chieco.2019.01.003.

Griswold, D. (2019, April 2). Is China a Non-market Economy? *The Bridge*. Mercatus Center George Mason University.

Hornby, L., & Zhang, A. (2017, December 4). China Hit by Gas Shortages as It Moves Away from Coal. *Financial Times*.

Huang, Y. (2017). *Cracking the Chinese Conundrum: Why Conventional Economic Wisdom Is Wrong*. Oxford: Oxford University Press.

Jin, J., Andersson, H., & Zhang, S. (2016). Air Pollution Control Policies in China: A Retrospective and Prospects. *International Journal of Environmental Research and Public Health, 12*(12), 1–22.

Johnson, K. (2018, February 2). Why Is China Buying Up Europe's Ports? *Foreign Policy*.

Kostecka-Tomaszewska, L. (2018). Economic Security of China: The Implications of the Belt and Road Initiative. *Optimum. Economic Studies, 4*(94), 166–182.

Lam, P. (2005). Energy in China: Development and Prospects. *China Perspectives, 59*, 14–25.

Lee, A. K. (2015). *China's Economy: The Hidden Truths—China's Economy Seen in the Undercurrent of Organized Unaccountability*. Global Era Public Interest Info Network.

Lee, I. H., Qingjun, X., & Syed, M. (2013, March). *China's Demography and Its Implications* (IMF Working Paper, WP/13/82).

Leonard, M. (2008). *What Does China Think?* London: Fourth Estate.

Li, Y. (2018). The Greater Euroasian Partnership and the Belt and Road Initiative: Can the Two Be Limited? *Journal of Euroasian Studies, 9*(2), 94–99.

Luo, B. (2015). China Will Get Rich Before It Grows Old: Beijing's Demographic Problems Are Overrated. *Foreign Affairs, 94*(3), 19–24.

Mehran H., Quintyn, M., Nordman, T., & Laurens, B. (1996). *Monetary and Exchange System Reform in China: An Experiment in Gradualism* (International Monetary Fund Occasional Paper, 141, 2).

Morrison, W. M. (2018, February 5). *China's Economic Rise: History, Trends, Challenges, and Implications for the United States*. Congressional Research Service 7-5700. www.crs.gov. RL33534.

Nan, Z., & Shuiyu, J. (2019, March 11). Reforms to Put SOEs in Key Role for Initiative. *China Daily*.

Ning, Z. (2018, June 13). Is China's Growth Model a Threat to Free-Market Economics? *The Economist*.

Perkins, D. H. (2018). The Complex Task of Evaluating China's Economic Reforms, Chapter 8. In R. Garnaut, L. Song, & C. Fang (Eds.), *China's 40 Years of Reform and Development: 1978–2018*. Canberra: ANU Press, The Australian National University.

Pradier, P. (2018, June 22). *The Chinese Hukou System Explained—What Is "Hukou" and How It Works*. New Horizons Global Partners.

Quinglian, H. (2018, October 22). China's Growing Unemployment Crisis. *The Epoch Times*.

Ren, B., & Chao, X. (2018). How Does the Urban–Rural Income Gap Affects the Quality of China's Economic Growth? *China Political Economy, 1*(1), 136–148.

Ross, J. (2013, May 7). *The Truth About China, Statistically Speaking*. www.china.org.cn.

Shazada, R. (2019, March 7). Communism Is Returning to China. *Daily Times*.

Shek, C. (2019, May 23). Aiming for the Top: Can China Escape the Middle Income Trap? *CKGSB Knowledge Magazine.*

Sheng, A., Edelmann, C., Sheng, C., & Hu, J. (2015). *Bringing Light upon the Shadow: A Review of the Chinese Shadow Banking Sector.* Hong Kong: Oliver Wyman and Fung Global Institute.

Sheng, A., & Soon, N. C. (2016). *Shadow Banking in China: An Opportunity for Financial Reform* (pp. 98–99). Cornwall: Wiley.

Shi, L. (2008). *Rural Migrant Workers in China: Scenario, Challenges and Public Policy* (Working Paper No. 89). Geneva: Policy Integration and Statistics Department, International Labor Office.

Shi, L. (2016). Recent Changes in Income Inequality in China. In *World Social Science Report: Challenging Inequalities, Pathways to a Just World.* Paris: UNESCO.

Shih, V. (2017, October 20). *Financial Instability in China: Possible Pathways and Their Likelihood.* Berlin: Mercator Institute for China Studies.

Song, L. (2018). *The Past, Present and Future of SOE Reform in China.* Canberra: Australian National University.

Tan, K. H., Ji, G., Chung, L., Wang, C.-H., Chiu, A., & Tseng, M. L. (2019). Riding the Wave of Belt and Road Initiative in Servitization: Lessons from China. *International Journal of Production Economics, 211,* 15–21.

Tan, Y. (2014). *Performance Risk and Competition in the Chinese Banking Industry* (p. 9). New York: Chandos Publishing.

Tang, X., McLellan, B., Snowden, S., Zhang, B., & Höök, M. (2015). Dilemmas for China: Energy, Economy and Environment. *Sustainability, 7,* 5508–5520. https://doi.org/10.3390/su7055508.

Taylor, T. (2019). http://conversableeconomist.blogspot.com/2019/02/chinas-high-savings-rate.html. Accessed 30 May 2019.

The Economist. (2000, December 21). *Go West, Young Han.*

The Economist. (2011, April 28). *Chinese Property and Investment: More on the Chinese Bubble Issue, by Buttonwood.*

The Economist. (2015, March 12). *A Tightening Grip.*

The Economist. (2019, April 20). *China's GDP: Growth in Train.*

The State Council Information Office of the People's Republic of China. (2018, June). *China and the World Trade Organization.*

Urban China. (2014). *Toward Efficient, Inclusive and Sustainable Urbanization.* Washington, DC: The World Bank Group.

van der Linden, R. W. H. (2010). Bank Strategy, Governance and Ratings, Chapter 12. In P. Molyneux (Ed.), *Palgrave Macmillan Studies in Banking and Financial Institutions.* London: Palgrave Macmillan.

van der Linden, R. W. H. (2013). Bank Performance, Risk and Securitisation, Chapter 11. In J. Falzon (Ed.), *Palgrave Macmillan Studies in Banking and Financial Institutions.* London: Palgrave Macmillan.

van der Linden, R. W. H. (2015). Lending, Investments and the Financial Crisis, Chapter 5. In E. Beccalli & F. Poli (Eds.), *Palgrave Macmillan Studies in Banking and Financial Institutions*. London: Palgrave Macmillan.

Vörös, Z. (2010). EU–China Relations: "Race" for Raw Materials. In Á. Tuka & I. Tarrósy (Eds.), *Borderless Europe: Challenges–Opportunities* (pp. 91–101). Pecs: Publikon Kiado.

Wang, Y., & You, J. (2012). Corruption and Firm Growth: Evidence from China. *China Economic Review, 232*(2), 415–433.

Wei, Z., Song, X., & Wang, D. (2017). Manufacturing Flexibility, Business Model Design, and Firm Performance. *International Journal of Production Economics, 193*, 87–97.

Weidou, N. (2007). China's Energy—Challenges and Strategies. *Frontiers of Energy Power Engineering in China, 1*(1), 1–8.

Weinland, D. (2019, January 23). China Bad Debt Disposals Hit Levels Not Seen for 20 Years. *Financial Times*.

Wildeau G. (2017, October 26). China Backs Away from Long-Term GDP Targets. *Financial Times*.

Wu, J., & Ma, G. (2016, May). *Whither China? Restarting the Reform Agenda*. University Oxford Scholarship Online.

Xing, C., Yang, P., & Li, Z. (2018, October). The Medium-Run Effect of China's Higher Education Expansion on the Unemployment of College Graduates. *China Economic Review, 51*, 181–193.

Yu, J. (2018). *The Belt and Road Initiative: Domestic Interests, Bureaucratic Politics and the EU–China Relations*. LSE Research Online. http://eprints.lse.ac.uk. Accessed 14 Apr 2019.

CHAPTER 3

China's New Style of Globalization as a Route to a More Sustainable Growth Path

Abstract This chapter describes the foundation for a new type of globalization whereby China positions itself in the center with BRI as the major infrastructural project. Finally, this should lead to a transition toward a more developed economy. In this chapter, the current trade war, i.e. the ongoing trade conflict between China and USA and related increase of inbound and outbound investments are explained to show the impact of China on the world economy and the changing role of the Chinese companies from global manufacturers to global investors. Since Chinese private-owned enterprises currently account for half of the China's outbound FDIs, the number and size of private-owned enterprises are growing and an increasing number of them are also joining hands with state-owned enterprises to expand globally. As a global player in terms of trade and investments, China's monetary and foreign exchange policy is playing a more significant role in the world as well with the largest stock of foreign exchange reserves and a currency listed on the IMF's reserve basket. China's new style of globalization is also described in a policy trilemma context. Although China never abandoned all its capital controls, there were numerous ways to move money into and out of China. At the same time, the RMB has started to float more against the USD and liberalized its interest rates without too much impact on the exchange rate. Thus, the policy makers made the argument that China negotiated between the three choices and in essence circumvented the logic of the impossible trinity. With the rise of China's shadow

P. Łasak and R. W. H. van der Linden, *The Financial Implications of China's Belt and Road Initiative*,
https://doi.org/10.1007/978-3-030-30118-7_3

banking since the global financial crisis and the desire for more RMB internationalization since the late 2000s, the increasing financial liberalization is at odds with the striving for more financial stability. The significant costs associated with the credit crisis added financial stability to the policy trilemma policy goals, modifying its framework into the policy quadrilemma. China and other emerging markets frequently coupled their growing financial integration with sizable hoarding of reserves, as a means of self-insuring their growing exposure to financial turbulences. Also, the impact of the BRI in the policy trilemma or quadrilemma is examined. China's new style of globalization to a more sustainable growth model is eventually described as the main feature of China's 'new normal' economy and as a way to avoid a 'middle-income trap' in the near future.

Keywords New type of globalization · Sustainable growth path · Inbound and outbound investments · Foreign exchange reserves · IMF's reserve basket · Impossible trinity · Policy trilemma and policy quadrilemma · RMB internationalization · 'New normal' economy · 'Middle-income trap'

3.1 China's Role in the Global Trading System

The contemporary economic globalization defines an unprecedented period in the postwar history. It has begun in the 1980s and the international trade constitutes the first phase of the process begun. Since the very beginning of the growth of international trade, apart from the flow of capital, changes in production systems and creation of global value chains have become one of the core elements of the globalization process including the reduction of (non)-tariff barriers. As a result, increasing trade liberalization, multilateral trade negotiations, and preferential regional trade arrangements have led to a more open global trading environment. In 1992, with his slogan 'getting rich is glorious', Deng Xiaoping provided an incentive to integrate China more into the world economy. The country was going through different stages and finally achieved its current status, becoming an important player in the current global trading system. Investment flows, technology transfer, and spread of knowledge were important factors which fostered the whole process. A key moment was the Chinese accession to the WTO in 2001 (see Sect. 2.1) which accelerated domestic reforms, lifted investor's

Table 3.1 Top trading countries by value and world share in world merchandise trade 2017 (excluding intra-EU trade)

Rank	*Exporters*	*USD bln*	*Share*	*Rank*	*Importers*	*USD bln*	*Share*
1.	China	2263	16.2	1.	USA	2410	16.9
2.	EU (28)	2122	15.2	2.	EU (28)	2097	14.7
3.	USA	1547	11.1	3.	China	1842	12.9
4.	Japan	698	5.0	4.	Japan	672	4.7
5.	Republic of Korea	574	4.1	5.	Hong Kong (China)	590	4.1

Source World Trade Statistical Review (2018), WTO

confidence to the economy and created new opportunities to the Chinese export. China was not only the major beneficiary of the globalization process, but also an active player, having a high impact on the global economy. Looking from today's perspective, it might be stated that China has enhanced its global interdependence to a degree never seen before (Drysdale and Hardwick 2018, p. 545). Apart from the high share in the global production chains, China has become an important trading partner for many other countries. The foregoing economic development of China is based on the export-oriented strategy adopted at the end of the 1990s. As Table 3.1 shows, China is the largest exporter and third largest importer in the world (China's export has a large import content) in comparison with the EU (28) as a trading bloc and the second largest importer after Germany in comparison with the individual EU countries. As separate countries, China and the USA are the world's largest exporter and importer, respectively, which partly clarifies the huge impact of the current trade conflict on the global economy.

Figure 3.1 shows the corresponding increase in China's export and import from the 2000s as a percentage of total world export and import, giving it an increasingly pivotal role in production and consumption decisions in other countries.

One of the most important advantages, assuring the leading export position for the economy are the investments in massive and integrated supply chain infrastructure which will make the Chinese companies faster and more reliable to foreign companies. The share of China's commercial services in trade has also risen sharply in recent years with the surplus in trade in goods partly offset by an increasing deficit in services trade

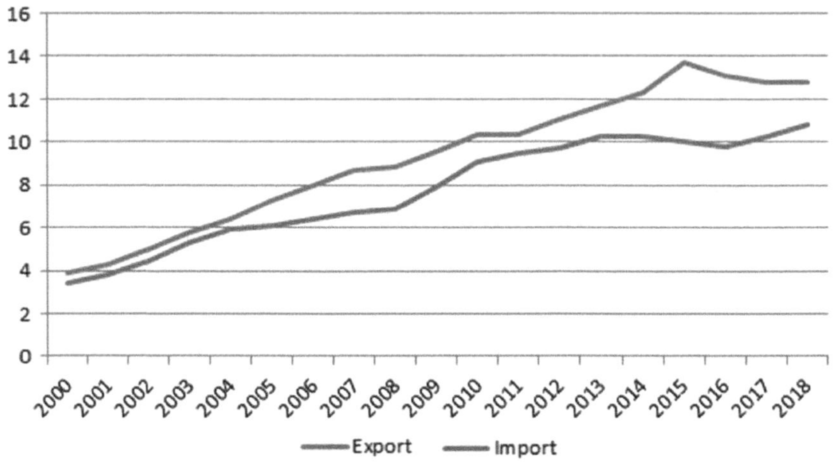

Fig. 3.1 Percentage of Chinese export and import of total world export and import (*Source* Own calculations based on UNCTAD statistics [accessed: 25.05.2019])

(see Fig. 3.2). This is mainly due to the enormous increase in China's tourism abroad. Over the past decade, the Chinese have been traveling more and more, with an estimated fivefold growth rate (*The Economist* 2019a).

Among the key dimensions of the foregoing Chinese economic development and expected position of the country in the future trade might be enumerated the following aspects:

- development of regional trade relations;
- the growing position as the major global exporter and importer;
- the main contributor to global trade imbalances;
- international trade conflicts.

Regionalization is the other significant process, which apart from globalization played an important role in the context of the Chinese international trade development. Even more, the process of regionalization has become a mechanism leading to linking the Chinese economy with the global economy. The Asian economic cooperation, especially the Asia-Pacific Economic Cooperation (APEC), fostered the internationalization of the economy. Since the beginning of the 1990s APEC becomes the main international

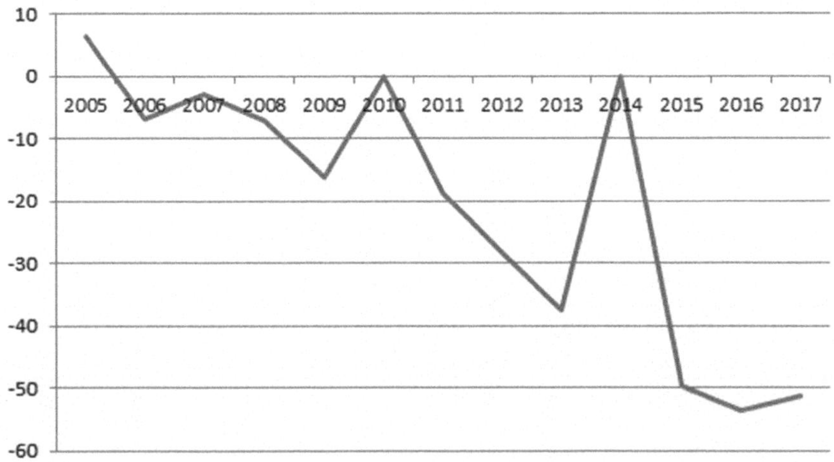

Fig. 3.2 Percentage of Chinese import of total world import of services (*Source* Own calculations based on UNCTAD statistics [accessed: 25.05.2019])

forum, facilitating China's liberalization (Drysdale and Hardwick 2018, p. 552). The cooperation with APEC was shaping China's path to the WTO accession. It has accelerated domestic reforms, lifted investor's confidence to the economy and created new opportunities to the Chinese export. Currently, China's production process is deeply integrated into Asian value chains and, together with other Asian countries, forms an integral part of supply chains that support economic growth in the region. It plays an important role as significant source of demand, especially for many Asian economies and commodity exporters (Dieppe et al. 2018, p. 38). The growing significance of the whole region is also visible during the US-China trade war which the US government started in 2018. As a result, the Chinese manufacturers, motivated by the growing tariffs imposed by the USA on Chinese products, relocate their production to the neighbouring countries (e.g. Cambodia, Thailand or Vietnam) (He 2019).

The prominent role of China in the international trade not only exerts a great impact on the development of the Chinese economy, but impacts the whole global economy as well. As a net-exporter, China has a high savings ratio, which has helped to build up large current account surpluses and, consequently, an accumulation of strong foreign exchange reserves (see Fig. 3.3). This boosted the economic development and created a buffer for unexpected international capital outflows, but it adversely

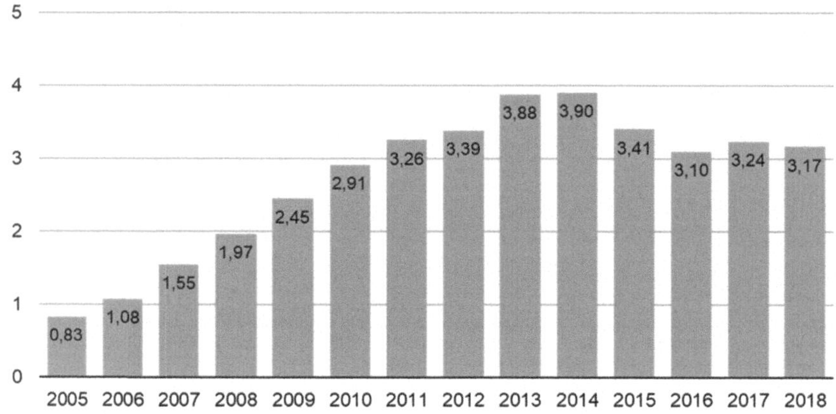

Fig. 3.3 China's foreign exchange reserves 2005–2018 (bln USD) (*Source* Adapted from World Bank database)

affected deficit countries, especially the USA, and can be treated as one of the causes of the global trade imbalances. It is also considered to be one of the reasons for the decline of Western manufacturing and the inflow of the excess savings to the US bond markets that fueled the subprime housing bubble. Although China is still a net-exporter, the current account surplus is decreasing and may even become a deficit in 2019 for the first time since 1993. This could mean that China is switching from a net-lender to a net-borrower to the world, which means it should gradually raise more foreign capital and liberalize its financial system (*The Economist* 2019a).

As China plays a crucial role in international trade, it is also considered as one of the most important players in international trade disputes. Some competitors such as the USA submit the arguments that nowadays China is moving away from the WTO principles in the sense, that it uses the trade policy for fulfilling its internal economic goals irregardless of the universal international trade values. The current US government in particular is accusing China's state capitalism which makes it a bad player in the global trading system. These accusations mainly concern the fact that China has remained wedded to the central planned industrial policies, supports SOEs and develops and protects the high-tech branches of industry. The country is being accused by the USA for an unfair approach in trade relations and the pointed issues, like intellectual property theft, subsidizing SOEs or forced technology transfers, are one of the most often highlighted disputed areas. Irrespective of the fact, that the Chinese trade surplus slowly becomes smaller, there is an active international debate about the growing risk of the trade war, in which China will play a crucial role. Particular attention is given to the complexity of the international economic relations and interdependencies. The main argument is that it does not regard only the trade, but also aspects such as flows of cash, people, and technology. The Chinese steps met with a deep concern in many Western countries. They highlight that the current Chinese industrial policy (especially based on the 'Made in China 2025' plan) poses a great threat to other economies. They emphasize that in the center of the plan is not only the ambition to make the Chinese economy a global high-tech manufacturing hub, but it is being implemented in an unfair way because of government subsidies, mobilization of SOEs, and the pursuit of acquisitions of IPRs (McBride and Chatzky 2019).

The recent US–China trade conflict has drawn growing attention and concern over its possible impact on the global economy, given that both countries are the world's two largest economies, accounting for about 40% of the global economy and over 22% of the world's export of goods. Chinese goods exported to the USA were mainly consumer and manufactured goods (e.g., computer equipment, toys, games, and apparel), while USA goods exported to China were mainly capital and intermediate goods (e.g., aerospace products, oil seeds, and soybeans). The existence of a trade deficit with China in goods has over the years been the concern of the USA. This is one of the reasons to restrict trade with China which earns cash from other countries and then did not spend it. This so-called global saving glut makes China's trade surplus the mirror image of the US trade deficits. Another argument from the US government to restrict trade with China is that the surge in Chinese imports had led to more unemployment in declining industries in the manufacturing sector such as the US steel, car, and shipping industry. Several studies have recently been published about this so-called China shock on US blue-collar workers which are inconclusive about the significance of this effect. However, a counter-argument is that increased trade ties with China had also brought number of benefits to the US economy, for instance by enabling US companies to tap into the Chinese market with a lucrative customer base and to offer lower prices of consumer goods through low-cost production. Despite trade negotiations between China and the USA since the beginning of 2017, the USA has nevertheless initiated announcements on all kinds of trade restricting measures in 2018 that affect China and other trading partners such as Canada, Mexico, and the EU as well. The USA has taken actions against China on the following three fronts, namely tariff increases on major goods import from China including those related to the 'Made in China 2025' program; WTO dispute settlements with respect to certain measures pertaining to the protection of IPRs and specific investment restrictions; and enhanced export controls for Chinese persons and entities related to the acquisition of industrially significant technology to protect national security. Obviously, this led to announcement of several counter trade measures imposed by China. This trade war has been escalated since the USA and China introduced new import duties on October 1, 2018, at 200 billion USD in Chinese goods and 60 billion USD in the US products, respectively, including threats of an increase in tariffs of 10–25%. Amid the trade conflict with China, the USA has also imposed punitive tariffs on products imported from the other major trading partners, including Canada, Mexico, and EU. These countries (and EU region) have responded by imposing retaliation tariffs on US goods. These 'tit-for-tat' actions have aroused concerns of some stakeholders in the USA, worrying that on the one hand US consumers and businesses will have to pay more for commonly used imported products and materials, while on the other hand US exported goods will become more expensive, resulting in sales loss and unemployment (Tiffany and Chung 2018). The USA and China have agreed to a temporary truce to de-escalate trade tensions at the G20 Summit in Buenos Aires on December 1, 2018. According to the agreement, both the USA and China decided to refrain from increasing tariffs or imposing new tariffs for 90 days (until March 1, 2019), as the two sides work toward a larger trade deal (Wong and Koty 2018). Although a trade deal and hence more equal competitive conditions would surely promote economic growth and better protect IPRs since March 2019, the US–China trade conflict is still going on. Both countries announced to impose new trade tariffs from September 2019—respectively: the USA additional 10% tariff on 300 billion USD goods and services coming from China, and China announced to impose retaliatory tariffs on 75 billion USD worth goods coming from the USA. Meantime the trade talks between both countries are continued and the situation is developing very rapidly.

The Chinese trade is strictly interconnected with the international situation and the government plans. The Chinese government is striving for a rebalance of the economy by shifting it from investment and export toward internal processes, especially consumption and services (see 'supply-side structural reforms' in Sect. 5.4). The main reason is the raising concerns that the economy is overinvested. The investments in the past were very often based on the indebtedness in the non-financial sector, what means that the rebalancing is necessary. The gradual rebalancing from investment toward consumption and the service sector has an impact on the trade situation. Weakening export impacts on the slower import growth, what exerts an effect on the Chinese trading partners (Dieppe et al. 2018, pp. 14–15). Simultaneously, the international situation and the current position of China in the global trade offers for the country an opportunity to step forward and further strengthen its position on that level. The USA via its President Trump reduces its leadership role, the EU has its own internal economic problems, so China emerges as the leader of the world trade. The support for WTO and the global trade system is very important for China, as its economic development is still largely based on the export (Davis 2018). The current development in international trade is a threat not only to the Chinese economy, but also to the entire world trade order. It is essential to avoid a corresponding economic downturn as during the Great Depression of which was partly caused by protectionism. With the rise of US protectionism and China's new style of globalization, the momentum has come to use the BRI to increase China's role in the global trading system.

3.2 China's Development of Inward and Outward Investments

The growth of Chinese trade has a huge impact on its investment trend in the country. China's global FDI inflows grew rapidly after it began to liberalize its trade regime since the launch of the 'open door' policy in 1979 and the accession to the WTO in 2001. Although China's inbound or inward FDIs are still rising and are not becoming less attractive to multinationals after the GFC, the outbound or outward FDIs have increased even more substantially over the past decade since Chinese firms are increasingly going abroad looking for brands, talent, and technology to bring back to the Chinese market. China's outward FDIs is largely concentrated in Asia, although investment has increased significantly in Latin America, Africa, and the EU over the past decade. In 2015, China's outbound has surpassed its inbound investment flows changing the role of the Chinese companies from global manufacturers to global investors (see Fig. 3.4). In line with the ongoing liberalization strategy, the focus of China's outward FDI is shifting from natural resources to high-tech- and consumption-driven sectors. Since Chinese

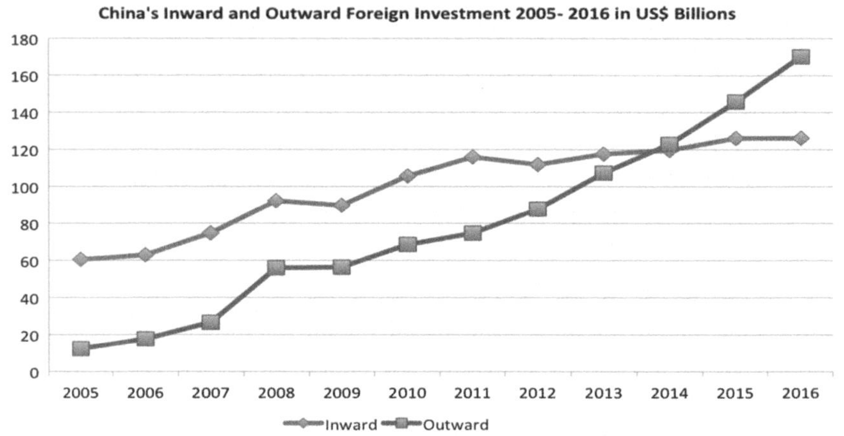

Fig. 3.4 China's inward and outward foreign investments (2005–2016) in bln USD (*Source* Adapted from National Bureau of Statistics, China, various years, 2019)

POEs currently account for half of China's outward FDIs, the number and size of POEs are also growing and an increasing number of them are also joining hands with SOEs to expand globally (Ernst & Young 2015).

As part of China's Go Global strategy, the government mobilized its policy banks, mainly China Development Bank and the Export–Import Bank of China, to enable outgoing capital flows. These banks increasingly support the foreign investments of Chinese companies, as well as mergers and acquisitions of foreign companies. From 2010, these state-owned policy banks have become very active in development finance, which gave China more opportunities to manage environmental and social risks associated with these investments during this decade. Furthermore, with the arrival of the BRI China has gained additional influence in development finance through the creation of the NDB, AIIB, and the Silk Road Fund (see Sect. 4.2).

There are several factors which have largely driven the sharp increase in China's outward investments since the late 2000s. First, the Go Global strategy is mainly driven by China's massive accumulation of foreign reserves from which a significant level has been invested in relatively safe, but low-yielding assets, such as US Treasury securities. Through investments in foreign companies, or acquiring them, the government wants to use FDIs to gain access to IPRs, technology, know-how, management skills, and world-famous brands in order to move Chinese firms (especially SOEs) up along the value chain in manufacturing and services, boost domestic innovation and development of their own brands, and help them to become major global competitors. Thus, Western countries with advanced technologies, stable economies, and healthy investment environments continue to be the most popular investment destinations. Second, China's slowing economy and rising labor costs have also encouraged greater Chinese overseas FDIs in order to help firms diversify risk and expand business opportunities beyond the domestic market, and, in some cases, to relocate less competitive firms from China to low-cost countries. Third is to obtain natural resources, such as oil and minerals, deemed by the government as necessary to sustain China's rapid economic growth. Fourth, increased FDI outflows may be the result of the Chinese government attempting to diversify its foreign exchange reserve holdings. Until recently, it appears that a large share of China's foreign reserves have gone to portfolio investments, especially US Treasury securities, which are relatively safe and liquid, but earn relatively small returns (Morrison 2018).

The increase in China's outward investments, which partly has been stimulated by the BRI, has been raising the question for a number of years why China is investing so much in other countries instead of developing its own internal infrastructure. There are various reasons for this. Firstly, its own industrial overcapacity can be digested in this way; secondly, China has an 'overemployment' problem that can be used relatively easily in this way in foreign construction projects to keep the surplus number of construction workers against unemployment. After all, the Chinese construction sector is largely owned by the government, so it is their responsibility to look after these employees. Thirdly, there are more and more industries with a saturated domestic market, whereby Chinese manufacturers try to sell cheap 'Made in China' products to mostly poorer surrounding, whether or not, BRI recipient countries where there is still market potential for this. However, partly through the enormous flow of inward investment of the last two decades, China is also developing its own internal infrastructure. For instance, this is reflected in the large number of bridges built to connect rural areas with urban areas. Also, although sometimes somewhat controversial, many dams have been built for local people to take advantage of natural resources and to prevent natural disasters. Another example is the Shanghai metro system with 15 lines and around 700 km which started out of nothing about 25 years ago and has now grown to become the world's longest metro network. The city recently unveiled plans for another 300 km as part of national pressure to boost infrastructure spending by 'digging deep for more growth.' Perhaps the most impressive domestic push is the network of high-speed railways (HSR) which accounts for around two-thirds of the world's HSRs in commercial services, the most extensively used HSR network built in almost one decade and the world's longest with an average of 3600 km annually over the past five years (*The Economist* 2019b).

Since the launch of BRI in 2013, China's outbound investments in recipient BRI countries have been mainly focused on construction and greenfield investments, while in non-BRI countries the emphasis is more on mergers and acquisitions (Chen and Kang 2018). It is likely that the BRI will enable businesses to access more diversified and emerging markets, which will provide impetus for the economic development of BRI countries. Chinese outbound capital restrictions appear to be more likely to be approved for OBOR-related transactions at the expense of non-OBOR outbound deals for foreign real estate for instance. The OBOR's emphasis on infrastructure has helped boost Chinese exports of construction-related goods and services. To what extent BRI-boosted outbound investments and the associated transportation corridors mature into economic corridors, depends on the effectiveness of its implementation. Chinese capital controls, while favoring outbound investment for OBOR-related projects, are still inefficient and overly restrictive for inbound investments. In addition to the financial-economic motives, the BRI aims for more exchange of ideas and knowledge are at odds with the current increase in nationalism and censorship in China. These current trends in China all contradict the BRI's expressed goal of improving global connectivity. In order to reduce the gap between the slowdown in inbound and significant increase in outbound investments, the government has already taken measures at the end of 2017 to ease restrictions on inbound FDIs and to regulate outbound FDIs. In the end, Beijing's dilemma is that greater connectivity fueled by BRI requires giving up some control (Hillman 2018). The Chinese authorities will always have to balance between, on the one hand, market liberalization stimulated by BRI and, on the other hand, social stability through government control. From the start of economic reforms in 1979, this meant in practice that the reins were sometimes tightened, while at other times they were released again or, in another metaphor, sometimes the oyster gradually opened and on other moments it closed again.

3.2.1 China's Foreign Exchange and Monetary Policy in a Global Context

The rapid growth of the Chinese economy was based on the monetary policy and exchange rate regimes which became the crucial aspects fostering the growth. From the postwar period, three periods with a different exchange rate system can be distinguished, namely the period of 'recovery and management economy' (between the end of the 1940s and the 1980s); that of the 'transition period of the economy' (1981–1993) and the period of the 'market mechanism' (1994–present). Although different phases and different approaches to exchange rate policy can be distinguished, this policy has always been rather evolutionary instead of revolutionary in nature. With the exchange rate regime to be determined, it always meant economic growth as the main objective of the policy with possible subordinate exchange rate adjustments if necessary.

During the first postwar period, China has a fixed exchange rate regime. The country was closed and did not develop its trade relations with other countries. This autarkic economy with a high level of regulatory constraints highly relied on self-sufficiency. The Chinese central government played a crucial role in setting the exchange rate and in many other aspects related to the economy (Gloria 2014). The RMB was kept overvalued to the other currencies. This approach has some advantages; for instance, it enabled import of machines and high-technology products, necessary for industrialization of the economy.

In contrast to the former autarkic period, the role of the exchange rate became a more important factor in the new mercantilist period under Deng which fostered the rapid economic development. There were set two crucial goals for the exchange rate policy in the country, namely to provide employment and to develop the industry. Such motives led to the loosening of foreign exchange controls which became very beneficial for Chinese exporters. The authorities adopted a dual exchange rate system—the official exchange rate and internal settlement rate (ISR). Through the official exchange rate, China has kept a fixed exchange rate of its currency, while the ISR was adopted to apply the truly neoliberal approach and to keep the currency on an undervalued level to make the Chinese export more attractive. In this way, the ISR enabled to maintain stability in the domestic economy by promoting export. Despite the dual exchange rate system, the government was determined to intervene in the currency, as it was doing in the previous approach. There was, however, a tendency for a small adjustment of the currency to the real (market) value. Finally, in 1985 the values of the two exchange rates merged, the ISR was abolished and the exchange rate system returned to a single currency system. In this stage, the market mechanisms were promoted by the CPC and the single currency system led the Chinese economy toward neoliberal economic principles. The government was determined to promote free trade and the exchange rate needed to be adjusted to the demand and supply forces (Gloria 2014). Moreover, the domestic banks were engaged in the sterilization operations[1] which limited their activity on the commercial market and undermined not only the typical banking activity, but also distorted the market mechanisms and impacted on the supply of money for the business. It stems from the fact that such instruments, like open market operations and reserve requirement ratio were adopted to sterilize the growth of RMB supply (as a result of foreign currency purchase and to absorb excessive liquidity in the banking system). Sometimes such operations are against the market trend and determine the needs of the real economy.

Since 1994, the 'economy transition period' has finished, and China entered into the 'market mechanism period' with less regulatory constraints. It means that the economy was under greater market pressure, although this was not applied to the same extent for the exchange rate system. The currency system during the 'market mechanism period' might be divided into two shorter parts, namely the period between 1994 and 2004, and the period since 2005 ongoing. The main cause of the first decade (1994–2004) is the consequences of the Asian financial crisis in 1997 whereby the RMB exchange rate was kept stable in order to break competitive devaluations of Asian currencies. At the time of the Asian crisis, China's authorities adopted fixed nominal exchange rate with the RMB fixed to the USD (the RMB was pegged to the USD at a rate of around 8.28) (Zheng et al. 2007). During these ten years, the cumulative nominal change of the RMB against the dollar has

[1] The sterilization operations involve the purchase or sale of financial assets by a central bank to offset the effect of foreign exchange interventions to limit the effect of inflows and outflows of capital on the money supply.

changed by less than 10% (Goldstein and Lardy 2008, p. 2).[2] Such policy posed some important challenges for the monetary authorities, as they had to keep the balance of the liquidity on the domestic money market (i.e., they applied the sterilization to open market operations to control the growth of the domestic liquidity in the banking and financial market) to prevent inflation. There is, however, a dilemma in this regard, since in the short term a better balance is achieved on the domestic money and currency market through sterilization operations, while at the same time greater currency flexibility is needed to mitigate the risks of macro-economic instability. Although sterilization as a monetary instrument is necessary to maintain the fixed exchange rate policy, there are also draw-backs to use this tool through the disruption of the interest and price mechanism. By keeping the exchange rate at an artificially low level the PBC (by selling RMB in exchange for foreign currencies) indirectly affected a lower level of interest rates which could lead to a higher financial risk and the possibility to create an asset bubble. Furthermore, the higher reserves of foreign currency are related to a higher risk of capital losses when the RMB will appreciate to achieve its optimum since the appreciation of the domestic currency will cause the relative depreciation of the foreign currencies held as monetary reserves.

China's exchange rate policy has important implications for the country's internal and external economic adjustments. Concerning the internal situation, it is argued that the flexible exchange rate is necessary to deliver an effective monetary policy. The continuation of the fixed exchange rate would lead to a distortional policy (financial repression and relatively closed capital account). In broader terms, it might lead to some other costs like keeping the real rate of return for savers on a very low level, provide cheap credit for inefficient SOEs and pose a higher risk that might lead to asset price bubbles. In the context of the external situation, the RMB revaluation or appreciation might lead to a reduction of China's net-export (i.e., a fall of the current account surplus) or at least constrain foregoing competitive advantages of the economy. It is important to reduce China's external imbalance and in this way reduce the global imbalances. It means that the stronger RMB should contribute to the global payments' imbalances reduction.

[2] It is officially argued that China suspended its 'dual exchange rate system' and implemented the fixed exchange rate since January 1, 1994, however, in fact the authorities adjusted the exchange rate continuously till October 1997.

The whole period between 1978 and 2005 is defined as the 'External Liberalization and Foreign Exchange Management System.' During this period, the Chinese authorities applied a comprehensive system of foreign exchange management. It enabled to govern foreign exchange receipts and payments, purchase and sales, borrowing and lending, facilitate cross-border transfers, international settlements, and organize the foreign exchange market. The restrictive control measures were intended to mitigate the risks for the economy, e.g., maintain the equilibrium of the balance of payments, keeping the independence of the monetary policy and prevent firms and financial institutions from taking excessive external risks (Zhao 2006, p. 8). The exchange rate policy was very important because in the Chinese circumstances the government had limited indirect tools to manage the business cycle and the private business and banks had a lack of capacity to manage the foreign exchange and financial risks.

The biggest problem in the 1990s and the first decade of twenty-first century was the undervalued RMB. China used the exchange rate policy together with the reform of the foreign trade system in the country as the main mechanisms fostering the growth of the economy. Such undervalued RMB was kept by the Chinese government up to the end of 2004. Despite some analysts argue that the Chinese government was focused on fostering the export competitiveness, during the whole time China has tried to realize a broad set of goals. The authorities focused on both internal and external targets such as macroeconomic performance, social development, international income and expenditure, progress of financial market reform, economic growth and employment, foreign trade, and business situation (Gujon and Guérineau 2006). Among the most important aspects were to keep the internal and external equilibrium of the exchange rate. The internal equilibrium is oriented on keeping macroeconomic balance with the intention to fulfill the highest possible employment. The authorities were concerned that the RMB revaluation will impact negatively on China's export and hence the economic growth and worsen the employment situation. The other crucial pressure was on the foreign investments. Revaluation might increase investment costs for foreign firms and discourage the investors. All these causes might have a rather short-term impact, but they were very important for the country's development. The external equilibrium goal was to maintain a sustainable current account and clear the balance of payments. The selected level of exchange rate helps to keep the stability of foreign exchange reserve, trade balance and the inflation on the modest level. A more flexible exchange rate regime helps to mitigate impacts of external shocks and the possibility of a currency crisis.

Over time the RMB exchange rate became a very important issue in international macroeconomics. It has attracted considerable attention due to China's large trade surpluses and its rapid accumulation of foreign exchange reserves. There was a heated debate in the global society, especially among the top Chinese trading partners, that the RMB was undervalued. The Chinese officials resisted the external pressure and the fixed exchange rate policy was continued until July 2005, when some important changes were implemented. It constituted the second part of the 'market mechanism period.' Since 2005 the exchange rate policy was officially shifted from fixed exchange rate to a managed floating system. The CPC announced that the exchange rate since the time will be managed with reference to a basket of currencies instead of being pegged to the USD (Das 2019). From that time the authorities tried to use the monetary policy and exchange rate policy as an effective instrument of macroeconomic management while maintaining a gradual pace of currency reform. The main promise was that the flexible exchange rate helps the PBC to absorb external shocks and use monetary policy for achieving the domestic goals. The crucial aim was to rebalance the sources of domestic economic growth (foster internal consumption and hinder the excessive trade and investment surpluses).

Overall, the dollar peg has served China well at a time when the economy was suffering from severe inflationary internal imbalances. The evolution of China's exchange rate system over the past 70 years of CPC reign has been a period of re-pegging, un-pegging and de-pegging (appreciation) of its currency. Now that consumer price inflation has been brought down to single digits, exports are increasing and further intensification of financial reforms will lead to further steps toward free capital movement, the case for the peg is less compelling. Moving into a managed floating exchange rate regime could stimulate a more independent monetary policy, although the banking system is still in a gradual process of transition to modernization and its capital account is not yet sufficiently open (van der Linden 2010).

Among the most important arguments leading to the strengthening of RMB was the assumption that the RMB was significantly undervalued. The appreciation of the RMB could contribute to China's transition to a more consumption-driven growth path. The stronger currency should limit the export and foster import, resulting in more balanced international trade. Moreover, the more flexible exchange rate policy should lead to a greater flexibility of the domestic interest rates and raising the lending rates. There was also a need for the greater RMB flexibility for the growing importance of the currency on the foreign exchange market. Since 2005 the RMB was valued with the reference to a basket of other currencies (the currencies were, however, not specified).[3] Originally the system was designed in this way that the RMB was allowed fluctuating in a daily band of ± 0.3% against the USD and 1.5% against other currencies. During the next months and years, the bands of fluctuations were widened, and after the GFC the PBC introduced a new rule for setting the RMB parity against the USD. The band of fluctuation against the USD was broadened, and finally in 2014, the RMB was able to fluctuate against the USD ± 2% and against other currencies ± 3%. The daily central parity was based on the previous day's closing rate of the interbank foreign exchange market. The official announcement described the new exchange rate system as an adjustable basked peg, but in practice, during the next decade, it was a crawling peg against the USD. Since the GFC the pressure on stabilization the currency to a central parity was back again. The RMB appreciated (in nominal and real terms) against other currencies in the period 2005–2015. After 2015 the Chinese growth and macroeconomic indicators deteriorated, what triggered a pressure on depreciation of the currency. The pressure was enhanced by the PBC which changed the RMB/USD parity. This approach shows that the exchange rate system in China is still being used as an important tool in the country's macroeconomic policy.

Although China promotes internationalization of RMB for the last two decades, especially since 2009, after the GFC, the authorities have introduced a genuine and relevant RMB internationalization policy. Since China has emerged as the world's second largest economy and the biggest exporter, its currency has been severely underrepresented in global trade and capital markets. Therefore, in light of the current trade war with a 'rising dragon and falling eagle' it seems natural to talk about RMB internationalization and its potential reserve currency role as a rival to the USD and other major currencies. The main aim of RMB

[3] In August 2005, the PBC published the composition of the currency basket, which included USD, Euro, Japanese Yen, Korean Won and the currencies of Singapore, UK, Malaysia, Russia, Australia, Thailand, and Canada (Zheng et al., p. 3).

internationalization is to promote the currency as a unit of account, means of payment and store of value for banks, firms and government and it should ensure greater independence for China from the USD. Until now the Chinese business and banks conduct their transactions mainly in the USD, so the businesses are potentially vulnerable to the changes of the USD/RMB exchange rate (Gwiazda 2017).

In addition, the RMB internationalization still has a number of advantages that, particularly since the arrival of the BRI project in 2013, have played an increasingly important role. First, the increasing use of the RMB in trade reduces exchange rate risks and provides greater convenience for Chinese exporters and importers whose other costs and revenues are mostly in local currency terms. Second, RMB internationalization reduces the exposure of China's tradeable sector to sudden falls in the global supply of US dollars. A reduction in US dollar liquidity during the GFC has contributed to a significant decline in Chinese exports at the time. Third, RMB internationalization reduces borrowing costs for Chinese firms by increasing access to offshore RMB funding markets. Borrowing offshore in local currency also reduces the exposure of Chinese firms to exchange rate risk. Although it is quite understandable from a historical point of view that China wishes to internationalize its currency due to its economic size, it should be noted that the authorities are still maintaining extensive controls on capital flows and a tightly regulated financial market. A true effective implementation of RMB internationalization also requires sufficient confidence in the currency and open financial markets. Therefore, it is likely that the push to RMB internationalization was driven by and tied to domestic development aims such as further opening of the capital account and the liberalization of the domestic financial system. In a similar way in which China's access to the WTO was also used for some domestic market reforms, which otherwise could have been politically difficult to achieve, the RMB internationalization is also used to accelerate China's capital account opening, which would in turn build pressure to introduce further financial reforms which had become politically difficult to progress in the aftermath of the GFC. Especially from 2009, the PBC has implemented the simultaneous pursuit of both interest rate reform, capital account convertibility and currency flexibility 'in a coordinated way' (Windsor and Halperin 2018).

After the GFC internationalization of RMB has been one of the most important aims for Chinese monetary policy. In the official declarations, the Chinese exchange rate policy has entered into a new phase, which is named 'new normal' paradigm. In such approach the Chinese economy has 'a two-way trading and foreign exchange volatility.' It means that due to the process of internationalization, the RMB is changing under the market conditions which have not existed yet in the postwar stages of the Chinese economic development (Lo 2015). In addition, as part of RMB internationalization, China has recently taken a number of important steps, including the creation of the AIIB and the inclusion of RMB in the Special Drawing Rights (SDR) in 2016.

Apart from the official government policy and the activities oriented on the internationalization of RMB, it is significant that there are some factors supporting and some other factors restricting the process of internationalization of the currency. China is a country with a politically stable government, large GDP, and a large share in the international trade. These factors are supporting the RMB internationalization. On the other hand, there are some important constraints in the process. The Chinese financial market is in the process of development to make it less bank-oriented with a more developed capital market. The RMB is still responsible for only a small part of all international payments tracked by the SWIFT and is not commonly accepted as a reserve currency held by the central banks. It is likely that commercial banks and foreign parties will be willing to use RMB if they observe that they can freely buy and sell this currency (Gwiazda 2017).

In 2015 China introduced a new exchange rate mechanism, which has made the currency more flexible and more susceptible to the global market trends. The international markets lead to the appreciation of the RMB. Looking at the strength of the Chinese currency from a broader perspective, it is obvious that for the future economic development the appreciation of RMB is beneficial taking into account nowadays the exchange rate policy has a broader impact on the whole economy as it had in the past. A stronger currency could lead to normalization of the Chinese trade relations with many countries (not only the USA but also with some EU countries, Brazil and India, etc.). Among the other important aspects, it also exerts an impact on China's economic performance, international markets' expectations, China's cross-border capital flows and some other factors such the confidence in the Chinese economy. The weak RMB could lead to a capital outflow and be risky for the financial stability of the Chinese system. A strong exchange rate can positively impact on macroeconomic and financial stability. In times of economic slowdown, apart from the demographic problems and higher wages, the next challenge for the economy is inflation. The natural response for such situation is to raise interest rates, which is strictly interconnected with strengthening of the currency. It means that the process of strengthening the currency will help to combat the negative consequences of a recession. The only precondition is that the appreciation of RMB must take place gradually. Too rapid change might be harmful to the Chinese exporters and could negatively impact on the foreign reserves kept by the PBC.

The interest rate policy is very strictly interconnected with the monetary policy. Especially during last several years, the PBC, by loosening the currency grip, gives more autonomy for the monetary policy in the country. More flexible exchange rate regime helps to improve the monetary transmission and makes the monetary policy more effective. Nowadays the monetary policy in China officially has numerus objectives, which are hidden under the general statement, that the policy is responsible for maintaining the stability of the value of the currency and promotion of the economic growth (McMahon et al. 2018, p. 5). The policy changes its role during the process of transformation of the Chinese economy. As a result of the rapid growth and increasingly becoming a market economy, China needs an effective monetary policy. It must be highlighted that the objectives of the PBC are not focused on inflation-targeting but are much broader, so the monetary policy has broader objectives. The policy should be adjusted to such goals as managing inflation and ensuring price stability, supporting sustainable growth, boosting employment and promoting a more balanced balance of payments account (Hu 2010). Currently monetary policy carries more system-wide implications and is more systemically important than the exchange rate policy. It impacts every part of the economy and has a huge influence on the micro-level. An important aspect is that the PBC does not have a full decision-making power over the money supply targets and interest rate policy, as well as it has the limited operational independence. All the key decisions must be approved by the State Council (China's equivalent to a government cabinet) (see Article 5 of the General Rules in the People's Bank of China Law).

Before the 1990s, the monetary policy in China was submitted to the rapid supply of RMB on the market. Over time, it obtained a more important role. Together with the banking system development and the gradual process of the Chinese financial system liberalization, the PBC developed its approach to the monetary policy. It has adapted some instruments such as open market operations and reserve requirement ratio. The balance of payments surpluses during many years resulted with inflow of foreign exchanges and forced the PBC to increase its foreign exchange reserves and in this way inject base money to the economy. The culmination of this approach was between 2003 and 2007, when the growth rate of foreign exchange reserves in China exceeded 35%. It was a consequence of the sterilization operations implemented by the PBC aimed at withdrawing excess liquidity from the market (BIS 2008, p. 148). Step-by-step the monetary policy became a more important guarantor of stabilization for the economy.

After the GFC the Chinese government implemented a relatively expansionary monetary policy. A relatively limited influence of the GFC on the Chinese economy led to a huge increase in foreign exchange inflows and as a result a substantial rise in liquidity with a risk of high inflation. Such situation created a need for a balance between the economic growth, further economic reforms, and a management of inflationary expectations (Hu 2010). One of the crucial aspects impacting on the monetary policy in China is the process of liberalization of the financial system in the country. In parallel with the RMB internationalization and accompanying liberalization of capital account transactions, the Chinese government is implementing the liberalization of interest rates in the country. It is based on the assumption that such approach should enhance the ability of interest rates to influence fund flows, and causes that investments are more sensitive to interest rate fluctuations, thereby increasing the effectiveness of monetary policy. Currently, China has an exchange rate system in which some, but not complete, fluctuation of the currency is allowed. A similar situation occurs in monetary policy with a certain, but not complete, degree of interdependence and effectiveness (Kwan 2018).

3.3 China's Challenge of the Impossible Trinity

The impossible trinity or triangle, also known as inconsistent or 'unholy' trinity or trilemma, is a policy-choice problem based on the traditional Mundell–Fleming paradigm developed in the 1960s. This hypothesis in international economics states one of the three aims is a trade-off with the other two aims and no one could reach all three aims simultaneously. Robert A. Mundell (1960) concluded that a country with free capital mobility or convertibility would be better off by adopting fixed exchange

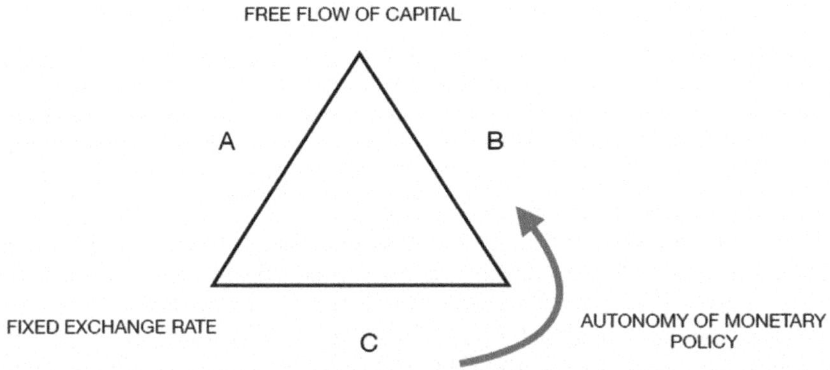

Fig. 3.5 China's gradual change from side C to B of the impossible triangle since the start of the millennium (*Source* Łasak and van der Linden 2019)

rates to avoid the dependency on interest rates to balance a too large deficit or surplus on the balance of payments of a certain country.

For decades after 1979, the PBC can manage its exchange rate without releasing its independent monetary policy, but only by maintaining controls on capital flows (so for many years the authorities pick side C of the triangle in Fig. 3.5). However, the last two decades when capital became substantially more mobile, China has experienced significant capital inflows mostly due to huge amounts of inward or inbound FDIs combined with huge outward or outbound FDIs since the last decade. Especially the speculative short-term capital movements can easily evade the capital restrictions. Although China has liberalized its capital flows over time, still the authorities prefer to have some control over the capital flows and its effects on domestic industries. It can be assumed that further progress of the BRI will exert a higher pressure on further financial market liberalization and result in higher openness for free flow of capital. At the same time, China's exchange rate is becoming more managed floating than fixed since the rising capital mobility has made the RMB more vulnerable to speculation, so the authorities gradually change from side C to side B of the triangle (see Fig. 3.5) which will ultimately stimulate more globalization and financial integration. The PBC tries to keep the exchange rate low and stable to remain competitive in the global markets, but as a matter of fact, the RMB has been rather undervalued for many years and the financial market forces continuously have given pressure for RMB revaluation. That is why the PBC let the currency float to the extent where it does not harm certain vulnerable domestic industries. The monetary sovereignty is also acquired to some extent since the PBC mainly uses it for the maintenance of the exchange rate. It may be presumed that fast growth of debt will necessitate some adjustments of monetary policy as well. It motivates the Chinese government to treat monetary policy as an important tool to provide stabilization to the economy. The last two decades, especially in the years before the GFC, Chinese authorities have tried several times to reach all the 'corners' of the triangle or step on all the 'horns of the trilemma' at the same time and it actually has at least some features of every policy. However, since the start of the GFC the focus is again more on currency stability combined with more capital mobility as a response on a rising RMB in the years before the GFC (a gradual move from side B to C in the triangle). On the other hand, from 2014 onward, the policy will change again to a combination of monetary autonomy with free movement of capital (a gradual move from side C to B in the triangle). Since the Mundell–Fleming model fails to consider monetary sterilization policy, e.g., using open market operations, the government was able to bend or circumvent the policy trilemma and in this way disprove the theory that the trinity is completely impossible. Although the authorities cannot defy this Mundell–Fleming model completely, since 2015 they have tried to bend this trilemma because the RMB is formally listed on IMF's reserve currencies in 2016. Since the IMF requires China to free its capital flows as the precondition of the listing this has huge implications for its economy and financial system.

Aizenman (2011) has transformed the policy trilemma into a quadrilemma by including the financial stability as an additional policy aim (see Fig. 3.6). This theory allows China to have a fixed (or in practice more managed) exchange rate, independent monetary policy, and free capital flows at least to some extent, but now it has to sacrifice financial stability mainly because of problems caused by volatile short-run capital inflows or 'hot money.' The tendency of the authorities to challenge the trilemma as much as possible will make it harder to keep the financial system stable and might lead to even bigger market distortions. The main problems of the Chinese economy could be related to the policy quadrilemma, so China could be better off if it would sacrifice one of the trinity aims and keep financial stability (Aizenman 2011; Aizenman and Sengupta 2012; Aizenman et al. 2013).

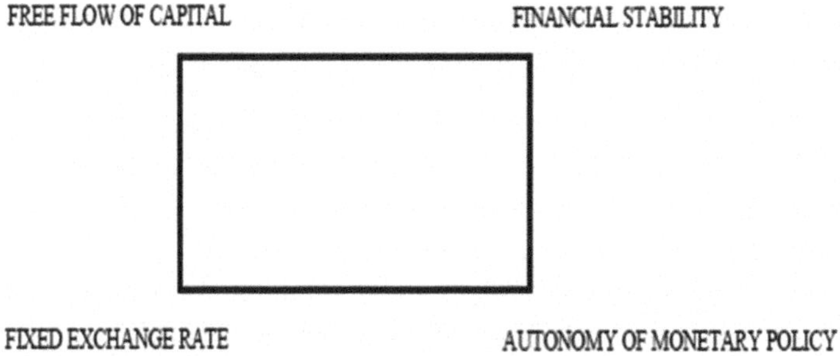

Fig. 3.6 The policy quadrilemma (*Source* Łasak and van der Linden 2019)

3.4 China's Next 'New Normal' Growth Model

As indicated in the 13th FYP, China is undergoing a difficult but necessary transition from a growth model that emphasizes heavy industry, construction, and exports, to a new development model that focuses more on services, innovation, entrepreneurship, and domestic consumption as a means of raising productivity and climbing up the global value chain. The large internal imbalances of savings, fixed investment, and consumption are caused by China's banking policies and the lack of an adequate social safety net. The Chinese government places restrictions on the export of capital. As a result, Chinese households put a large share of their savings in domestic banks. The Chinese government sets the interest rate on deposits as well, and often this rate is below the rate of inflation, which lowers household income. In addition, China's lack of an adequate social safety net such as pensions, health care, unemployment insurance, and education induces households to save a large portion of their income (Morrison 2018).

The 'new normal' economy embodies a focus on structural changes that can achieve still strong but lower economic growth of a much better quality in terms of its social distribution and impact on the natural environment. The structural reforms in many areas of the economy will address the 'middle-income trap.' In its 13th FYP, China sets a middle-high average annual 6.5% growth target despite slowing global and domestic demand, overcapacity, and rising debt. Moreover, the 13th FYP not only focuses more on supply side-structural reforms, but also enhances individual well-being through social welfare and health care reforms in order to reduce its relatively high savings ratio in favor of more consumption (Reeves and Hu 2015). The new development model also places a strong emphasis on reducing inequalities, especially urban-rural and regional inequalities, and environmental sustainability with a focus on reductions in air pollution and other forms of local environmental damage, as well as in greenhouse gas emissions (Green and Stern 2015).

This structural shift will likely be accompanied by further economic slowdown because the economy has become more mature and will be less predictable since markets and entrepreneurs, rather than directions from the center, are expected to play a larger role in the decision making. Since the government's legitimacy is closely tied to the creation of more employment and incomes, it has become more important than the economic slowdown remains within their target range. Also, the difficult process of transferring resources from declining manufacturing to growing services sectors of the economy would be easier if overall growth is strong. To support economic growth during its difficult transition, China has eased monetary policy in various ways while continuing a process of reforming and opening up its capital markets. Given the enormous amount of debt, Chinese debtors need low rates so as to help service interest payments and avoid bankruptcy. However, if Chinese households and corporate investors are offered lower rates in China and rising rates in the USA, they become increasingly attracted to overseas investment, which brings about capital flight and currency instability. If the PBC forgoes monetary independence and drives rates higher, Chinese debtors will face financial difficulties, thereby slowing economic growth. But if the PBC lowers rates too much, there may be a sizable capital flight that could quickly diminish China's foreign exchange reserves, ultimately forcing China to float its currency. An economy that is growing more slowly, and in which monetary easing by repeatedly injecting liquidity and using sterilization tools to offset capital outflows and economic slowdown, is not an economy that offers high returns to domestic savers. Consequently, Chinese households and firms are looking abroad for higher returns than the RMB-denominated investments. However, increased private capital outflows also constitute a flight from the RMB toward the USD and other currencies which puts downward pressure on China's exchange rate.

In the short run, the PBC can offset this pressure by selling some of its enormous stocks of dollar-denominated securities and buying RMB.

Although China should be able to defend its exchange rate for some time, but if this trend should continue, eventually China will run low on reserves and will no longer be willing or able to buy up RMB in the foreign exchange market with the risk that the RMB will fall too sharply. Moreover, the risk that the RMB might be significantly devalued in the future could accelerate the decline in reserves, by leading households and firms to sell RMB now to avoid capital losses from a possible future devaluation. This is the essence of the trilemma in the current Chinese economy: if China wants to use monetary policy to manage domestic demand and to simultaneously free up international capital flows, it may not be able to manage the exchange rate at current levels (Bernanke 2016). Given the desire for an ongoing financial, i.e., capital and interest rate, liberalization and the need for more currency flexibility for the purpose of the RMB internationalization, the three policy aims of the trinity are themselves more at odds with each other and will make it harder to maintain financial stability. However, in December 2016, the PBC has focused more on a policy of currency stability as an important tool to achieve the policy goals of the BRI, namely trade and investments. Facing higher US rates, the PBC effectively gave up monetary autonomy by implementing a more tight monetary policy. In a world of a relatively strong USD, the PBC may well need to maintain high rates for a prolonged period of time, or face intensified outflow pressure. At the same time, the PBC is also breaking the promises it had made to the IMF on RMB convertibility, erecting new barriers to the conversion of RMB in order to staunch capital outflows. Rather than circumventing the impossible trinity, China for now has sacrificed both free capital flows and monetary autonomy in order to preserve currency stability (Shih 2017).

References

Aizenman, J. (2011, March 1). *The Impossible Trinity: From the Policy Trilemma to the Policy Quadrilemma*. Santa Cruz: University of California.

Aizenman, J., & Sengupta, R. (2012). *The Financial Trilemma in China and a Comparative Analysis with India*. UCSC and the NBER India: IFMR.

Aizenman, J., Chinn, M. D., & Ito, H. (2013). The "Impossible Trinity" Hypothesis in an Era of Global Imbalances: Measurement and Testing. *Review of International Economics, 3*(21), 447–458.

Bernanke, B. (2016, March 9). *A Fresh Approach to Fiscal Stimulus Is China's Only Solution to the Impossible Trinity Devaluations and Capital Controls Won't Work*. Bloomberg.

BIS. (2008). *Financial Globalisation and Emerging Market Capital Flows* (Vol. 44).

Chen, S., & Kang, J. S. (2018, January). *Credit Booms—Is China Different?* (IMF Working Paper, WP/18/2).

Das, S. (2019). *China's Evolving Exchange Rate Regime* (IMF Working Paper, WP/19/50).

Davis, C. (2018, March 9). It Is Up to China to Save the Global Trading System. *Financial Times*.

Dieppe, A., Gilhooly, R., Han, J., Korhonen, I., & Lodge, D. (2018, January). *The Transition of China to Sustainable Growth—Implications for the Global Economy and the Euro Area* (ECB Occasional Paper Series No. 206).

Drysdale, P., & Hardwick, S. (2018). China and the Global Trading System: Then and Now. In L. Song & C. Feng (Eds.), *China's 40 Years of Reform and Development 1978–2018*. Canberra: Australian National University Press.

Ernst & Young. (2015, March). Riding the Silk Road: China Sees Outbound Investment Boom: Outlook for China's Outward Foreign Direct Investment.

Gloria, E. (2014). *China's Exchange Rate Regimes and Their Policy Implications*. Asian Center.

Goldstein, M., & Lardy, N. R. (2008). *China's Exchange Rate Policy: An Overview of Some Key Issues*. Washington, DC: Peterson Institute for International Economics.

Green, F., & Stern, N. (2015, June). *China's "New Normal": Structural Change, Better Growth, and Peak Emissions*. Centre for Climate Change Economics and Policy, Policy Brief.

Gujon, M., & Guérineau, S. (2006, March–April). The Modification of the Chinese Exchange Rate Policy: Its Rationale, Extent and Recent Developments. *China Perspectives, 64*, 1–14.

Gwiazda, A. (2017). The Sluggish Internationalization of the Renminbi. *Bank i Kredyt, 48*(5), 483–494.

He, H. (2019, May 22). US-China Trade War Manufacturing Exodus Creating Boom Time for Chinese Logistics Companies. *South China Morning Post*.

Hillman, J. (2018, January 25). *China's Belt and Road Initiative: Five Years Later*. Washington, DC: Center for Strategic & International Studies.

Hu, X. (2010, July 26). *Exchange Rate Regime Reform and Monetary Policy Effectiveness*. Beijing: People's Bank of China.

Kwan, C. H. (2018). Issues Facing Renminbi Internationalization: Observations from Chinese, Regional and Global Perspectives. *Public Policy Review, 14*(5). Policy Research Institute, Ministry of Finance, Japan.

Łasak, P., & van der Linden, R. W. H. (2019). The Effectiveness of the 'Belt and Road' Initiative in Tackling China's Economic Slowdown and Its Financial

Implications Within a Policy Trilemma Context, Chapter 12. In E. Gualandri, V. Venturelli, & A. Sclip (Eds.), *Frontier Topics in Banking: Investigating New Trends and Recent Developments in the Financial Industry*. Cham: Palgrave Macmillan.

van der Linden, R. W. H. (2010). Bank Strategy, Governance and Ratings, Chapter 12. In P. Molyneux (Ed.), *Palgrave Macmillan Studies in Banking and Financial Institutions*. London: Palgrave Macmillan.

Lo, C. (2015). *China's Impossible Trinity: The Structural Challenges to the "Chinese Dream"*. London: Palgrave Macmillan.

McBride, J., & Chatzky, A. (2019, May 3). *Is "Made in China 2025" a Threat to Global Trade?* Council on Foreign Relations.

McMahon, M., Schipke, A., & Li, X. (2018). *China's Monetary Policy Communication: Frameworks, Impact, and Recommendations* (IMF Working Paper No. WP/18/244).

Morrison, W. M. (2018, February 5). *China's Economic Rise: History, Trends, Challenges, and Implications for the United States*. Congressional Research Service 7-5700. www.crs.gov. RL33534.

Mundell, R. A. (1960). The Monetary Dynamics of International Adjustment under Fixed and Flexible Exchange Rates. *Quarterly Journal of Economics, 74*(2), 227–257.

Reeves, M., & Hu, D. (2015, December 7). What China's 13th Five-Year Plan Means for Business? *Harvard Business Review*.

Shih, V. (2017, October 20). *Financial Instability in China: Possible Pathways and Their Likelihood*. Berlin: Mercator Institute for China Studies.

The Economist. (2019a, March 16). *China's Current-Account Surplus Has Vanished*.

The Economist. (2019b, April 20). *China's GDP: Growth in Train*.

Tiffany, N. G., & Chung, K. (2018, July 17). *Trade Conflict Between China and the United States and Its Impact on Hong Kong's Economy*. Research Office Information Services Division Legislative Council Secretariat.

Windsor, C., & Halperin, D. (2018, September). *RMB Internationalisation: Where to Next?* Reserve Bank of Australia Bulletin.

Wong, D., & Koty, A. C. (2018, December 14). The US–China Trade War: A Timeline. *China Briefing*.

WTO. (2018). *World Trade Statistical Review 2018*.

Zhao, M. (2006, May). *External Liberalization and the Evolution of China's Exchange System: An Empirical Approach* (World Bank China Office Research Working Paper No. 4).

Zheng, Y., Yi, J., & Chen, M. (2007). *Revaluation of the Chinese Currency and Its Impacts on China* (China Policy Institute and Centre for Global Finance, Discussion Paper 24). University of Nottingham.

CHAPTER 4

The Rationale for the 'Belt and Road' Initiative

Abstract This chapter is related to the economic rationale of the 'Belt and Road' initiative. One of the crucial aspects of the initiative is its broad impact on the real economy in China by fostering coordination of the developmental policy, stimulating infrastructure development, enhancing trade and investment, reinforcing financial market liberalization, and increasing cooperation between people. The BRI can be compared to the historical 'Marshall plan,' which was treated as a solution fostering economic growth and development in Europe after the Second World War. The chapter highlights some similarities and differences between the two initiatives. The BRI project is not only oriented on strengthening the domestic economy, but also at successfully implementing the 'Going-Out' strategy aimed at intensifying foreign trade and investments. The chapter also elaborates on some financial aspects of the BRI. Especially important are the means of financing the projects. Some special institutions were created, dedicated for supporting the initiative, like AIIB and Silk Road Fund, but many other ways of financing are described as well, like the private sector, Multinational Development Banks, and others. It is likely that the possibilities and the way in which the BRI will have to be funded in the future will be decisive for its success. The BRI is focused on participation of many countries in the initiative, and the cooperation is very important aspect of the project. Foreign participation enables to develop many infrastructure projects over a long distance such as railways, ports, bridges, and others, which would never

P. Łasak and R. W. H. van der Linden, *The Financial Implications of China's Belt and Road Initiative*,
https://doi.org/10.1007/978-3-030-30118-7_4

be launched without the BRI. Despite many benefits, the initiatives trigger some adverse aspects as well such as the high debts, environmental problems, trade conflicts, and many others. Eventually it is essential that the BRI creates a 'win-win' cooperation for all participating countries.

Keywords 'Win-win' cooperation · 'Going-Out' strategy · Asian Infrastructure Investment Bank (AIIB) · Silk Road Infrastructure Fund · Multinational Development Banks · BRI participating countries · 'Marshall plan'

4.1 The Aims and Logic Behind China's Alternative 'Marshall Plan'

The framework of the BRI promotes common interests in all fields, including development toward prosperity with political trust, economic integration, and cultural inclusiveness. The starting point of BRI is not a geopolitical tool, but a platform for cooperation. The following five key goals or major priorities, originally from the National Development and Reform Commission (2015), are meant to 'break the bottleneck of connectivity':

- policy coordination;
- infrastructure connectivity;
- unrestricted trading opportunities;
- financial integration;
- people-to-people exchange.

The first priority of the BRI consists of the planning and supporting of large-scale development infrastructural projects of OBOR countries. This key goal comes down to sharing interests, build policy exchange and communication mechanisms, enhance mutual trust, and reach consensus to coordinate large-scale projects. The second major priority aims to improve connectivity through the building of infrastructure networks and construction plans along the 'Belt and Road' including infrastructure for energy, maritime, and communication. The third key goal aims to facilitate cross-border investments and supply chain cooperation. It intends to simplify customs clearance systems and minimize quarantine to have better access to the different markets and eliminate trade barriers.

Aside from that, it also includes the expansion of free-trade zones and ease for investments abroad. A fourth priority is to enhance monetary policy coordination and bilateral financial cooperation. The financial integration can be achieved through China's financial institutions that are built for the sake of the OBOR project as well as for the promotion of the RMB internationalization. The fifth key goal is the cooperation through media, culture, and friendship to engage in the public's support of the project itself in order to promote culture, science, health, tourism, and education including study abroad programs. An example of people-to-people exchange is the Alliance of Silk Road business schools founded in 2016, building a cross-border communication platform for students, scholars and entrepreneurs. Interconnectivity is the essence of the BRI and is in line with the old Chinese saying 'friendship between people is the key to good relations between states' (Northern Trust 2017).

China has developed an impressive reputation as the 'world's factory' over the last three decades. In recent years, however, its comparative advantages in manufacturing, such as low labor costs, have begun to disappear. For this reason, the Chinese leadership wants to capture the higher end of the global value chain and the BRI can play an important role in this. The primary goals are to make the country's manufacturing industry more innovation-driven, emphasize quality over quantity, and restructure China's low-cost manufacturing industry. The BRI can facilitate the export of higher-end Chinese manufactured goods and encourage the acceptance of Chinese technical standards. Apart from the high-speed rail sector, the Chinese government is also using the BRI to push for Chinese technical standards in other sectors such as energy and telecommunications. The Chinese plans are not limited to the traditional branches of industry, but they are targeted to the modern, technologically advanced branches as well. For this reason China defined an approach which is called 'Digital BRI' in an attempt to use 'big data' to address and solve some of the challenges in sustainable development. The strategy is dedicated mainly to the developing economies and its goal is to facilitate digital connectivity for such countries. Boosting connectivity has been one of the key aspects of the BRI since its very beginning, but over time the agenda of the 'Digital BRI' has become broader, and it embraces such areas as strengthening internet infrastructure (e.g. 5G networks), application artificial intelligence, deepening space cooperation, developing common technology standards, and many others (Deloitte 2019).

With the significant investments under the BRI, China also intends to compensate for the overcapacity that characterizes many sectors of its industry such as steel, aluminum, cement, machinery, turbines, heavy goods vehicles, and basic chemicals by transferring part of the production overcapacity of mainly SOEs to countries that are along the 'New' Silk Road. OBOR projects are currently too small to absorb China's vast glut of steel and other products. Instead, Chinese authorities want companies to move this excess production capacity through direct foreign investment to Asian countries who need to build their infrastructure. China exports high-quality production capacity, equipment, technical know-how, and developmental experience in terms of poverty reduction and improving health outcomes and in this way retains control over the import of raw materials needed to fuel its economy.

The BRI will enable Chinese companies to successfully carry out the Chinese government's 'Going Out' strategy through helping them to establish foreign trade strongholds or production bases along the routes covered by the initiative. It will also have a significant domestic focus since the authorities will also use the BRI as an addition, revival, and incentive for China's 'Going West' campaign that started in 2000 with the aim to close the development gaps between coastal and inland areas. For instance, the improved transport connections with the western province Xinjiang can be considered as a stimulus to alleviate poverty and hence reduce terrorism. Despite Beijing's preferential policies, large-scale fiscal injections, and state-directed investments, the western provinces' share of China's total GDP increased only marginally. A drawback of China's 'great western development' is the fact that there is little emphasis in the Go West campaign on measures to alleviate poverty, while the government is obsessed with gigantic, and correspondingly expensive, infrastructure projects. In order to implement the OBOR projects more effectively, the authorities have to take into account that heavy state subsidies in these western provinces have led to a high concentration of SOEs and low penetration of POEs (Cai 2017).

At least in theory, it is the intention that the BRI will lead to a 'win-win' situation for both China and the recipient countries. China has the financial means and the technical infrastructure expertise, while many of the BRI countries are fiscally constrained and lack infrastructure funding. For China, the BRI helps address its economic rebalancing priorities by exporting its own manufacturing overcapacity, while better infrastructure in recipient countries will enable local industrialization and business creation. Geopolitically, it supports a rise in China's foreign policy 'soft power.' For the smaller, recipient economies, this platform expedites a move toward a higher stage of economic development (Nomura 2018). China's ultimate aim is to make Eurasia dominated by China an economic and trading area to rival the transatlantic one dominated by America. If the BRI increases China's 'soft power,' it might give the authorities more 'leverage' in future negotiations about military conflicts (*The Economist* 2017).

Despite the equality in access to the project and declared similar treatment, some countries have a special importance for the success of the BRI. To such countries belong: some Central Asian countries (Kazakhstan, Kyrgyzstan, Tajikistan Turkmenistan, Uzbekistan), countries linking China with selected ports on the Sea Route (Pakistan, Myanmar) and the Central and East European countries (the group of 17 plus Belarus and Russia). The whole OBOR-conception makes no sense without these countries and they are especially precious for its success. Sometimes the states are not adequately appreciated and some of them fluctuate between full participation and selected involvement in particular projects. It is essential from the very beginning that first, different countries will participate and benefit from its membership in the BRI in different ways; second, the participation in OBOR projects must create a 'win-win' cooperation; third, beside many advantages, OBOR brings some shortcomings (see Sect. 4.4) as well and participant countries must be active to deal with them; fourth, it is very difficult to predict in advance the exact result of the whole BRI and the net impact on the member countries. Although breaking the bottlenecks of connectivity is considered the general main objective of the OBOR project, a detailed blueprint about its performance in terms of the billions of dollars to be spent, the amount of kilometers of track to be laid or how much new port capacity to be built including a time-plan is lacking (*The Economist* 2018).

Some countries will benefit from the BRI at the very beginning of the initiative, especially developed countries like the USA, some EU nations, and Japan. The OBOR project is requiring some global industries and services providers. China and other BRI participants need services like master planning, design, architectural services, consulting, project management, legal and financial services. All of them are provided by the developed countries and their industries. The BRI might be beneficial economically for the developing countries as well.

It increases economic activity, facilitates the trade and by attracting foreign investments simultaneously creates jobs in the countries and enables access to foreign production chains. All of that minimizes the threat of internal unrest by offering the possibility of hinterland development (Krukowska 2016).

The role of the Silk Road is intended to meet the interests of all participant countries and to provide a 'win-win' cooperation for all the participants. The positive aspect of the cooperation stems from some features of the BRI, namely:

- participating economies are very often complementary;
- China is able to invest abroad with a positive impact on the other countries;
- participation enables BRI countries to utilize their geographic advantages.

Cooperation in the BRI is treated as the mechanism to achieve strategic goals by member states. Many of the infrastructural projects (roads, energy pipelines) are unable to be accomplished by a single country or through bilateral efforts, and they require participation of a bigger group of countries. For many countries the participation in the BRI might lead to diminishing their dependence on the traditional, low value-added industries (agriculture, mining, etc.) and develop other branches of industry, diversifying the factors of development and attract more technologically advanced investments. All the factors will help to boost the participating countries' economies. Additional benefit is that OBOR will turn many informal ways of cooperation (e.g., international trade) into formal ones, which will lead to reduction of accompanying obstacles. The great example of a 'win-win' cooperation is the energy market and cooperation between China and Russia in the field of trade cooperation (Li 2018).

Since the BRI was referred to as 'China's Marshall Plan without a war' on the South China Morning Post (Sabine 2017) the question arises to what extent, the BRI and the US-led Marshall plan for post-war destroyed Europe are comparable. Both USA after the Second World War and China after the GFC have an interest in its neighbors getting richer and importing more goods from USA and China, respectively. Although the two infrastructural projects differ in terms of capital involved and geographical focus, in both projects political and economic problems are interlinked perhaps with a different causal relationship. Nonetheless, there are five core similarities in the background and purposes of the Marshall and OBOR plan by their initiating countries, namely increasing exports; exporting the domestic currency; countering a rival; fostering strategic division; and the removal of diplomatic support.

First, just like the USA at the end of the Second World War, China after the credit crisis is a strong but somewhat saturated manufacturing country equipped with high industrial capacity. In both countries, the inevitable economic slowdown of the domestic market and failure to export excess capacity caused economic growth to stagnate. In order to cope with the postwar economic transformation and the overcapacity problem, the USA was forced to seek foreign, initially European, markets for their products. Accordingly, China needs to export excess capacity, resources, and labor through foreign investment in order to become a high-income advanced economy. A corresponding postwar economic imbalance between the USA and Europe also occurs between China's strength in infrastructure building, and Central and Southeast Asia's lack of infrastructural investments. Just as the US foreign investments were accompanied by the US export to Europe, China also hopes to secure its exports through the strong growth of outbound investments (see Fig. 3.4). Therefore, China oversaw the establishment of the AIIB in accordance with the BRI in order to promote 'Made in China' in Central and Southeast Asia.

Second, both the Marshall and the OBOR plan encourage to export the domestic currency. In order to stimulate more market mechanism within the framework of the Party, China has long been working to gradually internationalize its currency. This RMB internationalization ultimately led to the RMB being included to the IMF's Special Drawing Rights basket of currencies in October 2016. However, the most effective way to promote cross-border circulation of the RMB is still regional economic cooperation. The RMB is regarded as the strongest currency among the major regions of the OBOR initiative and through OBOR could be more used as the settlement currency of large-scale commodity trade in the region, and at the same time, the engagement of Chinese capital investment in infrastructure building should be increased and promote cross-border payments by RMB. The RMB through OBOR can allow China to challenge the US's leading role in the international arena, just as the status of the US currency was consolidated through the Marshall plan.

Third, the Marshall plan provided a blueprint for undermining the influence of the Soviet Union. Similarly, China's OBOR targets the USA as a potential competitor. The emphasis on interconnection stresses the construction of onshore energy pipelines as well as harbors. By importing energy through dispersed channels, China can lower the strategic risk of energy imports and enhance control over Indian Ocean shipping routes. At the same time, the consolidation of trade relationships among China (with its exports of manufactured goods), the Middle East and Central Asia (energy exports) and Southeast Asia (exports of raw materials) can counterbalance the US rebalancing strategy and reduce the economic dependence of China on the USA.

Fourth, the Marshall plan can be viewed as a factor that contributed to the division of West and East Germany. Similarly, the BRI may lower the solidarity of Asia-Pacific integration organizations headed by the USA and Japan, such as APEC. By searching out APEC member states which desperately need infrastructure, the BRI allows China to foster bilateral integration with those member states. That, in turn, will undermine the significance of APEC and delay these states' entry in the original US-led Trans-Pacific Partnership (TPP). The US decision to withdraw from the TPP can be seen as a signal of a considerable weaker position of the USA in Asia. Though APEC countries will still keep diplomatic ties with the USA, the BRI limits the chance of forming of coalitions against China, such as the US-India and US-South Korea coalitions in the past.

Fifth, in the period shortly after the Second World War, the US hoped to use the economic development of Western Europe as an incentive that could increase US influence in Eastern Europe. In a similar way, China wishes to intensify relations with traditional US allies in Western Europe, which in turn undermines US influence in the region. Recent frequent interactions between leaders of China and major Western European countries as well as decisions by the UK, France, and Germany to join AIIB despite the US objections seems to indicate the decline of US influence. If economic integration and strategic integration are achieved between Asia and Europe, China may become the center of the world, leaving the US marginalized (Shen and Chan 2018).

Unlike the USA and Europe, China uses aid, trade, and FDIs strategically to build goodwill, expand its political sway, and secure the natural resources it needs to grow. In this context, the BRI could be seen as umbrella initiative of current and future infrastructure projects. In the next decades, China plans to build a thick web of infrastructure around Asia and, through similar initiatives, around the world (Manuel 2017). The historical comparison between the postwar Marshall plan and the current OBOR plan shows that when a new world power emerges, the large-scale investment in new infrastructure is an important indicator and vehicle for further influencing this development. An OBOR project that succeeds on China's terms could revise a new and more equitable economic order to reflect Chinese interests. Changes would be seen in supply chains for goods, from manufactured products to energy and other resources. China's currency would become more widely used. Chinese technical standards, for everything from high-speed railway systems to wireless networks, would become more widely adopted, as would Chinese preferences for environmental and social safeguards. All these changes could push the USA away from its current position in the global economy and move China toward the center (Hillman 2018). In four decades, China has gradually become the second-largest economy and the world's largest trading nation, and its largest bilateral lender to others, similar to as in the postwar US situation. Now it's China's turn, the time has come to make the transition to a high-income country via a 'new normal' growth model, and using the OBOR project to quietly reshaping the world's economic order.

4.2 The Financial Means and Options for the 'Belt and Road' Project

One of the most important issues related to the BRI is to find the ways of financing the project. The way the BRI is financed could be the most important factor in terms of the sustainability of the entire initiative. It is estimated that the total investment needed to cover the transport and infrastructure (excluding power, water, and other infrastructure) for the coming 5 years is estimated between USD 1 and USD 8 trillion (Hillman 2018; PwC 2016; Ho 2017). Collecting such an amount of money involves joining together many different sources. The transcontinental development projects related to the BRI, which already have been announced, are estimated on over USD 900 billion (Chatterjee and Kumar 2017). The most important question related to the plans is to how to provide a sustainable financing for such a large project. So far, it is known that the entire OBOR project will be financed from the following sources (PwC 2016):

- 50% National budgets;
- 20% National Development Banks;
- 25% Private sector;
- 3–4% Multilateral Development Banks;
- 1–2% South-South flows.

Despite resistance from Western countries due to their overlapping purpose with IMF, three financial institutions have been built in order to fund this project, namely Silk Road Infrastructure Fund, Asian Infrastructure Investment Bank (AIIB), and New Development Bank (NDB). For the BRI, especially important is the AIIB. The AIIB is a multilateral development bank (MDB) aiming to support the building of infrastructure, especially in Asian countries. It was launched by Chinese President Xi Jinping in October 2013 and started its operations in January 2016. Despite the fact that the official aim of the institution is to finance the infrastructure in Asia, sometimes it is treated as a key instrument of China's foreign and development policy (Stuart-Haentjens 2017). Irrespective of the varied aims, so far both initiatives, BRI and AIIB, are operating in significant synergy, and it is expected that the AIIB will serve as one of the most important funding sources for the infrastructural investments. Since 2016, when AIIB began its operations, it has approved over thirty projects of the BRI initiative. They are realized in different countries which acceded to the New Silk Road and are related to different sectors of the economies (see Table 4.1). The bank is very helpful in leveraging capital from its member countries to finance infrastructure projects.

One of the most important problems related to the fast-economic development of Asian countries is the infrastructural gaps. They are obstacles between countries and markets for the transfer of goods, services, capital, information, and people, as well as fostering the further integration. The AIIB is an important initiative which responds on the poor institutional environment in this region and is oriented on building new infrastructure in Asia, and linking the continent with Europe, Africa, and the Middle East. The AIIB's role is to support the infrastructural projects. It proposes a coherent and transparent set of policy frameworks,

Table 4.1 Some of the amazing projects achieved worldwide under the BRI

Project name	*Country*	*Project type*	*Year*
Jakarta-Bandung high-speed rail	Indonesia	Railway	2015
Abuja-Kaduna railway	Nigeria	Railway	2016
Ethiopia-Djibouti railway	Ethiopia	Railway	2016
China-Laos railway	Laos	Railway	2016
Colombo port city	Sri Lanka	Port	2019
Piraeus port	Greece	Port	2016
Doraleh multipurpose port	Djibouti	Port	2017
Zeebrugge terminal	Belgium	Port	2018
Muara port	Brunei	Port	2017
Gwadar port	Pakistan	Port	2016
Temburong bridge	Brunei	Bridge	2014
Peljesac bridge	Croatia	Bridge	2018
Padma bridge	Bangladesh	Bridge	2016
Punta Sierra wind farm	Chile	Industrial project	2018
Yamal LNG project	Russia	Industrial project	2017
Isimba hydropower station	Uganda	Industrial project	2015
Uyuni 350KTPA Potash Plant	Bolivia	Industrial project	2018
China–Belarus Industrial Park	Belarus	Industrial park project	2012
China-Egypt Suez Economic and Trade Co-operation Zone	Egypt	Economic and trade co-operation zone	2016
Djibouti International Free-Trade Zone	Djibouti	International free-trade zone	2017

Source: *China Daily*, May 2, 2019 (https://www.telegraph.co.uk/china-watch/business/belt-road-projects-list/)

with multilateral governance oversight of the lending principles. Some of the features of the AIIB are the well-defined and transparent set of governance policies applying best practices; formal cooperation with other MDBs; the status of multilateral institution which enables a high degree of legitimacy and reduces some (political) risks and the institution guarantees that the implemented projects will serve the sustainable growth for the participating economies (Wilson 2018).

An important advantage for financing the BRI by the AIIB is the transparency provided by the institution. The bank provides higher transparency, comparing to bilateral government-to-government negotiations with China. As an international institution, the AIIB must fulfill the binding standards and regulatory requirements and watch over their application for all funded projects. The bank follows a clear and well-defined approval process before financing projects. It provides that the accepted projects are viable, and the participants will comply with the international standards. The AIIB is complementing the institutional deficiencies of other MDBs. Among others might be indicated here the need for new funding instruments for the Asian countries (László 2018). It should be highlighted that the AIIB plays a complementary, not a substantial role in the international financial system. Moreover, in terms of cooperation, it rather strengthens the South-South cooperation instead of the traditional North-South one.

Before the establishment and start-up of the AIIB activity, there was a fear that the bank would influence the existing multinational institutional order and that the bank's main role would be to strengthen the Chinese position in the global economy. It is argued that China is trying to reorganize the international institutional system as the Chinese interest in postwar Bretton Woods institutions such as the IMF is too limited in terms of, for example, voting rights in proportion to the size of an economy. With the creation of the AIIB, the Chinese authorities have attempted to balance the importance of new emerging economies even though there is some controversy about it. After the AIIB started its operational activities, the status of this multilateral institution that does not conflict with the existing international institutional system was increasingly respected, so that gradually more (Western) countries joined this institution with 97 (prospective) members with total investments of USD 8.48 billion as of July 13, 2019. As a multilateral bank, the AIIB borrows on international markets to finance its operations, so must respect the standards and norms ruling these markets. It becomes clear that its aim is to meet the development needs and complement the international institutional order. The advantage of the AIIB is that some of its member countries, even if opposed to the BRI, being members of the AIIB and in this way moderate their attitude against the BRI. On the other hand, the AIIB holds the most controversial projects, as the consensus of all its member countries must be achieved. Ultimately, the influence of the AIIB on the BRI reduces the risks associated with the BRI. In addition to the AIIB, the Silk Road Infrastructure Fund, the NDB, and other MDBs, the Chinese financial sector itself is also an important source of financing for the BRI. For the coming decade, it will be quite a challenge to investigate the feasibility of financing the BRI, including the role of the Chinese banking system and that of the recipient countries.

4.3 'Belt and Road' Infrastructure Projects as Tools in a New Development Stage

The rapid development of the Chinese economy leads to the idea of rebalancing the country's position in the global economy. The new development phase is more focused on deepening participation in global governance whereby China has changed from a 'rule-follower' to a 'rule-settler' with a proactive role in finance, oversees capital expansion, and production outsourcing (Li 2019, p. 32). The most important features of this development phase are the adjustments of the structure of the industry and extending the production factors to domestic interior provinces and abroad (Ohashi 2018). The concept of strengthening the Chinese presence on some foreign markets and to develop a new area of international cooperation was part of the strategy. While in the past China was mainly focused on pursuing high-economic growth, the focus is now more on entering new markets, foreign investments, RMB internationalization and maintaining diplomatic relations.

The political foundation of the BRI assumes that the whole project is deeply anchored in the Chinese vision of economic growth. It is important that the BRI is recognized in a similar way by the participating countries as a Chinese development style that contrasts with the Anglo-Saxon neoliberal development model that was partly responsible for the problems during the GFC. The Chinese model offers a competing vision and geopolitical clout to gain cooperation between participating countries. Moreover, if the economic situation in Western countries will not improve, China will have more power to implement the BRI on its own terms and in this way to amplify its power in the global economy. According to this vision, China is a center of economic gravity which will lead to the creation of a big community of countries interlinked by a common strategy of economic development and cooperation.

In recent years, there have been increasing numbers of developing countries from all parts of the world who want to attract Chinese investment and thereby seek closer economic cooperation with the country (Ash 2018). The BRI has thereby strengthened the connectivity of institutional cooperation and policy, rules and standards cooperation. Compared to the Anglo-Saxon approach, the BRI proposes a new approach to deals that can be better adapted to different cultures, regions, and political systems. An important feature is that the BRI idea combines mutually beneficial cooperation, peaceful rise and common stakes in the future ('community common destiny,' i.e., the profits and market values are not the most important determinants of the project). The main idea behind the initiative is regional integration and a vision for a new regional order (Wuthnow 2017, p. 9). Although the BRI is not only aimed at the Euro-Asian region and this 'platform' should give access to all interested participating countries, it is obvious that the BRI is more a Sinocentric than a Western-oriented project.

The aim for the Chinese authorities in pursuing the BRI is not only to exert impact on the international economic order and to promote the Chinese values and style of development, but also the BRI is considered as a new tool for further economic development in China. The BRI is a crucial driver of the opening-up policy implemented by the Chinese authorities. The commitment to the creation of the international economic order embraces, among others, the growing role of China in the international trade, investments, and the international currency regime. The cooperation, however, is extended behind the traditional economic channels of trade and investment. In the contemporary economic conditions, the BRI concept offers a very strong focus on the new technology development and cooperation. It embraces such areas as cyberspace, space development, bioethics, and technology.

Through the BRI, China promotes its own investments and thereby creates a new economic order that frees up more space for realizing China's own interests. The BRI is aimed at combating the current problems in the Chinese economy and creating opportunities for further Chinese industrial development. It works three-dimensionally because this project makes it possible to develop parts of China that were previously underdeveloped; it makes it possible to adjust industrial overcapacity and the BRI encourages the transfer of some industries abroad. In a sense, the GFC has created a great opportunity for Chinese policy makers due to the significant slowdown in the global economy following this financial crisis.

During this decade, many Chinese financial institutions have become involved in all sorts of major infrastructure projects around the world under the BRI. Table 4.1 provides an overview of twenty different types of projects, such as railways, ports, bridges, industrial (park) projects and even involvement in the cooperation and introduction of economic free-trade zones. In some cases, the projects listed in Table 4.1 are not actually new phenomena under the BRI, but this initiative largely involves a massive rebranding of existing projects to satisfy management. BRI was officially launched in 2013, but some projects started years earlier are often counted. For example, Gwadar, the port built in Pakistan from 2001 to 2007, became a focal point of the BRI.

It can be concluded that without the BRI some infrastructural projects might never have been launched. Even if they were, their scale, speed, and international interconnectedness would never be similar, as the current ones. Financing infrastructure always needs a state support, and very seldom is possible to accomplish them in accordance with the commercial basis. Some of the projects are of regional and global significance. It is possible to indicate some crucial projects of such an importance. The five main projects of the BRI distinguished by the South China Morning Post are the following (*South China Morning Post* 2019):

- Railway to London (Yiwu–London route: a two-week train ride from China to the West);
- Gwadar Port (the nexus between China and the Middle East: China-Pakistan Economic Corridor);
- Railway to Iran (a key access point to the Middle East);
- Central Asia–China natural gas pipeline system needed to feed China's growing appetite;
- Khorgos gateway connects Kazakhstan to China by rail (the biggest dry port in the world).

The changes in the national economies and on the international level underline the importance of the BRI. One of such examples is the Brexit, which leads to deepening the trade ties between China and the UK. The railway between Zhengzhou (major national railway hub in China and easy reach of Beijing, Xian, and Hong Kong), the Chinese industrial belt (cities: Baoji, Tianshui, Lanzhou, and Zhanye), then Kazakhstan, Russia, and some Central and Western European countries (Belarus, Poland, Germany, Belgium, and France) finally reach the UK. For China, it is an important land cargo corridor.

The second very significant project is the China–Pakistan Economic Corridor. This project is estimated as the biggest project under the whole BRI. It connects Kashgar, the trading post of the historical Silk Road, with Gwadar Port in Pakistan. It is estimated that the connection should reduce transport cost by 50% and provide shipping route from China to the Middle East.

The third important connection under the BRI is between western region of China unto Teheran. The most important part of the project is the link between Almaty in Kazakhstan and Teheran. Such connection offers the second option for the cargo from Zhongzhou to London—in Almaty is the fork of the rail to the Central Asian countries—via Uzbekistan, Turkmenistan, with destination in Iran. The main goal is not only to offer Chinese goods to the Middle East countries, but also to provide for China greater access to oil. Iran hopes to become the major Eurasian trade hub. Except from oil, an important source of energy for China is the natural gas. The need defines the fourth strand of the BRI—gas pipeline between China and Central Asian countries (Kazakhstan, Turkmenistan, Uzbekistan, Kyrgyzstan, and Tajikistan). It is expected that the Central Asian Gas Pipeline will be a win-win cooperation. It will help China to meet its energy demands and be a much-needed boost for the Asian countries.

The fifth most important project is the Khorgos gateway. Khorgos, situated in the border between China and Kazakhstan, is turning to become the world's biggest dry port. The significance of the project is that it is situated in the epicenter of the BRI. There are two main goals of the project—first to boost not only the Chinese economy (cargo transport corridor to Europe), but also to allow Kazakhstan to take advantage of the BRI (especially from Chinese manufacturing and technology imports).

BRI exerts impact not only on the enumerated projects and countries which are crucial for the initiative, but has influence on many other countries, and on the whole global economy. It is estimated that so far China has signed 173 cooperation agreements with more than 120 countries. In result over 240 thousand jobs were created outside China (Ndegwa 2019). Despite this direct impact on participating countries, the whole initiative impacts on many countries in indirect way as well. There is something what can be called 'the BRI spirit.' It can be explained in some extent by the examples of cooperation between China and such countries as Cook Islands, Italy, Latvia or New Zealand. Despite formal Memorandums of Understanding between China and these countries, they might be not legally obliged to abide their term, and lead rather to indirect cooperation. On the other hand, such agreements are strengthening the cooperation in many areas—not only trade and transportation, but agricultural technology, culture, and tourism as well. The soft approach is sometimes called 'mutual learning between civilisations' (Ng 2019).

4.4 The Drawbacks of the 'Belt and Road' Initiative and Its Impact on Recipient Countries

Despite many benefits for the recipient countries of the BRI, it is important to realize that there is a clear economic dominance of China in mutual cooperation with the other BRI countries. It remains to be seen whether it is attractive for the BRI participants to simply accept China's unwanted industrial capacity. The project does not solve the deteriorating domestic demand in China, but is instead focusing on finding new yet still 'unstable' export regions. More concerns come upon the fact that there are no real customers that actually come to the newly developed infrastructures in the Silk Road, such as the shopping malls developed in the desert that has almost no buyers and just several shops that all sell the same product.

Another concern is that China wants to export its industrial overcapacity which was built during years of stimulus spending, and have them rebuild abroad with all the connected adverse consequences (*The Economist* 2018). This approach might lead to the situation when the Chinese industrial surplus will become a contagion spread across the economic 'belt.' Many BRI recipient countries are not enthusiastic about accepting China's excess capacity because in several sectors of their own industries they are competing directly with China.

It is significant, that most of the financial Chinese funds will come from loans, not from grants, which might create heavy debt burden for some countries. It means that if the receiving country will not be able to pay them back in the future, China can acquire the infrastructure built with the funds. Some of the Chinese loans are not transparent, which makes it more risky comparing to loans from other sources. Additionally, the Chinese inexpensive import might displace local firms and thus hurt employment in small enterprises. It is still unclear how the cooperation will impact on living standards and there are some concerns that the BRI will be beneficial only to the upper- and middle-class and will not have a positive impact on ordinary people (Hurley et al. 2018).

Another complaint is that BRI has mainly benefited China's SOEs which on average are extremely highly leveraged. Although the BRI's initial focus was on energy and infrastructure with a huge involvement of SOEs, it is now widening in trade, manufacturing, internet, and tourism as part of the BRI's key goals with more possibilities of participation of POEs and multinational corporations in the BRI as well

(Deloitte Insight 2018). As more resources are spent to boost the POEs, SOEs may see their access to capital curtailed in the long run. However, because SOEs face stronger urge to meet political targets and come under close government oversight, they are more likely to follow the government's lead and invest in the BRI. In contrast, POEs have greater freedom to avoid financially risky BRI projects, despite Beijing's efforts to enlist the support of China's growing private sector. Despite the rapidly changing financial environment in China and the continuing pressure of SOE reforms, the SOEs are not yet deterred by investments in the surrounding BRI countries. This could lead to 'moral hazard' concerns and hence inefficient allocation of resources if SOEs make more risky investments knowing that the Chinese government will bail them out anyhow. The absence of concrete support from POEs to increase their participation may exacerbate the moral hazard issues and undermine Xi's ability to fully mobilize domestic resources to deliver his aims behind the BRI. The growing cautiousness of the authorities to inject extra money into the BRI due to the continuing trade conflict and shrinking foreign exchange reserves could further reinforce this misallocation of sources (Li and Zeng 2019).

Also, the forecasted debt growth is considered as a shortcoming of the BRI. It is predicted that the BRI will not be plagued with wide-scale debt sustainability problems for its participants, stemmed especially from over-investing in some infrastructural projects. On the other hand, it is unlikely to avoid any instances of debt problems among some participating countries. Current research from the Center for Global Development shows that the problem might involve especially eight countries: Djibouti, the Maldives, Laos, Montenegro, Mongolia, Tajikistan, Kyrgyzstan, and Pakistan. Those BRI countries risk piling up dangerous amounts of debt, which some fear is designed to give China a strategic hold over them. In a certain way, the BRI can be seen as an effort to commit to the Chinese influence around the world by financially binding countries to Beijing by way of a 'debt trap diplomacy' (Pakistan as a vassal state is seen as an example). In response to this negative debt scenario, China is providing some debt relieves in an ad hoc manner and is trying to implement a greater coherence and discipline in order to avoid unsustainable debt among the BRI countries (e.g., implementing risk controls for overseas banking activities) (Hurley et al. 2018). Also, Chinese policy banks funding the BRI are pursuing partnerships with international lenders to improve financial governance and manage debt and investment risks (Xu and Chen 2019).

Another challenge for developing economies is that they must take advantage of this opportunity and climb up the global value chains, building their own comparative advantages. It means that with time some developing countries must shift their orientation from energy carriers to the production of goods and services of higher added value, some others must plug its production systems and own business into the international trade system. If they will fail to do so, they could be marginalized in the whole project and will serve always as suppliers of raw materials for China (Královičová and Žatko 2016). On the other hand, it might be difficult to develop a strong industry, separately for the core BRI, as the Chinese projects sometimes have some strings attached, like special concessions for Chinese entrepreneurs, some requirements to use Chinese contractors, labor and machinery, and what is limiting the contribution of these projects to local economies. The other risk is that some investments might become unsustainable or generate low returns in the future, which will impact the participants. Some projects regulations shift the accompanying risk to the state where the project is being implemented (Szczudlik 2017).

A general problem of the entire BRI is that some ambitions may contradict others and different motivations might lead to conflicting interests which ultimately might have a delaying effect on the implementation. There is infighting between the most important Chinese institutions involved, including the ministry of commerce, the foreign ministry, the planning commission, and China's provinces.

Furthermore, China is finding it hard to identify profitable projects in many BRI countries, and is facing a backlash against some of its plans. The examples are the elected governments in Sri Lanka and Myanmar which are repudiating or seeking to renegotiate projects approved by their authoritarian predecessors (*The Economist* 2017). Several failed projects are being canceled, renegotiated, or delayed (see Table 4.2) due to disputes about costs or complaints host countries get too little out of projects built by Chinese companies and financed by Chinese loans that must be repaid (e.g., a USD 15 billion high-speed railway in Thailand was suspended in 2016 following complaints too little business went to Thai companies). This will downgrade China's credit rating; however, authorities are renegotiating to give local contractors a bigger role.

Basically the BRI has the potential to promote connectivity and free flow of economic factors, highly efficient allocation of resources and deep

Table 4.2 Examples of OBOR projects' problems

Country	*Project*	*Year*	*Description*
Pakistan	Diamer-Bhasha dam project	2017	Pakistan dropped its bid to have the dam financed under China-Pakistan Economic Corridor framework. The reason was that Beijing placed strict conditions including ownership of the project, operation, and maintenance cost. They were unacceptable for Pakistan
Sri Lanka	Hambantota port project	2016	The port was funded by EXIM Bank of the People's republic of China. Sri Lanka borrowed funds with own interest rate of 6.3%. The interest rates of soft loans from the World Bank and ADB are 0.25–3%. The port incurred heavy losses making debt repayment unable for the country. As a solution, it was proposed to convert the debt into equity (debt-for-equity swap). It may lead to Chinese ownership of the project funding
Bhutan	Doklam plateau	2017	There is a political pressure from China which challenged Bhutan's sovereignty by attempting to extend a road into disputed territory leading to a military standoff with India. The behavior triggered a very negative signal to China's neighbors that it will aggressively behave to take over the control over disputed territories
Mongolia	Egiin Gol hydropower project	2016	In 2015, China and Mongolia decided to develop a large hydropower project, which was treated as an essential part of the OBOR initiative. Its main investment was a dam on the Eg River (one of the main water sources of Lake Baikal). It was planned to fund the investment by the China EXIM Bank. After Russian complaints, the China's National Development Reform Commission in 2016 suspended the project due to environmental concerns (threat to the Baikal Lake's ecosystem). The case highlighted that the OBOR so far lacks of environmental safeguards and specific green development guidelines

(continued)

Table 4.2 (continued)

Country	*Project*	*Year*	*Description*
Thailand	Bangkok–Nong Khai railway project	2016	In 2012, China and Thailand agreed to build high-speed railway from Bangkok to Nong Khai on the border with Laos. In 2016 the Thai government has rejected the accomplishment due to complaints that not enough Thai business will participate in the project and Chinese land rights requests. The Chinese part wanted to achieve the rights to develop commercial property at the stations and along the whole rail track. Finally, after additional negotiations, the countries agreed for new contract. The new conditions projected that for the investment China will provide expertise and supervision, while Thailand provide equipment, materials, engineers, and architects

Source Tracy et al. (2017), Wood (2017), Sajjanhar (2017), Rana (2017), Choudbury (2017)

integration of markets. In the many speeches during the Second Belt and Road Forum for international cooperation in April 2019, the BRI was called, among other things, an 'alternative to Western hegemony,' a 'way to modernize mulilateralism' and a 'new version of the globalization strategy'.[1] However, it is difficult to predict the exact result of the BRI as it requires deep collaboration between member countries. The OBOR project is still characterized by many political, financial, technical, environmental, and social uncertainties, and there is a fear that the BRI will end up producing a scattering of large, abandoned 'white elephant projects' along the 'belt and road' routes. What is essential is that the project must prove profitable for all partner countries, not only for China. However, up to now there is no blueprint to measure the BRI's performance (*The Economist* 2018).

[1] Following the inaugural Forum in May 2017, President Xi Jinping organized a Second Belt and Road Forum for international cooperation in April 2019. The following topics were discussed here: a more concrete roadmap for the development of Belt and Road; an evaluation of Belt and Road five years later; focus on implications for business; the direction of globalization; and a direct response to criticisms about BRI (see the drawbacks of the BRI).

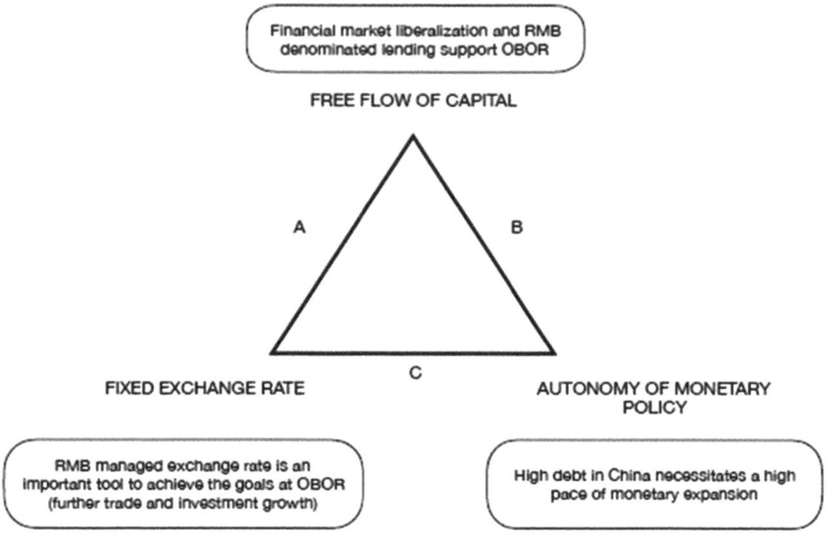

Fig. 4.1 The impact of the 'Belt and Road' project on China's policy trilemma (*Source* Łasak and van der Linden 2019)

It must be clarified that all the Chinese joint investments with its partners are related to the policy trilemma in three dimensions (see Fig. 4.1). First, financial market liberalization and RMB-denominated lending will support the BRI and hence free movement of capital. Capital flows accompanying the pursuing investments impact on greater financial openness. The different sources of financing the investments are an important contributor to the free flow of capital. Second, implementation of the BRI will expand the debt burden which requires a high pace of credit lending. A rise of shadow banking will push financial liberalization at the expense of monetary autonomy. Third, being open to cross-border capital flows may result in the loss of control over national credit conditions which might be harmful for the domestic consumption. Fourth, RMB managed floating exchange rate is an important tool of the BRI to promote trade and investment growth.

In 2013, the OBOR project was launched with great enthusiasm as the 'new Marshall plan without a war.' However, taking into account all the delaying factors that the OBOR implementation entails, the Chinese proverb 'loud thunder, small raindrops' might well apply or more ironically expressed OBOR is sometimes called 'one road, one trap.' With the arrival of the BRI, the aim of RMB internationalization has become even more necessary, if in the future the AIIB or Silk Road Fund would like to implement the RMB-denominated lending against investment of infrastructure. However, assuming the BRI will be accompanied by the necessary delays and that the drastically reduced foreign reserves will be used even more to finance the OBOR projects, aggressive foreign investment of infrastructure, RMB internationalization, and implementation of a more flexible market-oriented financial policy are three goals which could not be realized anymore. Even though the authorities have been able to circumvent or bend the impossible trinity with many policy adjustments during the last decade, eventually out of these three goals only two could be realized simultaneously.

4.5 Conditioning of 'Win-Win' Cooperation Under the 'Belt and Road' Initiative

Just as the UK was the growth engine of the global economy before the First World War, and this position was gradually taken over by the USA in the following period, so China is increasingly taking over this role in the current global economy. In this context, it is clear that the BRI has become the most important driver, not only for China, but also for the other participating countries[2] (*The Economist* 2016; Liu 2016). The OBOR project will not only exert a direct impact on the participating countries, but also an indirect impact on the global trade and production taking into account that the BRI is open to all countries which are ready to join. Since the BRI regards all regions of the world as a single area, it can be useful to tackle contemporary international trade problems through this approach and to rebalance the current global trade situation.

The BRI is a broad-scale initiative, involving infrastructure development and investments in more than 150 countries and international institutions. Xi Jinping declares that one of the crucial features of the project is the bias toward cooperation between the participating countries. He highlights that the member countries create a 'community

[2] In the current era of new protectionism and declining US hegemony, the BRI is also seen as an alternative approach to a Chinese style of globalization. For some Asian countries such as India, the BRI is considered a hegemonic project that not only challenges the current global order but also seeks to replace it with a Sinocentric.

of common destiny.' It means that there is an increased emphasis on 'win-win' cooperation and joint development, especially in the economic sphere (Beeson and Li 2016). The cooperation is not only limited to the economic aspects, especially the international trade, but indirectly promotes peace and stability as well by building appropriate rules, norms, institutions, and partnerships.

The 'win-win' concept of the BRI is not based on profit-maximizing behavior, but refers more to globalization characterized by infrastructure development and regional connectivity. It implies that except from financial results, the 'win-win' approach is defined by a mutual understanding, mutual satisfaction, and fulfillment of non-material values such as peace, freedom, justice, and democracy. These non-material values are also based on co-humanity (i.e., being human together), collectivism, and multiculturalism, which are often in contrast with some Western values such as individualism (Khan et al. 2018, p. 4). As the BRI approach will lead to greater openness, integration, and interdependence, it is important that the Chinese approach to 'win-win' benefits for all participating countries will be shared as evenly as possible. In order to identify cooperation between participating countries, it is useful to distinguish between the following geographical areas and the different levels of possible cooperation.

The cooperation in the Southeast Asia region:

- connection between China and Central Asia, Africa, and Middle East;
- cooperation between China and Russia;
- cooperation in the dimension 17+1;
- cooperation between China and the European Union (EU).

Considering the dimension of cooperation there are such areas as:

- trade and investments (establishment of infrastructure for transportation and energy transmission);
- currency internationalization (the broader aim to replace the ongoing rules of international monetary system and its impact on the international trade);
- technological cooperation;
- cultural and political cooperation;
- digital connection.

Both enumerated ways of dividing the scope of cooperation under the BRI show the complexity of the entire initiative. The level of complexity confirms that the initiative is not based mainly on a single country but requires a cooperation between numerous countries. The impact of the initiative on a country (or region) is being established according to the position of the country (or region) to China, which creates the center of gravity. The strongest influence of the BRI is exerted on Southeast Asian economies, then on the Central Asian countries and Russia, further on Africa, Central and Eastern European Countries (CEEC) and the EU, and with the weakest impact to the rest of the global economy. However, this concerns the direct impact, while a more indirect BRI influence on participating countries can also distinguish many other hierarchies (e.g., the trade chain influence differs from the cultural impact and from the expansion of technology). In fact, the abovementioned geographic hierarchy defines the main structure of influence of the BRI on participating countries and regions.

4.5.1 East and Southeast Asia

The key aspect of the cooperation between China and Southeast Asia is the awareness that the cooperation is pivotal for the success or failure of the whole OBOR project. Among the crucial BRI members of the region might be mentioned countries such as Cambodia, Laos, Malaysia, Myanmar, Singapore, Thailand, and Vietnam. The successes of cooperation between China and these countries, achieved under the new vision of an Asian community and the defined goals of the integration, will be shared by all the participating countries. There are some important motives for cooperation, like the economic growth stimulation and integration or political stability. The BRI plays a crucial role in stimulation of trade and investment in the East and Southeast Asian region. It was especially important in some sectors of the industry (Tables 4.3 and 4.4).

The economic growth is interconnected with the bilateral and multilateral agreements binding closer the neighboring countries. The intensive cooperation under the BRI is focusing especially on investment projects. The member countries understand the 'win-win' situation when they have a high degree of exchange of both the inputs into economic activity and the outputs from the activity. The trade is important for the region, and especially in the low-cost economies, the outsourcing from China became fundamental (CIMB 2018, p. 5). Among the main areas

Table 4.3 Imports of goods from China into ASEAN in the period of 2014–2017 ($ mln)

Sector	*2014*	*2015*	*2016*	*2017*
Organic chemicals	4739.2	4261.9	4298.8	4954.5
Chemical products	2735.4	2551.9	3145.4	4484.9
Stone, plaster, cement, asbestos, mica	573,151	646,982	696,175	815,592
Ceramic products	1479.1	1592.2	1670.5	1745.0
Glass and glassware	1208.3	1329.8	1718.5	1762.8
Iron and steel	13,131	13,549	14,747	13,359
Iron or steel articles	7137.4	8182.9	7542.0	7993.8
Copper and articles thereof	1377.9	1468.4	1704.1	1771.5
Nickel and articles thereof	577,373	125,620	26,085	38,790
Tools implements of base metal	715,078	747,068	836,455	969,988
Metal, products of base metal	1103.7	1207.0	1383.5	1579.4
Nuclear reactors, boilers	39,270	39,673	39,284	42,008
Railway, tramway locomotives, etc.	305,342	629,942	589,549	317,017
Vehicles, other than railway	4277.0	5632.5	5056.2	5437.5

Source CIMB Asean Research Institute (2018, October), *China's Belt and Road Initiative (BRI) and Southeast Asia*, Kuala Lumpur, p. 14

Table 4.4 China FDI inflow into ASEAN in the period of 2014–2017 ($ mln)

Investment sector	*2014*	*2015*	*2016*	*2017*
Construction	197.19	80.59	661.82	719.50
Wholesale and retail trade	269.02	564.69	1766.85	2783.75
Transportation and storage	−303.74	168.09	−57.60	1.04
Accommodation and food service	23.63	46.80	809.02	28.67
Information and communication	−2.93	3.40	29.05	144.90
Financial and insurance	1844.84	1678.39	3441.17	1607.30
Real estate	2105.65	2005.29	2418.03	3053.43
Proof, science and tech	23.50	12.34	53.14	58.78
Total	6254.64	6620.07	11,275.50	11,295.27

Source CIMB Asean Research Institute (2018, October), *China's Belt and Road Initiative (BRI) and Southeast Asia*, Kuala Lumpur, p. 13

of such activity are the low cost-sensitive parts of electrical and machinery assembly, food processing, cloth manufacturing, etc. The richer countries are key exporters to China, providing for instance microchips, chemicals, plastic, or other higher value-added components.

Some of the joint projects between the enumerated countries go beyond the trade and investment area and embrace such aspects as financial markets standards, agricultural policy, and environmental sustainability (Parameswaran 2019). It must be highlighted that China had to suit to its neighbor's concerns and adjust to some of their expectations. Under the 'win-win' approach, it is important that BRI will lead to an advantage for all the participating countries. Among the benefits for the Southeast Asian countries are the railway connections and energy infrastructure (e.g., hydro powers) and digitalization of economics (increasing the role of digital technologies in commerce and industry) (Vinels 2018). There are, however, many obstacles for the project. The BRI originators in Beijing have already realized that the success of the project might be unrequited by other participating countries, because it brings for them not only profits but some serious risks as well. The countries of the region are concerned about excessive debt mechanisms accompanying the BRI projects as described in Sect. 4.4. Moreover, they are worried about the growing economic and political influence of China over the Southeast Asian region. The BRI is criticized as well for its lack of transparency and inclusivity. After six years of the BRI functioning, there are articulated such aspects that almost 90% of all contractors participating in the projects are Chinese companies. It has also been found that the workforce involved in OBOR projects is mainly of Chinese origin, which is not perceived as a way to improve the fifth key goal of people-to-people exchange to 'break the bottleneck of connectivity' (see Sect. 4.1). As a reaction, the Southeast Asian countries try to elaborate mechanisms of assessing the risks accompanying their presence in the BRI projects, which in their opinion would help to reduce the uncertain economic and political mechanisms.

Very different from the experience of abovementioned countries is the nature of relations between China, Japan, and South Korea under the BRI. For Japan, the participation in BRI is like reemergence of the values of common historical heritage and cooperation between Japan and some other BRI members. Japan is ready to assist the other member countries in their process of economic growth. Its assistance is oriented on three areas, namely political dialogue, economic cooperation and cooperation in peace-building areas and fostering stability. As the Japanese understand, the processes should lead to maintaining a long-term perspective and be based on mutual benefits (Dadabaev 2018, pp. 35–36). In the cooperation between Japan and China, both countries share the same approach that companies should take the lead in facilitating economic projects with the need to facilitate transport connectivity. Moreover, there are many other similarities regarding the political approach of China and Japan to other countries. In contrast to Japan, the South Korean approach is more pragmatic. The country defines its possible participation in many projects, like building railroads, participating in power generation plants, etc. Looking at the cooperation between China, Japan, and South Korea, it is important to remember, that the BRI strengthens the former initiative of free-trade agreement, undertaken between these three countries. It seems that South Korea and Japan will benefit from the progress of BRI. The aims of the Chinese approach are not only related to economic processes, but they aim to strengthen the 'soft power' in the Central Asia as well (see Sect. 4.1).

4.5.2 *Russia*

The cooperation between China and Russia is on different level comparing to the Southeast Asian countries. Russia does not want to offer its resources and territory for China-led projects at any costs, which might make Moscow more dependent on Beijing. Moreover, the Russian government wants to preserve its own initiative, the Eurasian Economic Union (EEU), which was created between Armenia, Belarus, Kazakhstan, and Kyrgyzstan. It does not mean that the BRI is outside the Russian areas of interest. Russia is very interested in participation in BRI, but the key issue is to get the respect from its partners for its own interests. The situation means that the main dimension of the 'win-win' cooperation between China and Russia is to 'harmonise' the EEU and BRI relations. The 'win-win' approach is undoubtedly the biggest advantage of the BRI and ultimately determines the Russian participation in the project. Such an approach highlights that the Chinese aim is not to use the initiative for maximizing the profits for one country, but to develop the cooperation and to achieve mutual benefits. Another important factor from the Chinese side is that it's not oriented on forming a small group of beneficiaries, but to relate a big group of participating countries which will enable to achieve the level of harmonious co-existence (Li 2018, p. 95). Moreover, Russia is not competing with China for a global primacy. Both countries achieved an advanced level of partnership built on a range of shared interests.

Since 2013, the future cooperation and development of the Arctic route have been on the agenda of the BRI. After a long period of discussion, in 2017, Chinese and Russian leaders jointly proposed the Ice Silk Road (ISR) with the aim of promoting 'win-win' cooperation and development in the Arctic without geopolitical thinking, at least in theory. In 2018, China and Russia, together with some other Arctic countries, achieved significant progress in their cooperation on the Arctic gas field and many cooperation agreements were reached on the construction of Arctic waterway infrastructure (Zhang 2019).

The relations between China and Russia are on an even keel from other reasons. Due to economic sanctions, Russia has had a poor relationship with Western countries in recent years, so the partnership with China is an excellent alternative for further Russian economic development. Strong partnership with China in global issues is a major Russian asset in its foreign policy. Thanks to the cooperation with other BRI countries, Russia will be a more active economic player. The OBOR project gives the country a great opportunity for attracting foreign investments, and on the other hand, Russia benefits from cargo transit through its territory. The geographic position between the EU and East Asia is an important advantage and has a special value for Russia (Feng et al. 2019). Thanks to the position the country strives to keep the balance between benefits from participation in BRI and keeping its independence from China.

4.5.3 *Africa–China Relations*

The BRI is not only focused on Asian cooperation, but also on the participation in the cooperation of other countries including the African member countries. China emphasizes the former cooperation with Africa and pledges further alignment, which will be based on a 'win-win' approach and to foster the conditions for achievement of sustainable development of the African region. Among the most important areas of cooperation are enumerated joint investment initiatives, special economic zones, and industrialization projects. For the African continent, sustainable development is based on three crucial factors. The continent is suffering such shortcomings as backward infrastructure, lack of professional and skilled personnel, and a shortage of capital sources. The OBOR project offers the possibility to combat the three constraints of development, and in this way to provide the 'win-win' circumstances. Moreover, for African countries the possibility for cooperation with

China is very symbolic and positive since it is always juxtaposing the past, colonial approach from Western countries. The narration with a peace and cooperation is a very positive impulse for the stronger relationship. Many African leaders believe in result they can achieve and that sustainable development and provision of common interests are beneficial for all the participating countries.

The Africa–China cooperation matches the strategy of a 'win-win' cooperation. For the last ten years, China is Africa's largest trading partner and crucial foreign investor. For China, the African continent is equally important as well. Africa has not only an abundance of natural resources and is an important market for Chinese export, but it has also a young labor force and good demographic prospects (it is forecasted that Africa will have the largest increase in size of its population during the next two decades, and in 2050 will have almost 2.5 billion inhabitants). All these factors have a strong influence on the Chinese pressure for more and better cooperation with African countries via the BRI (Cookson 2019; Wang 2019).

With regard to the BRI cooperation between China and other countries, another important feature can be emphasized, namely the major influence of the BRI on developing countries. Based on this feature, it might be concluded that the initiative symbolically shifts the power from the North to the South. While in the past the Western economies were the crucial countries in the global economy, in the last decade it has been mainly the BRICS countries and some other newly emerging developing countries such as Vietnam, Nigeria, Turkey, and Bangladesh. The BRI creates a great opportunity for strengthening the process. It is called 'South-South' cooperation and is being contrasted to the 'North-South' cooperation between developed and developing economies. It is likely that in the long run the BRI will contribute to a more balanced and efficient global economic system (Taidong and Haibing 2018). On the other hand, most of the 'south' countries are the African ones. The relations between China and Africa and China and Southeast Asia define the 'South-South' dimension of economic cooperation.

4.5.4 *The 17+1 Group*

Apart from the regional cooperation in Asia, and between China and some African countries, another important group was created by CEEC. During the visit of Chinese Prime Minister Wen Jiabao in Poland in

2012, the countries set up a '16+1 group'.[3] Since then the group elaborated and accepted a joint framework of cooperation. The main reason for creation such a group was the deepening economic relations between the member countries and strengthening their cooperation with China. Among the main goals were enumerated enhancement of connectivity, cooperation, trade, and cultural exchange between China and CEEC. The 'win-win' is one of the core principles, lying across the cooperation. The agenda is being discussed in annual summits. In every such a meeting the Chinese Prime Minister highlighted the equal treatment, 'win-win' results, and common development as a key element of the China-CEEC cooperation (Pepermans 2018; Chen and He 2018). In 2019 a further step of the cooperation was made, because the '16+1 group' was broadened and converted into '17+1 group', as Greece joined the initiative. The decision was made during the eighth meeting of the China-CEEC countries, which took place in the Croatian city Dubrovnik. By joining to the group, Greece becomes an important member, which supports the Balkans and Central European countries to encourage the trade and investment between China and Europe.

The real benefit, which is important for the whole group of CEEC, is the financial investment. The countries have strong ties with the EU, but the GFC has forced them to search for capital outside Europe. The cooperation under the BRI is a great opportunity for increase of investments in the CEEC.

The data related to FDI show that the CEEC region has still a great potential for the investment as compared to the Western European countries. The value of the Chinese investments in this region is still below 10% of the value of the investments of the country in the whole EU (Table 4.5).

Among the main priorities are transport, infrastructure, technology, and ecology. Another important field in this regard is science, education, and cultural exchange. Despite the persistent trade imbalances and huge deficits, the CEEC are much stronger supporters of the BRI than many other Western EU members. Such approach leads to implementation of many infrastructural projects in these countries.

[3] The "16+1" group was created by China and CEEC countries: Albania, Bosnia and Herzegovina, Bulgaria, Croatia, the Czech Republic, Estonia, Hungary, Latvia, Lithuania, Macedonia, Montenegro, Poland, Romania, Serbia, Slovakia, and Slovenia. Since April 2019 the group "16+1" changed into group "17+1", as Greece became its member.

Table 4.5 The value of Chinese FDI stock in the EU in 2015

EU-15	*EUR mln*	*New EU Member States*	*EUR mln*
Great Britain	12,212	Estonia	23
Ireland	99	Latvia	3
Netherlands	2997	Lithuania	30
Belgium	928	Czech Republic	138
Luxembourg	432	Poland	453
France	5907	Hungary	1891
Spain	1096	Romania	733
Portugal	5138	Slovenia	8
Italy	4202	Croatia	4
Greece	405	Bulgaria	207
Germany	6827	Cyprus	31
Denmark	134	Malta	69
Sweden	1522	Total	3590
Finland	102		(7.8% of total EU)
Austria	436		
Total	42,437		

Source Own calculations based on Richet (2016)

Among them might be enumerated projects that are finished, projects under way, and some plans for the future (e.g., express ways between Montenegro and Albania, highways: 'Hemus,' 'Black Sea,' 'Kičevo-Ohrid,' 'Miladinovci-Štip,' 'Podgorica-Kolašin,' construction of power plants: MW Tuzla, MW Banovivi, MW Stanari, railways: Wuhan-Pardubice, Chengdu-Łódź, and many others) (Zakić and Tešić 2018, pp. 98–103). On the other hand, the cooperation between CEEC and China has also had adverse consequences, including the increasing trade deficits and the financial imbalances in Chinese participation in infrastructure projects in the CEEC countries. It should be highlighted that many of the planned projects meet with difficulties in financing, some of them are wrongly estimated, vulnerable in many areas, or there is no progress in their implementation. One of the examples of pitfalls in the cooperation between China and CEEs under the BRI is the railway line between Budapest and Belgrade. The project to build 336 kilometers of rail line linking Serbian and Hungarian capital cities was originally announced in November 2014 (Góralczyk 2017). Since the time many obstacles occurred, which impeded the accomplishment of the project (e.g., lack of transparency, cultural, mental and technological obstacles, and the pressure from the EU to limit the cooperation with China). Another example of improper cooperation is the Chinese investment in Poland, aimed at construction of highway connecting Warsaw and Łódź. Originally the project seemed like win-win cooperation, but the Polish government decided to cancel the contract. The main reason was the financial difficulties in which ran COVEC (China Overseas Engineering Group) once the construction get underway (Cienski 2011).

One of the greatest risks for cooperation between China and the CEEC is the fragmentation of the European countries. The CEEC are very diversified, with different economic conditions and different needs of individual states. It creates a great asymmetry between China and the diversified European region. Different economic conditions, needs, and priorities, together with all the constraints lead to a loss of confidence among the countries and might have an important impact on further cooperation if China will not attach greater importance to the 'win-win' cooperation approach and the necessity for mutual benefits as defined during the joint summits. Moreover, it is essential for the cooperation that most of the CEEC are EU members which means that the cooperation under the BRI should provide a 'third win'- situation throughout EU (Huang and Liu 2017).

4.5.5 EU-China Relations

The cooperation between China and EU has a great potential in the areas of trade and investment, peace, security, and people-to-people exchange. There are many other issues behind the economic fields, like finance, environment, and technology. It is important that the EU is China's biggest trading partner, and China is the EU's second-largest trading partner (Misiągiewicz and Misiągiewicz 2016).

Chinese companies have invested heavily in key sectors of the EU over the past decade including stakes in most of UK's leading banks, Sweden's largest carmarket, robotics in Germany, power utilities in Portugal, high-tech manufacturing and power grid in Italy, solar farms in Hungary, roads and railways in Serbia, Montenegro, Bosnia-Herzegovina and North Macedonia and the aforementioned majority stake in the Greek port of Piraeus (Xu and Chen 2019). The cooperation between China and the EU is probably one of the most complicated relationships. On the one hand, the EU market is very important for China and vice versa. On the other hand, for many EU countries, like France, Germany, and some others, the BRI project consists of all kinds of shortcomings. In addition to all the BRI disadvantages mentioned in Sect. 4.4, there can also be mentioned the market-distorting practices and the strong trade competition between the USA and China with an adverse effect on the entire global economy.

The main problem related directly to the China-EU cooperation is created by the lack of a comprehensive uniform strategy presented by the entire EU. Some EU members, like Greece, Italy and the CEEC mainly support the BRI, while other EU members present more a toned-down approach. However, the official relations between China and its separate EU countries can be misleading and sometimes contradictory. The statistics reveal that the main beneficiaries from Chinese direct investments are not the CEEC, but the core ones—UK (23%), Germany (19%), Italy (13%), and France (11%) (Kavalski and Mayer 2019). It became obvious that the BRI is increasingly embraced by European countries and cooperation is playing more and more important role in deepening China-EU comprehensive strategic partnership (*China Daily* 2018).

The EU-China relationship characterizes the complicated BRI in the background. On the one hand, the governments of the EU countries are concerned about the implications of Chinese investment in European ports, energy, technology, and agriculture, but at the same time they make joint plans for further cooperation.

References

Ash, M. (2018, October 18). *China's Belt and Road Plan to Reshape the International Order.*

Beeson, M., & Li, F. (2016). China's Place in Regional and Global Governance: A New World Comes into View. *Global Policy, 7*(4), 491–499.

Cai, P. (2017, March). *Understanding China's Belt and Road Initiative.* Sydney: Lowy Institute for International Policy.

Chatterjee, B., & Kumar, S. (2017, July 18). *Promises and Pitfalls of the Belt and Road Initiative.* Asia Pacific Bulletin, No. 388.

Chen, X., & He, Z. (2018, November). *16+1 Cooperation and China–EU Relationship.* Budapest: China-CEEC Institute.

China Daily. (2018, March 18). *Europe on Path of Expanding Cooperation on BRI.*

Choudbury, D. (2017, May 25). UN Warns About Financial Risks in China's One Belt One Road project. *The Economic Times.*

Cienski, J. (2011, June 15). Poland to China: You're Fired. *Financial Times.*

CIMB Asean Research Institute. (2018, October). *China's Belt and Road Initiative (BRI) and Southeast Asia.* Kuala Lumpur.

Cookson, C. (2019, June 17). Africa to Propel World's Population Towards 10bn by 2050. *Financial Times.*

Dadabaev, T. (2018). "Silk Road" as Foreign Policy Discourse: The Construction of Chinese, Japanese and Korean Engagement Strategies in Central Asia. *Journal of Euroasian Studies, 9,* 30–41.

Deloitte. (2019). *BRI Update 2019 - Recalibration and New Opportunities.*

Deloitte Insight. (2018). *Embracing the BRI Ecosystem in 2018: Navigating Pitfalls and Seizing Opportunities.*

Feng, Y., Gabuev, A., Haenle, P., Bin, M., & Trenin, D. (2019, April 8). *The Belt and Road Initiative: Views from Washington, Moscow, and Beijing.* Beijing: Carnagie-Tsinghua.

Góralczyk, B. (2017). China's Interests in Central and Eastern Europe: Enter the Dragon. *European View, 16*(1), 153–162.

Hillman, J. (2018, January 25). *China's Belt and Road Initiative: Five Years Later.* Washington, DC: Center for Strategic & International Studies.

Ho, D. (2017, September 27). Cost of Funding 'Belt and Road Initiative' Is Daunting Task. *South China Morning Post.*

Huang, P., & Liu, Z. (2017). *How the 16+1 Cooperation Promotes the Belt and Road Initiative.* China-CEEC Think Tank Series. London: Pathe International Ltd.

Hurley, J., Morris, S., & Portelance G. (2018, March). *Examining the Debt Implications of the Belt and Road Initiative from Policy Perspective* (CGD Policy Paper No. 121), 15–18.

Kavalski, E., & Mayer, M. (2019). *China Is Now a Power in Europe, but Fears of Interference in the EU Are Simplistic and Misguided.* The Conversation.

Khan, M. K., Sandero, I. A., Pratt, C. B., & Farid, T. (2018). China's Belt and Road Initiative: A Global Model for an Evolving Approach to Sustainable Regional Development. *Sustainability, 10*(11), 4234.

Královičová, M., & Žatko, M. (2016, August). *One Belt One Road Initiative in Central Asia: Implications for Competitiveness of Russian Economy* (Working Paper No. 2016/9). Maastricht School of Management.

Krukowska, M. (2016). China's 'One Belt, One Road' Strategy and Its Implications for the Global World Order. *International Business and Global Economy, 35*(1), 157–168.

Łasak, P., & van der Linden, R. W. H. (2019). The Effectiveness of the 'Belt and Road' Initiative in Tackling China's Economic Slowdown and Its Financial Implications Within a Policy Trilemma Context, Chapter 12. In E. Gualandri, V. Venturelli, & A. Sclip (Eds.), *Frontier Topics in Banking: Investigating New Trends and Recent Developments in the Financial Industry.* Cham: Palgrave Macmillan.

László, G. (2018, May 16). The Effects of the AIIB on the Multilateral Development banks' System. *GAGEO Geopolitikai Kutatóintézet.*

Li, L. (2018). *China's Manufacturing Locus in 2025: With a Comparison of "Made-in-China 2025" and "Industry 4.0"*. Technological Forecasting and Social Change No. 135.

Li, X. (2019). *Mapping China's 'One Belt One Road' Initiative.* International Political Economy Series. Aalborg: Palgrave Mcmillan.

Li, X., & Zeng, K. (2019, March). To Join or Not to Join? State Ownership, Commercial Interests, and China's Belt and Road Initiative. *Pacific Affairs, 92*(1), 5–26.

Liu, Z. (2016, October 23). China Ocean Strategic Industry Investment Fund to Promote 'Belt and Road' Initiative. *Global Times.*

Manuel, A. (2017, October 17). China Is Quitely Reshaping the World. *The Atlantic.*

Misiągiewicz, J., & Misiągiewicz, M. (2016). China's "One Belt, One Road" Initiative—The Perspective of the European Union. *Annales Universitatis Mariae Curie-Skłodowska, XXIII*(1), 33.

National Development and Reform Commission. (2015, March 28). *Vision and Actions on Jointly Building Silk Road Economic Belt and 21-st-Century Maritime Silk Road, National Development and Reform Commission (NDRC)*, Ministry of Foreign Affairs and Ministry of Commerce of People's Republic of China, with State Council authorization.

Ndegwa, S. (2019, April 25). Belt and Road Initiative a Global Game-Changer. *Business Today.*

Ng, N. (2019). *The Possible Impact of China's Belt and Road Agreement with Italy.* https://p.dw.com/p/3F4S2.

Nomura. (2018, April 16). *Belt and Road: Globalisation, China Style.* Global Markets Research Anchor Report.

Northern Trust. (2017). *One Belt, One Road: A Global Overview.* NTAC: 3NS-20.

Ohashi, H. (2018). The Belt and Road Initiative (BRI) in the Context of China's Opening-Up Policy. *Journal of Contemporary East Asia Studies, 7*(2), 85–103.

Parameswaran, P. (2019, May 15). Southeast Asia and China's Belt and Road Initiative. *The Diplomat.*

Pepermans, A. (2018). China's 16+1 and Belt and Road Initiative in Central and Eastern Europe: Economic and Political Influence at a Cheap Price. *Journal of Centemporary Central and Eastern Europe, 26*(2–3), 181–203.

PwC. (2016, February). *China's New Silk Route: The Long and Winding Road.* PwC's Growth Markets Centre.

Rana, S. (2017, November 15). Pakistan Stops Bid to Include Diamer-Bhasha Dam in CPEC. *The Express Tribune.* tribune.com.pk.

Richet, X. (2016, May 9–10). The Belt & Road Initiative and EU–China Economic Relations: Trade, Finance, FDI. In *Presentation on the Turin Center on Emerging Economies Conference*.

Sabine, P. (2017, March 28). Belt and Road is 'Marshall Plan Without a War', Analysts Say, as Beijing and Banks Woo Private-Sector Investors. *South China Morning Post*.

Sajjanhar, A. (2017, November 28). *China's Belt and Road Initiative: Prospects and Pitfalls*. Institute for Defence Studies and Analyses.

Shen, S., & Chan, W. (2018, March 27). A Comparative Study of the Belt and Road Initiative and the Marshall Plan. *Palgrave Communications, 4*(1), 32.

Stuart-Haentjens, R. (2017, July 6). *China and the AIIB on the Belt and Road: Power Sans Control*. Global Risk Insights.

Szczudlik, J. (2017, November 30). China's 16+1 Poses Few Risks to Europe.

Taidong, Z., & Haibing, Z. (2018). China's Belt and Road Initiative: An Opportunity to Re-energize South-South Cooperation. *China Quarterly of International Strategic Studies, 4*(4), 559–576.

The Economist. (2016). *Our Bulldozers, Our Rules*.

The Economist. (2017, May 13). *What Is China's Belt and Road Initiative? The Many Motivations Behind Xi Jinping's Key Foreign Policy*.

The Economist. (2018, July 26). *All Under Heaven: China's Belt-and-Road Plans Are to Be Welcomed—And Worried About*.

The Five Main Projects of the Belt and Road Initiative: A Visual Explainer. (2019). *South China Morning Post*. https://multimedia.scmp.com/news/china/article/One-Belt-One-Road/index.html.

Tracy, E. F., Shvarts, E., Simonov, E., & Babenko, M. (2017). China's New Eurasian Ambitions: The Environmental Risks of the Silk Road Economic Belt. *Eurasian Geography and Economics, 58*(1), 56–88.

Vinels, P. (2018, December 15). *Advancing ASEAN's Digital Economy* "East Asia Forum".

Wang, L. (2019, March 23). *China–Africa Cooperation Under the Belt and Road Initiative (BRI): Africa Sees the Way Forward*. Global Research.

Wilson, J. (2018). *Connecting the Asia-Pacific: Australian Participation in China's Regional Infrastructure Initiatives*. Broadway: Australia–China Relations Institute (ACRI).

Wood, A. J. (2017, August 25). *China-Thailand Rail Connection: A Silk Road Tourism Legacy*. https://www.eturbonews.com/162675/china-thailand-rail-connection-silk-road-tourism-legacy.

Wuthnow, J. (2017). *Chinese Perspectives on the Belt Road Initiative: Strategic Rationales, Risks, and Implications*. Center for the Study of Chinese Military Affairs, Institute for National Strategic Studies, "China Strategic Perspectives", No. 12.

Xu, S., & Chen, L. (2019, August 15). *China's Belt and Road Initiative: Recalibration and New Opportunities*. Deloitte Insights.

Yongquan, L. (2018). The Greater Eurasian Partnership and the Belt and Road Initiative: Can the Two Be Linked? *Journal of Eurasian Studies, 9*(2), 94–99.

Zakić, K., & Tešić, K. (2018). Managing Regional Development in CEE Countries – The Example of Initiative 16+1. *Progress in Economic Sciences, 5*, 95–109.

Zhang, Y. (2019, April 7). Ice Silk Road Framework Welcomed by Countries, Sets New Direction for Arctic Cooperation. *Global Times*.

CHAPTER 5

China's Financial Deepening and Its 'Belt and Road' Funding Dilemma in a Global Context

Abstract In this chapter, the contemporary development of the Chinese financial market is presented. Financial opening and liberalization of capital flows are necessary for China for its further successes on the international level. The BRI exerts a great pressure for the processes of domestic financial market growth, cross-border financial transactions increase and RMB internationalization. All of these processes can be described from two dimensions: the development of financial architecture (what is related to broadening of the scope and size of the financial market) and as important multidimensional contributors to the economic growth. A special consideration is given to the Mundell–Fleming policy trilemma. It means that fostering a 'Going-Out' strategy will exert an impact on further liberalization of the financial market with consequences for monetary and foreign exchange policy. China must define its priorities in the three areas, but there are possible several options to cope with the trilemma in the 'new normal' economic development. The best option is strictly related to the effective implementation of the BRI project. The rapid development of the Chinese financial market, together with an unstable international background, leads to the necessity to carefully balance the trade-off between financial liberalization and financial stability. The rapid liberalization and development of the Chinese financial markets have led to the expansion of the unregulated shadow banking system. The system is an important alternative for the traditional banking and offers many lending options. It became an important contributor to

P. Łasak and R. W. H. van der Linden, *The Financial Implications of China's Belt and Road Initiative*,
https://doi.org/10.1007/978-3-030-30118-7_5

both the encouragement of financial liberalization in China and enhancement of the BRI financing. The BRI poses many financial pitfalls to the economy. Among them are the growth of unsustainable debt as a consequence of the undertaken investments, lack of transparency and unpredictability of the investments in the long term, and some specific problems of participating countries. The successful strategy requires from the Chinese government not only the choice of a balanced policy, but also implementation of an associated effective regulatory environment.

Keywords Financial deepening · Financial liberalization · Financial stability · Mundell–Fleming policy trilemma · Shadow banking in China · Chinese financial market regulatory environment

5.1 The Impact of the Chinese Financial Market's Liberalization on the Policy Trilemma

An important condition for the success of the BRI is financial opening and liberalization of financial flows in China. This is considered to be one of the main goals defined in China's Financial Roadmap from the CPC Central Committee reference including the following main areas:

- Further open up the financial sector by allowing small, privately owned banks to participate in the market;
- Liberalize cross-border financial transactions;
- Promote the Chinese bond market development and fostering development of bond markets in other Asian countries;
- Promote equity market development and supporting equity finance in China;
- Encourage financial innovation through diversified financial products (Hsu 2015).

Although financial sector reforms started in China in the early 1990s, the current macroeconomic imbalances are still largely due to the problems with its financial system. Firstly, the low return on savings deposits and high risk associated with anything associated outside banks partly explain the high gross savings rate, consistently above 45% of GDP for the last decade with a declining trend. With limited other financial options, it is understandable that there is a preference to invest in real estate, one of the few seemingly 'safe' assets households can access. Secondly, a substantial part of corporate savings is reinvested in real assets of the company itself. Furthermore, POEs know that financing from either the stock markets or the state-owned banks is still rather uncertain (van der Linden 2008). Although the fixed-investment rate is currently slightly below 45% of GDP with a declining trend and several policy measures have been taken to improve an efficient allocation of savings into more productive investments, a further deepening of a fast-paced financial reforms will be critical to ensure sustainable growth in a global world. In that context, further development of China's real economy depends to a large extent on its financial market reforms. These reforms will especially support the development of SMEs and be favorable to individual borrowers and investors. Important steps have already been taken to push forward these reforms, for instance through the possibility of foreign listings (IPOs) in RMB-denominated assets on the Chinese stock markets and the creation of the China Banking Regulatory Commission (CBRC) established in 2003 by the State Council and merged with the China Insurance Regulatory Commission (CIRC) to form the China Banking and Insurance Regulatory Commission (CBIRC) in April 2018. The BRI itself might act as a drain on China's financial resources with negative consequences for the domestic market and economy, whereas the financial liberalization will lead to the increase of financial resources and to stabilize the internal development processes. The downside of the situation is that the liberalization of the financial market, together with more managed floating than fixed exchange rates excludes the PBC's monetary autonomy.

The financial liberalization will encourage not only the domestic economy but also the OBOR project. In order to facilitate different sources of financing (public and private, domestic and foreign), China must foster its financial cooperation with other states participating in the project. For this reason, it is necessary to create the institutional structure capable for combining funds from different sources. The Chinese financial market especially must be able to service the financial instruments from developed countries. To be able to fulfill this requirement, the market must have the necessary breadth, depth, and liquidity. China is the initiator and leading country for the BRI and having this position must have the abilities to manage the cross-border capital flows. It is necessary for the country to improve the institutional infrastructure facilitating the cooperation, including entities from different countries.

Financial market liberalization in China might impact the BRI especially in three ways:

- the process will facilitate economic growth;
- it will favor the development of the financial infrastructure, will broaden the scope and size of the financial market and in this way enable participation of investors from different countries;
- financial opening is important for the Chinese participation in the global economic governance.

Taking into account the great importance of the BRI, it is necessary to reduce the interest rate regulations in China and to create market mechanisms that allow financial institutions to set the interest rates according to the supply of and demand for funds. Only the market mechanism of interest rates settling will provide that intermediaries of funds are efficient. In conjunction with the interest rates liberalization, it is essential to create credit rating institutions who independently will be able to rate the creditworthiness of not only the 'Big Five' regulated banks, but also the growing shadow banking sector.

In the past, China's financial markets used to be mainly based on the banking system. Therefore, it is essential to develop other sectors of the market, especially the capital market with the capability to issue public, corporate and project bonds. The qualified Chinese financial institutions and companies should be able to issue bonds not only in RMB, but in foreign currencies outside China as well. There is a need to collect funds in countries along the BRI project.

In order to encourage FDI inflows to the BRI countries, it is necessary to adjust the Chinese law. The country must encourage private investment funds to participate in the key projects of the BRI, and it requires application of common international standards. On the other hand, it is necessary to develop some technical solutions, e.g., the ability to create public-private partnerships (PPPs). Many of the projects related to the BRI will generate lower returns. Financing them by commercial banks or other private investors is not appropriate because the low return might impact negatively for the financial situation of such institution. The PPPs are the most suitable way of funding such projects, which means that there should be created a sufficient legal and institutional environment for such possibilities.

As described in Sect. 4.1, the BRI requires a high level of connectivity. Open capital flows are one of the crucial dimensions which enable to intertwine different economies. For this reason, China must invest in infrastructure with the aim to support capital flows. It is necessary to create a credit information system and cross-border payment system, which will enhance private business engagement. A greater transparency, higher interconnectedness between different institutions and a more mature capital market will likely expand investment opportunities and enable acquisitions of stable and long-term funds.

It is evident that the financial market liberalization will increase free flow of capital in China. Such process seems to be deepening of inflow (and outflow if there will be any economic problem) and accelerating within the next years. It is the consequence of liberalization and deregulation, which enhances the free flow of capital. It should be stressed that further financial liberalization is necessary for fostering the BRI. If the PBC and the CBIRC will continue the regulatory policy implemented in 2017 and 2018, aimed at reining the highly leveraged financial sector, it might have a dampening effect on further investments within the next several years.

Another very important aspect of financial liberalization is the RMB internationalization. It can be treated as a separated political goal, but the BRI strictly impacts on the Chinese currency internationalization and helps to achieve by using the RMB the status of a global reserve currency (Djankov and Miner 2016). There are three dimensions of such process:

- the BRI will boost export of goods and services to the member countries. As a consequence, there will be an increased demand for RMB trade settlements.
- the Chinese investments occupying the OBOR project will entail capital flows denominated in RMB. As more and more infrastructure projects are undertaken, there will be a proportional outflow of the Chinese currency, which will strengthen its internationalization.
- the Chinese currency might be treated as a reserve asset. It is likely that it will increase the demand for RMB-denominated products in offshore markets. The status of the currency as the reserve asset was bolstered by its inclusion to the SDR basket in October 1, 2016.

The RMB internationalization will be very beneficial for the OBOR project in other ways as well. It will reduce exchange risk and costs of related investments, promotion of the development of the financial market and assist overseas expansion. The international status of the currency will be helpful for reducing China's reliance on the USD. All of these aspects are very important for the Chinese investment purposes (Zhang and Tao 2014). In order to challenge the USD dominance even more, the ambitions for RMB internationalization go even further since the PBC is ready to release the Central Bank Digital Currency (CBDC), digital yuan or e-RMB. With the possible support of large payment services of large companies such as Alipay, the PBC could be able to distribute the CBDC relatively easily. Especially for the BRI participating countries, this CBDC could improve the convenience of RMB cross-border payments, enhance the RMB as a tool for international trade pricing and payment settlement, and increase the functions of the RMB as a store of value and a reserve currency. Furthermore, the introduction of the digital yuan can also have a major impact on the monetary policy in countries with close trade relations with China. Unlike most central banks in the world, the PBC does not earn any fee income when issuing money (so-called seigniorage-effect), because the RMB is not used for trade settlement. This means that if Chinese tourists go abroad, they exchange RMB for the local currency and in this way indirectly pay the local central bank. Assuming that local traders and central banks will accept the digital yuan, this CBDC can stimulate the RMB cross-border payments by enabling Chinese citizens to pay abroad for local goods in Chinese money. The idea of issuing a digital currency in order to increase the RMB circulation is part of the BRI, but the flip side of this development is that smaller neighboring countries of China, such as Thailand and Vietnam, are threatened in their monetary sovereignty, a similar development as seen with the dollarization of some Latin-American countries (DigFin 2019).

Regarding the policy trilemma, it should be highlighted that a transition from a fixed to a more managed floating exchange rate system has an uncertain impact on the BRI (China's participation in the globalization processes including further trade and investment growth) and on the monetary autonomy at the same time (stimulus for the domestic economy). The model with free movement of capital, more managed floating exchange rates and monetary autonomy, i.e., a gradual change from side C to side B of the triangle in Fig. 3.5 in Sect. 3.3, originally gives the idea that during the period of prosperity, the more flexible exchange rate will conform the flows of capital and provide the expected monetary autonomy. However, this model might be harmful because RMB internationalization (attached to the free float exchange rate) might impact on the currency stability and will adversely affect other economic conditions. For instance, a depreciation of RMB will cause an outflow of capital from the country and will adversely affect the financial means for the OBOR project. Such a situation should result in some actions undertaken with the intention to limit the RMB fluctuations. Ultimately, it depends on the extent to which the PBC allows the currency to float freely or prefers to impose a return to a more managed exchange rate approach. By contrast to the presented model, it is worth to consider a different one, which seems to suit better the BRI and allows China to integrate more with the globalized world, but does not exert such harmful impact on the domestic economy taking its economic slowdown and debt problems into consideration. Such approach assumes that the fully liberalized capital flows are associated with lack of monetary policy autonomy and a more pegged exchange rate regime (i.e., a gradual shift toward side A of the triangle). Accordingly to the proposal, in the contemporary Chinese economic condition the most important need is to adjust and consolidate financial and economic systems and fully liberalize interest rates (step one), then allow more mobility of capital (step two, with some time delay to the step one) and finally the pegged exchange rate must be kept but there might be allowed a greater float. Such an approach is not only more beneficial to the BRI (gives necessary free flows of capital), but also enables the economic transition in China and eliminates some shortcomings of the free-floating exchange rate (e.g., a harmful effect of RMB appreciation in the long term) (Sun and Payette 2016).

5.2 China's Shadow Banking and the 'Belt and Road' Initiative

Apart from the traditional financial market, which is still underdeveloped, an important feature of the Chinese financial market is its large unregulated shadow banking. The shadow banking system is at the moment the most rapidly growing part of the financial market in China and the OBOR project might strengthen this process through demand for further investment financing. There are three important dimensions, which exert a great impact on the links between shadow banking and the BRI:

- China's bank-based nature of the financial system and its level of development (and the consequences as: limited supply of loans, important role of off-balance sheet instruments, interconnectedness between banks and unregulated institutions, etc.);
- the financial liberalization process and accompanying growth of financial innovations;
- the core position of China in the OBOR project and its shrinking financial resources for his purpose.

The Chinese banking system is still in the phase of its dynamic development, measured as an annual growth (FSB 2018) and an outstanding value of unregulated banking products. In the past, it used to be monolithic, and the government started to opening it up in the 1980s. Nowadays it is still state-dominated what impacts on the pattern of investments and limits the size and scope of credit supply. It also has an impact on the efficiency of the loans (the so-called loan-and-build model)[1] and undermines the financial feasibility and profitability of the investments. As a consequence, there is a large field for the development of private financing. This kind of financing, although economically more justified, allows to circumvent financial regulations and contributes to the development of the shadow banking system. Many entities with restricted access to SOBs loans are willing to pay higher interest rates for the shadow bank intermediaries which is an important factor spurring the growth of shadow banks in China (Sheng and Soon 2016).

The liberalization of the Chinese financial market, which enables financial innovation development is closely related to shadow banking. Innovation can help contribute to financial deepening, which will increase the amount of capital financing for the OBOR project. On the other hand, innovation generates shadow banking related to Fintech (e.g., mobile payments, online lending, and online investment) which might have an impact on the BRI in many aspects, especially enhancing the process of investment financing and broadening the international trade relations. While the traditional banking sector is relatively heavily regulated, the new technology is one of the most important channels for the unregulated financial development (*The Economist* 2017). The financial digital systems are very closely interconnected and at the same

[1]This model relates to the feature that borrowers do not think like investors and the commercial logic (rate of return) is secondary to political motivations.

time they constitute a bridge between mainland China and other OBOR countries (Sabine 2016). On the other hand, the BRI will be a catalyst for financial innovative investments (e.g., syndicated loans and infrastructure bonds and SWIFT, a global financial messaging service provider).

A very important driver of the shadow banking is China's borrowing options. Due to the BRI, China has become a major international lender, and for some countries it has become their most important source of long-term investment funds. The state-regulated Chinese financial system is over-extended by debt and the 'loan-and-build' model will deepen the debt and its costs. The shadow banking system will become an alternative for the traditional sources of credit. Nowadays China's traditional banks are big drivers of shadow banking. The data related to the structure of the shadow banking in China shows that among the largest part of the system which developed during the last few years are *entrusted loans* and *other shadow debts* (see Fig. 5.1). Entrusted loans are inter-company loans facilitated by financial institutions (very often there are banks involved), whereas other shadow debt include debt assets (very often bank-originated loans), letters of credit and other non-standard types of debt assets (Bowman et al. 2018).

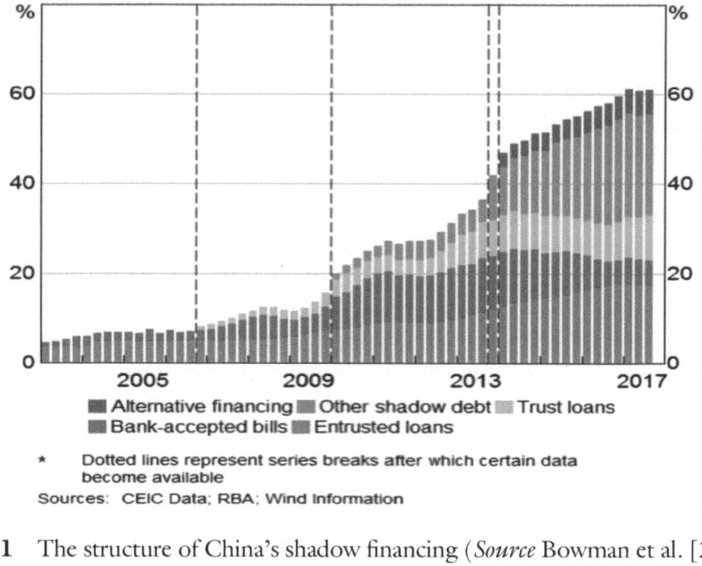

Fig. 5.1 The structure of China's shadow financing (*Source* Bowman et al. [2018])

The BRI can deepen the cooperation between different financial institutions on the Chinese market. The cooperation increases the banking activity not only for the domestic market, but also in foreign markets. On the other hand, it enhances the development of shadow banking and in this way poses a great risk on the investments being parts of the BRI. Some forms or instruments of shadow banking such as WMPs, trust and Fintech products are unguaranteed and opaque and as such do not only pose systemic risks to the banking sector but also raise concerns about consumer protection in the shadow banking sector at large. They are interconnected with other instruments and link up different sectors of the Chinese financial market and the markets of other OBOR member countries; for example, banks use trust companies as intermediaries of many of their activities. Usually, they are financed by banks and then they lend money to other entities like SMEs, local governments, etc. The growing imbalance between the investment needs and safe credit growth makes the BRI financing unsustainable. Binding different markets, the Chinese shadow banking system is able to trigger international financing crisis and affect the real economies in China and many other countries.

The growth of shadow banking in China is an important contributor of two processes: development of debt market (together with the erosion of monetary policy autonomy) and encouragement of financial liberalization in the country. The development of unregulated banking activities in China (e.g., off-balance-sheet banking operations, trust companies activities, etc.) enables to erode the controlled deposit ceiling rate, offers much higher rate of return than traditional deposit rates and develop the debt market in this way. Further pressure on the market is putting by Internet-based financial products. They not only have an impact on the debt market, but enable credit intermediation outside the regulated banking sector (channeling large amounts of deposits to other financial institutions) and in this way encourage the financial liberalization (intermediating private funds among different enterprises).

As a result of the abovementioned processes, the shadow banking development might be an important contributor for the BRI success. The rapid growth of the system makes the whole Chinese financial system more competitive on the international level and increases the probability to find funds for the BRI investments. It means that when considering the policy trilemma model, one side of the desired option is the free flow of capital (equated with the shadow banking growth). The other feature of the model is the lack of the monetary autonomy.

It stems from the fact that the important condition for the further development of the traditional banking sector in China (which is an essential counterbalance for the shadow banking system) is the lack of interest rates restrictions (lower government impact of the monetary authority). The monetary autonomy, as it used to be in the past, might lead to the situation that government-regulated interest rates are creating a 'financial repression regime' which might penalize some of the financial market participants. Full liberalization of the interest rates is a better option. This rationale leads to the managed exchange rate as well, which should be the second side of the desired model. The possibility of interventions in the exchange rate regime ('managed floating') makes the debt market more secure and creates more stability for the foreign currency-denominated debt. Taking the trilemma options into consideration, the most preferred solution for supporting the BRI is to pick side A of the triangle in Fig. 5.2.

Taking into account the idea of policy quadrilemma, the conclusion is similar to the trilemma, i.e., the Chinese authorities need to consider to sacrifice the monetary autonomy. It means that they should try to provide the free capital flows, together with the focus on financial stability and a fixed exchange rate regime. As regards the financial stability in relation to the shadow banking sector development, it is evident at the moment that the shadow banking market, together with the government debt in China, is still manageable. They will be challenged in the future, but there is a possibility that proper regulations (embracing the shadow

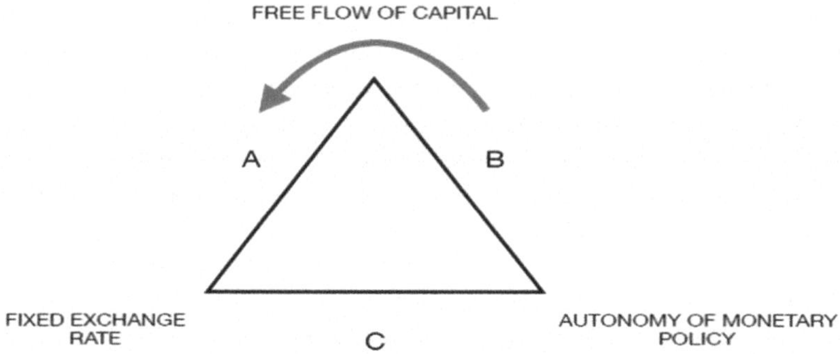

Fig. 5.2 Recommended policy approach: a gradual shift toward side A of the impossible trinity (*Source* Łasak and van der Linden [2019])

part of the financial market) together with the proper monetary policy will provide further sustainability for the system. On the one hand, it will be a costly process, but on the other hand, the lack of monetary autonomy means that the liberalized interest rates will create opportunities for some entities, e.g., the SMEs, to have an access to loans from traditional banks and be less dependent on the shadow banking sector.

5.3 The Financial Pitfalls of the 'Belt and Road' Initiative

The BRI initiative exerts a great impact on the member countries because it requires large financial resources for its implementation. As it was stated in Sect. 4.2, the cost of the initiative during the next five years is estimated up to USD 8 trillion. Collecting such amounts not only requires coordination of many sources, but will also have an influence on the BRI recipient countries with further consequences in terms of their ability to raise sufficient capital and in a broader perspective to actively foster the BRI in the context of many other internal economic and social objectives. Very important are the threats related to the different aspects of the OBOR project as described in Sect. 4.4.

One of the biggest challenges for the BRI is the debt risk stemmed from the project. The high leverage, created by mechanisms of fund collections, may cause harm for the countries and institutions supporting the BRI and financially participating in the initiative. It is especially dangerous if the political goals, backing the initiative, are not correlated with commercial viability. It is a likely scenario, that many countries participating in the BRI are only being lured by the argument that it enables to have a better access to international trade. In the future, the projects might turn to offer poor return to the invested money and simultaneously have a huge negative impact on the participant countries' public finances. There were such scenarios in the past, when some of the member countries in joint projects were not financially sound, and China acted as a 'lender-of-last resort' for these countries (e.g., Kyrgyzstan or Tajikistan). The list of such beneficiaries is longer and among the main capital receivers from the Asian region are enumerated Laos, Vietnam, Indonesia, Pakistan, Malaysia, Cambodia, Thailand, and many more (see Table 5.1). Most of these countries are developing economies with a lack of financial services and funding. They need foreign capital for the development of their economies and for building infrastructure.

Table 5.1 Top construction and investment recipients in the BRI project during 2014–2018 (H1)

Construction		*Investment*	
Country	*Volume ($ billion)*	*Country*	*Volume ($ billion)*
Pakistan	31.8	Singapore	24.3
Bangladesh	18.1	Malaysia	13.2
Egypt	17.0	Russian Federation	9.9
Malaysia	15.3	Israel	9.8
Indonesia	15.2	India	9.0
Russian Federation	13.4	Indonesia	8.7
Laos	12.6	South Korea	8.1
UAE	12.2	Pakistan	7.6
Iran	11.3	UAE	5.6
Saudi Arabia	9.7	Laos	4.7

Source Jay-Pèrez and Scissors (2018)

At the same time, they have problems to acquire loans from international institutions as well as from Western countries, due to financial difficulties and low sovereign credit ratings. Moreover, they are the necessary members of the BRI, and it is difficult to imagine the success of the project, without their participation. Among countries which benefit from the Chinese financial support appear some developed economies as well, not only Asian ones, but from other parts of the globe. Good examples are Greece and Italy, which benefits from the participation in the BRI (He 2019; Giuffrita 2019). Due to the OBOR project, they have relatively easy access to Chinese loans for the infrastructure investments, which are treated as part of the BRI.

It is a potential danger for these economies, especially smaller countries from South and Central Asia, like Bangladesh, Kazakhstan, Pakistan, or Uzbekistan, to use the borrowed money, which they must repay in the future. At the same time when they get an access to the foreign loans, the value of undertaken or planned investment is too high compared to the size of their economy. Moreover, in many of these countries the economic indicators are weak, e.g., the current accounts have deficits, the ratios of public debt-to-GDP are very high and the foreign currencies reserves are very small. It creates a risk that any deterioration in trade balance will undermine stability in such countries (Choudbury 2017). In this context, there is a possibility that the debt problems might lead to foreign control of their critical assets when debtors will default. It is a result of applied solution that when problems occur, a debt is converted into equity. Finally, it leads to the lender's ownership (mainly Chinese) of these projects. The other option is to lease the infrastructure to the lenders, as did Sri Lanka with the port of Hambantota in 2017, which was leased to China Management Port Holdings for 99 years, due to the inability to repay the debts (Chiang 2018; Hornby and Zhang 2019). Such a possible scenario, when the ownership changes occur, leads to a conclusion that for many countries the foreign loans should be treated as a 'debt trap'. Much better way is that the BRI projects financing is not unilateral financing or based mainly on debt, but when all its members participate in sharing expenses and taking risks. Moreover, it is important that a greater role is undertaken under market-based financing (He 2019).

The second challenge of the BRI is the expectation that the accompanying projects gather more privately owned capital and are based more on market-oriented sources of financing as a more efficient way of financing. Such approach very often turns out to be illusive and many of the OBOR projects rely too much on the support of government policies. This results from the fact that trade connectivity, building infrastructure and energy supply are usually considered as the main motivations of the BRI investments. The financial aspects of the initiative are in the second place among the initiator's motives. As a result, not all BRI investments are set up in the same economic sense. For example, some of the rail transports are heavily subsidized by local and regional governments with the main aim to demonstrate commitment to the project from the member countries instead of sound financial planning (Farchy 2016). Such approach means that the BRI might encounter a serious problem in the future, because the lack of efficiency of the fundings and the low rates of return should be undermining the success of the project. It is likely that the rationally thinking banking sector will not be very helpful in this situation. Despite investing hundreds of billions of dollars, Chinese banks might also fail to identify profitable projects, and to properly manage the risks related to these investments. The argument behind the presumption is that the Chinese banks have failed in the past in allocating resources efficiently at home, so they are unlikely to do it better oversees, when operating on unfamiliar markets (Wells and Weinland 2017). Moreover, the Chinese banks for several years are burdened with NPLs at home, and the engagement in infrastructure building abroad and lending for foreign governments may lead them to higher financial problems (Weinland 2017). In addition, there is another dimension to this issue, namely as a result of the slowing growth at the domestic market, the Chinese SOEs are forced to search investment opportunities abroad. The BRI is a great opportunity for them to reduce overcapacity. As a result, most of the investments of the BRI are made by Chinese SOEs. Unfortunately, based on the previous experiences these investments are not profit-seeking, but accustomed to a state support if the SOEs are in financial problems. It is likely that when the SOEs are investing abroad, they do not have the same conditions and financial support as they have at home. It means that they must consider to aim for more profit maximization, which will change the financial risk assessment, and causes a potential financial, mainly default and market, risk on these enterprises (Jay-Pèrez and Scissors 2018, p. 3).

The third challenge is related to the sources of funds used for financing the BRI and the mechanisms which are involved in the financing. Since the beginning of the BRI, China used its foreign exchange reserves as one of the main sources of funding the initiative. By investing in infrastructure, the Chinese authorities expected to take advantage of a more profitable market for China's vast foreign exchange reserves, as they did in the past. In the past, most of the Chinese investments were denominated in low-interest-bearing American government securities. Nowadays, the investment into infrastructural projects is in their opinion a better option. However, it is a very risky approach to exchange the American securities into Central Asian low-profitable infrastructural investments. Moreover, since the launch of the BRI in 2013, the external environment has changed a lot and since the early 2000s China's foreign exchange reserves increased continuously with a peak in June 2014 of around USD 4 trillion (see Fig. 3.3). Therefore, it was understandable to invest some parts of these reserves into infrastructural projects during the last six years. Since then the inevitable economic slowdown and some other internal factors, such as an appropriate anti-corruption campaign, have triggered a capital outflow from the economy. The central bank was forced to spend more than USD 1 trillion from its foreign exchange reserves in order to guarantee the stable value of the currency. In addition, the current economic slowdown and trade conflicts will probably dampen the export and hence impact the Chinese balance of payments. It is unlikely that a similar foreign exchange reserves accumulation as during the last two decades will be generated again in the near future. On the other hand, the PBC might be forced to use the foreign exchange reserves to defend its currency in order to maintain investor's confidence to China's economic stability (Pei 2019).

There is also another problem related to the Chinese foreign exchange reserves. It is the China external debt, which exerts a huge impact on the country's exchange rate. The external debt is accounted for nearly USD 2 trillion. It is estimated that about 60% of the debt is short-term which means that almost USD 1.2 trillion must be rolled over per year by the Chinese monetary authority (Balding 2019). Such amount represents about a third part of the whole Chinese foreign exchange reserves. Moreover, the Chinese government increased its debt abroad in dollars when there was 3–5% spread between USD and RMB. Nowadays the spread almost disappeared, and the pressure for RMB depreciation means that refinancing in USD has become riskier. Some part of the debt is related to BRI which means that China borrowed dollars on international markets and spend the money for the infrastructural projects. The long-term nature of the investments and short-term sources of their funding causes that rolling over the existing debt is inevitable. It is likely that the PBC will use a part of its foreign exchange reserves, borrow money on international markets, and/or apply a mixed approach. This creates additional costs, but simultaneously reveals the currency risk incorporated into the mechanism of financing the OBOR projects. On the other hand, there is no real, short-time option for a change and increase in the share of RMB-denominated financing of the BRI projects (Richter 2019).

The next, fourth problem, is related to the BRI project's lack of transparency, unpredictability and long-term of investments. Transparency should be the main principle of every investment. China treats the BRI as its main economic and political goal, but in the meantime it is a centrally run mega-project. Among the participants are state-backed companies, public sector banks and central and regional governments from many participating countries. They are participating as well some regional development banks and multilateral financial institutions like Asian Development Bank, the European Bank for Reconstruction and Development and the World Bank. Such a combination of participants made the whole project non-transparent (Crabtree 2019). Lack of transparency undermines market-based financing, because for the private companies BRI seems to be highly fluid and murky. Especially the Western lenders expect market-based principles and clear terms of their contracts, before they enter a project. Another obstacle is the expected length of the participation in the BRI. It is the feature of investments into infrastructural projects, that it requires a large amount of funds, but offers slow and long-term return. Additionally, they relate to many non-financial risks like political, operational, and cultural ones (Li and Jin 2018).

The fifth challenge related to the BRI project is that the Chinese government put too much emphasis on the benefits for China itself. It calculates only the profits of the project, neglecting the impact on the local governments, local communities, and local businesses in host countries. In assessing the financial aspect of the project, it is very important to take into consideration the interests of various stakeholders. If the project is oriented on building a community of common destiny, it must be based on mutual benefits for all participating parties. The BRI member countries cannot participate incurring negative economic and financial consequences, irrespective if it happens now or in the future. The same conclusion refers to the situation of China. In the long run, the country must benefit as the initiator of the whole project and cannot incur future excessive economic or financial risk, without assurance that the situation will not deteriorate.

The conclusion is that one of the best solutions leading to the OBOR project sustainability is to provide an adequate level of financial regulation and incorporate pre-warning systems for financial risks. It is essential not only to build financial regulatory and supervisory system, but to strengthen policy of communication and coordination, and to increase collaboration related to many aspects of the initiative, last but not least, equally important is to achieve a balanced structure of the BRI funding mechanisms.

There are three dimensions to achieve these abovementioned goals. The first one is to secure sustainable development of the Chinese financial market. The second is oriented on the due diligence in implementing the joint initiatives related to the BRI. The third means that all the processes related to the BRI should trigger a positive impact on the economies of member countries.

It is important that the further opening-up of the Chinese financial market must be accompanied by progress in exchange rate regime reform in the country. The exchange rate regime should assist the processes in the real economy, especially leading to balance of the current account of the country. Moreover, the financial regulatory capacity should match the openness of the financial sector to prevent financial risks. It is also important rebalancing the structure of the Chinese financial market by greater development of regulated capital market, in comparison with the banking sector.

The BRI is an important initiative not only for China and other individual countries, but it is crucial for the whole regional economy in Asia, and the international economy. For this reason, many international organizations and forums (e.g., G20, APEC, United Nations, ASEAN, Silk Road Fund, AIIB) must take part in coordination of the BRI activities. The importance of such cooperation, coordination, and supervision was highlighted by creation in 2017 Asian Financial Cooperation Association (AFCA). It is a non-governmental and non-profit organization, intended for building an exchange and cooperation platform for strengthening exchanges among regional financial institutions and financial resources integration, jointly safeguarding regional financial stability, and supporting the development of real economy in the region (www.afca.org).

The BRI must be beneficial for all the member countries. It should not expose them on a danger. It means that all the entities participating in the project must have the proper approach to financial sustainability and prudent risk management. Additionally, there must be implemented solutions protecting the participating countries in case of imbalances or financial failures, for instance debt forgiveness measures, insurance policies, and effective communication networks. Only such complex and coordinated approach may lead to reductions of the biggest financial pitfalls accompanying the BRI project.

5.4 Possible Policy Options to Cope with China's Policy Trilemma in a 'New Normal' Economy

The ongoing capital liberalization combined with a more managed floating currency and market-oriented interest rates means that China needs to bend the impossible trinity in order to maintain a 'new normal' sustainable growth model. Meantime the PBC seeks to limit the effects of capital flows on the money supply and tries to stabilize the value of the currency. A common form of monetary action to fine-tune the conflicting aims of the policy trilemma is a monetary sterilization policy through a purchase or sale of securities by the central bank. However, this approach cannot go on forever because the costs of sterilization might become unbearably high over time. These costs come mainly from interest payments to banks' required and excess reserves, PBC's bills and selling reverse repurchase agreements or open market operations.

If these costs in relation to GDP growth will become unsustainable, this means that retaining both monetary autonomy and currency control will become unsustainable too. From a macroeconomic perspective, sterilization intervention (and the BRI export boost) also leads to serious misallocation of resources by subsidizing the export sector at the expense of the rest of the economy. Especially the SMEs that mainly produce non-tradable goods are still denied much-needed funds and rely more on finance from shadow banks (Lo 2015).

China has for years been pursuing the policy trilemma, but it is likely that the country can bend the trinity which will come with costs in the form of lower official reserves and will lead to a policy quadrilemma. For decades, China has been hoarding reserves which have been increasingly used to bend the trinity in order to remain financial stability at the expense of declining reserves which have fallen with around 1 trillion USD since June 2014. The policy makers can keep going for a while, but at a high price and with the knowledge that ultimately its efforts will be doomed to fail. Consequently, the authorities are looking for possible policy options to escape from an economic downturn via a quadrilemma in light of a 'new normal' economy. The following policy options can be considered to reduce a possible further decline of monetary reserves or to fight the quadrilemma:

- effective implementation of the BRI project;
- capital controls and monetary policy tightening;
- more controlled freely floating currency;
- targeted fiscal policy;
- supply-side structural reforms 'with Chinese characteristics.'

An effective implementation of the BRI project will depend on to what extent the return of the BRI project will exceed incurred costs in terms of capital assigned to the OBOR investments; the implementation of the BRI project will not further increase Chinese credit overhang and debt problems and finally, the planned investments will be viable from an economic and political point of view. The effectiveness of the BRI requires a simultaneous occurrence of the following preconditions: First, a more flexible market-oriented financial policy and hence a monetary policy better adjusted to market conditions with market-conform interest rates which implies less monetary sovereignty; second, more free movement of capital since the scope of BRI projects forces to open the financial markets; third, the achievement of a high level of financial stability; fourth, RMB internationalization and a more free-floating exchange rate system needed for this. However, taking into account the possible adverse effects of too much currency flexibility and the growing impact of China's shadow banking on its financial system, it is advisable to keep the capital flows free and to give up some monetary autonomy combined with more managed floating exchange rates. The free flow of capital is necessary both for the BRI and further institutional development of the Chinese financial markets which is necessary for the PBC and the CBRC to be able to regulate the process of the financial intermediaries development (especially the Fintech side which is developing rapidly and in an uncontrolled way). The monetary autonomy will become less important in the context of the huge debt and the rapid growth of the shadow banking system. The question is what is the best policy option regarding the exchange rate system. On the one hand, it must be further internationalized, but on the other hand it is possible to keep the more managed floating rate in order to avoid the threats of the unfavorable appreciation in the long run, which would be harmful to the further development of the economy and might surpass the positive effects of the BRI. As indicated earlier, this ultimately means a gradual shift toward side A of the triangle (see Fig. 5.2).

Besides an effective implementation of the BRI, another possible option is to impose tighter and broader capital controls which received some support from the IMF and the Bank of Japan. For instance, by slowing capital outflows via reintroduction of restrictions on outbound FDIs, the pressure on China's reserves and on the exchange rate will mitigate. Although this will allow China to operate safely with fewer reserves, it will also put a halt to China's intention to integrate its currency more into the global markets, not only as a payments and trading currency, but also as a reserve currency. Also, as long as China maintains its openness to trade and inward investment, there are potentially many ways for households and firms to evade capital restrictions. Also, a more restrictive monetary policy could be implemented. For instance, China could raise interest rates, which might encourage capital inflows and discourage outflows, but this would hurt growth in an already declining economy. Almost two decades the opening of the capital movement in China has been accompanied with a monetary policy which sometimes loosens and sometimes tightens its reins, so it is likely that small steps forward or backward will be implemented in the near future as well.

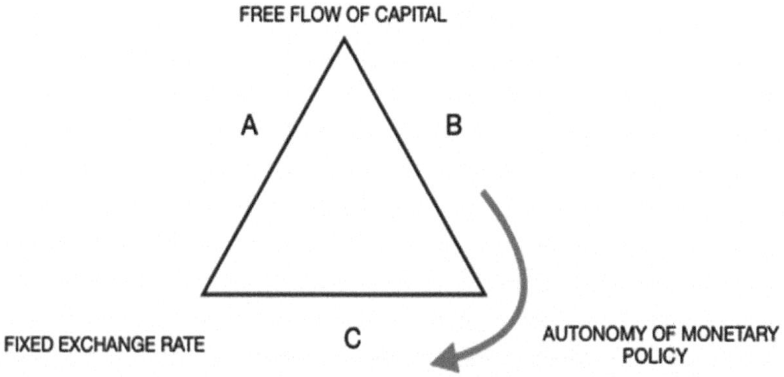

Fig. 5.3 The scenario with capital controls and monetary policy tightening: a gradual shift toward side A of the impossible trinity (*Source* Łasak and van der Linden [2019])

At the same time, it is also likely that the IMF reserve currency inclusion and the OBOR-initiated pursuit of more globalization will have to make capital flows more freely. From the theoretical point of view, the scenario with capital controls and monetary policy tightening leads to a shift back toward side C of the triangle (see Fig. 5.3). It means a return to a policy of the fixed exchange rate implemented together with the stricter monetary stimulus.

Another option is to allow the RMB to gradually float more freely, i.e., allow a more managed floating exchange rate, which would give back control of monetary policy to the central bank and eliminate the need to run down reserves to support the currency (the gradual shift toward side B of the triangle in Fig. 5.4). The price that China is paying for maintaining currency stability is that the central bank has not been able to ease monetary policy more strongly, so it is likely the PBC will have to make the RMB a more controlled free-floating currency. However, that option exposes China to the risk that the RMB will plunge, thereby hurting confidence in the currency and creating a death spiral. It could also create more speculation in the global financial markets with a growing number of risky investment funds that bet against the RMB (Steil and Smith 2016). Such scenario would be less favorable for the BRI comparing to the option with free flow and fixed exchange rate, when taking into account the export-oriented policy and

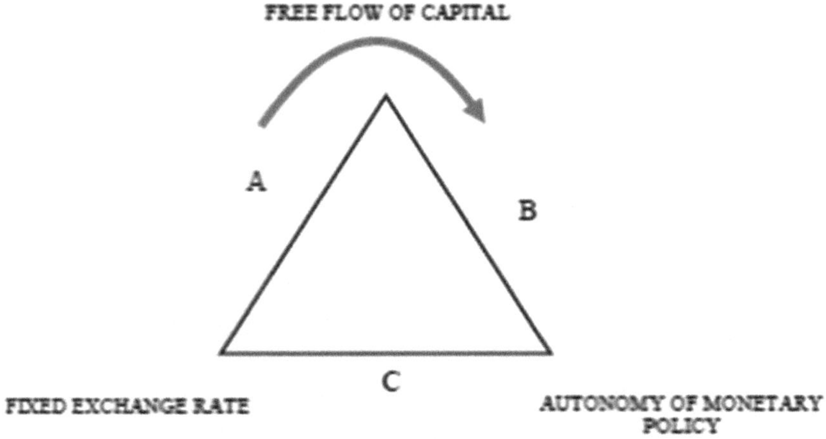

Fig. 5.4 The scenario with controlled freely floating currency and monetary policy tightening: a gradual shift toward side B of the impossible trinity (*Source* Łasak and van der Linden [2019])

the possibility of exchange rate stimulus. On the other hand, more free float exchange rate is better for the RMB internationalization, which is also essential for further OBOR investments.

An alternative option is to target fiscal policy, i.e., government spending and tax measures aimed specifically at supporting the transition into the 'new normal' economy. For example, the lack of a strong social safety net combined with an aging society implies that Chinese citizens are mostly on their own when it comes to covering costs of health care, education, and retirement and is an important motivation to use China's relatively high household savings rate. Also, the recent reversal of the 'one-child' policy and transition to a 'two-child' policy might partly address this problem. Fiscal policies aimed at increasing income security, such as strengthening the pension system, would help to promote consumer confidence and consumer spending. Likewise, tax cuts or credits could be used to enhance households' disposable income, and government-financed training and relocation programs could stimulate the labor transition from slowing to expanding production sectors. To what extent it is effective to subsidize the services sector should be further explored, but the reduction of existing subsidies to the heavy industries and SOEs combined with efforts to promote entrepreneurship would certainly be useful (Bernanke 2016). The impact of such scenario on the BRI may be different depending on the strength of the change, but finally it should lead to a 'new normal' growth model more based on the domestic market than on the foreign investments. On the other hand, building an efficient model based on the domestic market is time-consuming, so it should be accompanied by the continued development of the BRI projects.

Another alternative policy option is to focus on supply-side structural policy reforms to support the transition in China's 'new normal' growth model as a logical response to the failure of existing reforms and restructuring after the GFC. The Chinese government insisted during the 12th FYP period on an economic development strategy of enlarging domestic demand. To some extent, this move inhibited the economic slowdown, but economic growth nevertheless dramatically declined. The ineffective demand-side stimulus gave rise to the introduction of supply-side structural reforms as a main feature of the 13th FYP. Since November 2015, the Chinese government has been implementing supply-side structural reforms to improve the Chinese companies' productivity, to win the competition in a global market, further release the reforms, offset downward economic pressure, better meet the needs of the society, and promote sustained and sound economic and social development. These structural reform policies are executed in many areas, including price formation, tax regulation, financial and investment regulation, and de-monopolization with the final aim to further embrace a more competitive market mechanism (Reeves and Hu 2015).

The China-specific supply-side structural reforms include the following elements: elimination of excess capacity; reduction of the housing surplus or inventory; deleveraging or restructuring debt; cost reductions and restoring weak growth areas. As the Chinese economy has slowed, heavy industrial capacity has continued to grow, and the result has been massive overcapacity in many industries such as coal and steel. Firstly, to tackle overcapacity, the focus is on increasing mergers and decreasing bankruptcy and liquidation. Secondly, the reduction of the housing surplus is mainly focused on fulfilling the housing demand of new urban residents. In practice, this means reducing inventory of unsold housing in second- and third-tier cities. While housing markets in top-tier cities like Beijing and Shanghai are relatively healthy, smaller cities still have an enormous excess of unsaleable housing. The supply-side policy will include efforts to make them affordable to rural–urban migrants.

Thirdly, the restructuring of China's debt will involve to prevent systemic and regional risks and will be a complicated task since its debt burden is not only huge, but also difficult to trace and locate in the economy. The banking system is certainly at the center of the debt problem, but other parts of the financial system are also involved. Closing down loss-making SOEs means writing-off their debts, including debts to banks, local governments and other obligations in the capital markets (Naughton 2016).

Another way to address the corporate debt problem is the introduction of debt-for-equity swaps for state-owned banks with many NPLs. These banks would obtain equity stakes in corporations that have borrowed and cannot service their loans. This could lead to a 'win-win' situation for the banks in the form of lower bad debts, and for the firms the interest payments could be reduced. However, making credit decisions for companies in which banks have a stake might lead to a conflict of interest (Kalish 2016).

A consideration of the pressure from the non-banking financing in China leads the authorities to implement some regulatory reforms on the sector. Among the most important goals is to expand the sector to SMEs, rural businesses, and households and increase the systemic safety for the system. It is important not to reverse the increasing consumer access to the financial services during the process of regulating the non-bank part of the Chinese financial market. The consumer safety should be improved and non-bank financial institutions more carefully and comprehensively regulated, but at the same time encouraged for further support for the real economy (Elliott and Qiao 2015). Together with the abovementioned, the Chinese regulator must limit the corporate debt. This category of debt accounts for over two-thirds of total debt in the country, and comparing to other markets, Chinese companies are among the most indebted in the world (Duceux 2018).

The reduction of redundant capacity and restructuring the debt would allow firms to reduce their costs. This additional fourth element refers to further policy measures that would help firms to reduce costs and increase competitiveness. To lower costs, comprehensive measures are put in place, including systemic transaction costs, cutting tax burdens for enterprises and reductions in burdensome regulation and reductions in social security contributions although this latter will conflict with the targeted fiscal policy aimed at increasing income security. The final element to improve weak growth areas implies that effective supply will be enhanced through poverty alleviation, cultivating newly emerging industries, etc. It is important that all key tasks of the supply-side structural reforms will be carried out together in a coherent way (Naughton 2016).

Although there are some similarities between Chinese and Western supply-side structural reforms with regard to lowering tax rates, for the rest they have little in common. The 'Chinese characteristics' of supply-side structural reforms emphasize cutting overcapacity, a specific aim of the BRI as well, and increasing effective supply to a large extent guided by heavy government intervention, while Western supply-side proponents prefer to avoid heavy involvement of demand-side policies. As a matter of fact, China's supply-side reforms could be considered as an umbrella term for the pragmatic approach to solve its structural problems. The abovementioned elements make it clear that it could mean different things at different times, and the temptation to rely on demand-side management remains overwhelming. As long as the current authorities are bounded by the existing political institutions, their approach to solve economic problems has not fundamentally changed. Step-by-step further institutional reforms are required to effectively push through the structural reforms that China urgently needs and to carefully balance the trade-off between financial liberalization and financial stability (DBS Group Research 2016).

Implementation of the financial stability to the main policy aims in China means that there is a change from the policy trilemma to the policy quadrilemma (see Fig. 5.5). At the present time, in the context of BRI it means that the free capital flows and financial stability are given. The authorities have a choice between fixed exchange rate and

Fig. 5.5 The change from the impossible trinity to the policy quadrilemma (*Source* Łasak and van der Linden [2019])

independent monetary policy. This choice leads to the conclusion that the main dilemma is if the policy is aimed more on supporting the BRI or more on supporting the supply-side structural reforms in China.

It must be highlighted that even having defined the possible scenarios, it might be very difficult to implement them in the current circumstances. Lo Chi (2015) argues that it will be a great challenge to find an equilibrium between the necessary monetary autonomy and exchange rate control when the capital account is fully opened. There are a few reasons for this. The main problem is that the PBC has a multiple policy goals but is short of policy instruments. The second challenge is the great instability of the economy and is still unanswered if the PBC will be able to cope with the mounting debt problems. And the third, and probably the most important one, the PBC treats the secrecy of its policy as the power to move markets and influence economic behavior. Many other central banks abandoned such policy during the last three decades. They argue that in the age of systemic risk the policy transparency and communication with the markets is the best approach (Lo 2015). It poses a new challenge for the Chinese policy.

5.5 China's Revised Regulatory Framework of the Financial Sector

The financial market in China has been developing in a coordinated way under the CPC supervision, however, during the last decades the authorities fostered the innovative approach to its further expansion. Since the 1980s was initiated in China the process of creation market-driven financial system. Both, the money market including the interbank lending market, and the capital market including bond and equity (or stock exchange) market have been rapidly developing. An important feature of the financial market's development is the process of its internationalization. China fostered the opening of its financial sector by establishing financial institutions able to operate on international level, extending the business scope and accepting foreign ownership. As a result, many former restrictions for foreign banks have been removed. During the last years, after the GFC, the reforms have not slowed down, but rather accelerated. Among the most important evidence can be enumerated the RMB internationalization process and implementation of a state policy announced by President Xi Jinping at the Boae Forum for Asia Annual Conference in March 2019, oriented on further reform and open the financial sector. The reforms were oriented on fostering opening-up of the financial sector in such areas as payment and clearing, bond market, credit rating, and credit reference (Yi 2018). As a result, financial institutions in China are growing stronger and becoming more globalized.

The rapid development of the different parts of financial market in China requires ensuring the necessary security in the form of an appropriate institutional structure of the financial safety net. The Chinese regulatory and supervisory architecture was created at the turn of the twenty-first century. Finally, the structure was formed in 2003, when was created CBRC, an independent banking regulator. The whole structure was called 'one bank and three commissions,' because the key role in the regulatory environment of China's financial industry was determined by the following institutions (Lan 2018):

- The People's Bank of China (PBC);
- The China Banking Regulatory Commission (CBRC);
- The Chinese Securities Regulatory Commission (CSRC);
- The China Insurance Regulatory Commission (CIRC).

The CBRC, CSRC, and CIRC were centralized and unified regulators, dedicated to the selected sectors of the financial market. Among their rights and responsibilities were formulations of supervisory policies, rules and regulations, authorizations of the financial institutions, conduct on-site examinations and off-site surveillance of the institutions, guarantee the financial health of the institutions, conducting enforcement actions against rule-breaking behaviors and preparing public statistics and reports of the banking, insurance, and capital market.

The GFC and its adverse impact on the Chinese financial markets stressed the importance of regulatory changes which was necessary after a period of a relatively loose regulatory approach during the development of the Chinese financial markets. Former lax supervision created a potential for financial abuse and danger triggered by the financial intermediaries. Especially in the period directly before the GFC, the Chinese regulatory system was characterized by a strong fragmentation, which made it attractive for many financial market participants to use the gaps and loopholes in the system through various arbitrage strategies. The goal of the regulatory changes was to reduce the overlapping competencies, which increasingly failed to provide necessary safety to the rapidly developing Chinese financial markets. The regulations of the financial market in China after the GFC are oriented on the further liberalization of the market to foreign investors, regulation of the shadow banking sector and tightening up control over the asset management business.

The regulatory reforms involved some institutional changes. The first initiative undertaken by the PBC, upon the requirement of the State Council, was the establishment of the Inter-Ministerial Joint Meeting for Financial Regulation and Coordination in August 2013. The next major step was the decision of July 2017 to set up the Financial Stability and Development Committee under the State Council. Among the main goals of the Committee are the prevention and defuse of systemic financial risks. The Committee supervises China's monetary policy and financial regulation. Moreover, it defines policies on systemic financial risk and is responsible for financial security on the Chinese economy. The Committee has also the power to supervise financial regulators and local governments in China (Zhou 2018).

Apart from the establishment of the Financial Stability and Development Committee, the following regulatory initiatives for the Chinese financial markets have been introduced after the GFC:

- creation of the deposit insurance system in 2015—since that year businesses and individuals have their deposits guaranteed up to 500 thousand RMB per bank. The solution provides a 'level playing field' between smaller and larger banks for deposit protection;
- implementation of regulations for risk management of capital market securities;
- removal by the PBC the floor on bank lending rates in July 2013 and lifting the ceiling on bank deposit interest rates in October 2015. It was an important step of deregulation of the lending market and leading to higher competition between banks, but there's still a huge gap in liberalizing interest rates between China and mature markets, because the domestic banking system remains dominated by SOBs[2] (Kwong and Poon 2019, pp. 126–127).

Moreover, there were introduced some other reforms related to the Chinese financial market, like allowance for municipal bond issuance,

[2] China still to a certain extent uses a 'dual-track' interest rate system, with deposit and lending rates set with reference to benchmark rates while money market rates are decided entirely by the markets.

stock connect systems and reform of the stock IPO system. These reforms were not only focused on providing safety for the market, but rather for the market development and creation of necessary facilities for the development.

The development of financial market in China poses several risks to the Chinese financial system, and then to the whole economy. One of the risks is the growth of the debt-to-GDP ratio, of which the corporate debt and the local government debt are the most vulnerable components (see Sect. 2.4). The local government debt might be to a higher degree confined by the central government policy and its regulators together with local governments' actions (He 2018, pp. 349–355), whereas the corporate debt creates a big risk and must be kept by other mechanisms than direct government guidelines. Moreover, over 80% of the corporate debt in China is financed by the regulated and shadow banking sector (Li 2017, p. 7). All the features of the Chinese debt, the rapid speed of its growth, a relatively high and persistent level of NPLs in the banking sector, and risks created by the shadow banking sector have a potential danger of ultimately unleashing a systemic risk in the financial system. This in turn could create a danger for the stability of the whole real economy. From this perspective, it is clear that the reform of, in particular, the regulation and supervision of financial markets will become essential.

The reforms of the Chinese financial market safety implemented after the last financial crisis can be divided into two parts: The first one is related to the reshaping of the financial market supervisory structure; the second one concerns the changes in financial regulations. It must be highlighted that the financial regulations are dedicated not only to the traditional financial institutions, but to the previously unregulated shadow banking sector as well. The main reform of the supervisory architecture in China was implemented in March 2018. It changed the old structure of the regulatory bodies and reshaped the regulatory architecture. In 2018, an arrangement was adopted in China under which the PBC is responsible for drafting important laws and regulations concerning banking and insurance sectors and designing the prudential regulation system. It is responsible for formulation a development strategy for the financial industry. Moreover, the National People's Congress decided to delegate more authority to the PBC. Such a decision was important to change the sectoral- or organization-based regulation that existed in the past to a more functional-oriented regulation where several regulatory bodies may oversee the operations of banks and other financial institutions, depending on the types of products and services they offer. The PBC took over the legislative and rule-making functions of the CBRC and CIRC (Chorzempa 2018). The other financial regulators focus their attention on enforcement and working out meticulous regulations and ways of their implementation to subordinated sectors (Hongyuran et al. 2018).

The reshaping of the financial market regulatory structure in China embraced the changes of the structure of the regulatory commissions, for instance, as mentioned in Sect. 5.1, two of the previous commissions were merged to form CBIRC (see Fig. 5.6). The merger of CBRC and CIRC is considered as one of the biggest reforms of the structure of China's financial regulatory system in the last fifteen years. The aim was to tighten the oversight over the banking and insurance sectors in China with the intention to crack down the efficiency and coordination of Chinese financial regulation and improve the supervision of the 'integrated' nature of China's finance sector and the overlap between banking and insurance operations (Moody's Analytics 2018). The new body is

Fig. 5.6 The structure of China's financial regulatory system at the end of 2018 (*Source* Own elaboration on the basis of public news)

responsible for supervising the establishment and ongoing business activities in both sectors of the Chinese financial market, namely the banking and insurance market. Moreover, it is responsible for taking enforcement actions against regulatory violations in these sectors.

In the first part of 2018, the Chinese authorities announced the intention of relaxing restrictions for foreign investments on the Chinese financial market. On 27 April 2018, various financial regulators in China promulgated new measures further opening-up the financial services industry to foreign investment, regulating non-financial entities to invest into financial institutions and tightening up control over the conduct of asset management business by financial institutions (Norton Rose Fulbright 2018). This intention was entitled 'Open-up Initiative' and is related to the following aspects (EY 2019):

- facilitating foreign investments (e.g., removal caps on the foreign shareholding ratios in domestic financial institutions or the removal of restrictions on foreign investment in the banking industry);
- providing the same rules for foreign and local investors;
- relaxing the requirements on establishing foreign branches on the Chinese financial market;
- optimizing supervision over the foreign financial institutions.

As regards the asset management business, the first guidelines in the area appeared at the end of 2017. They were oriented on unifying the types of products offered on the Chinese market, limiting the amount of offered products and minimizing the regulatory arbitrage.

As described in Sect. 5.2, China's shadow banking has developed very strongly over the last decade, but this has not been accompanied by professional national oversight for this specific part of the financial sector. These shadow banking institutions which provide similar to banks deposit and loan services or other intermediary services, but are not registered as banks, insurance companies, or institutions of the capital market, are not regulated in proper way. Institutions like local governments, police officers, or even the local departments of the Ministry of Commerce can regulate and supervise the institutions which offer the financial services without proper license. They are, however, not able to do it on the same level of professionalism as typical financial supervisors (Gao 2017, pp. 410–411). It creates a regulatory loophole for shadow banking institutions, when comparing to the other institutions of the financial market. This can be considered as a heritage of the previous regulatory system, which was more focused on institutions or sectors instead of their functions in the financial business industry, and less interested in supervising shadow banking and thereby excluding shadow banking from the formal regulatory system (Gao 2017).

After the GFC, there was a reflection that the rapid development of shadow banking creates many unintended consequences to the whole Chinese economy. One of the biggest was an explosion of credit and the related debt problem. Regardless of these problems, China's unregulated shadow banks have always been strongly associated with formal financial system and were useful in times of an economic upturn, but less effective in times of economic decline (Hsu 2019). The authorities realized that there is a necessity for a regulatory reform of the shadow banking system. The shadow banking poses a systemic stress when the interconnectedness between the regular and shadow banks continues to grow, increasing the lack of confidence in the whole economy. This observation is also stressed by international bodies like Financial Stability Board or the group G20. They highlight that China's shadow banking sector ranked fourth globally, after the euro area, the USA and UK (Binham 2018; Financial Stability Board 2018).

The regulatory actions for the shadow banking system in China took place in the period of 2011–2015. The undertaken actions were aimed at:

- creation an institutional supervisory regime dedicated for the shadow banking sector;
- implementation rules aimed at improving transparency in the shadow banking market;
- regulatory actions referring to institutions and products (Łasak 2015, p. 313).

Especially dangerous became the threats from the excessive credits and growth of NPLs. The evidence shows that the lion's share of such credits was created by the alternative funding (shadow banking). The system became an important credit intermediation outside the regular Chinese banking system. It stems from the fact that the linkages between the formal and shadow banking sectors are stronger in China than in other countries (Ehlers et al. 2018, pp. 7–12). The implemented regulations are intended to providing more transparency in the banking sector as regards the ownership structure (interconnectedness between bank and non-banking financial institutions) in the banking industry (Reuters 2018). The second aim was to reduce the banks' activity on the entrusted lending business (Weinland 2018). Banks have been pressured to stop making shadow loans backed by high-interest offerings known as WMPs (Lelyveld 2017).

The rapid development of China's shadow financing is closely related to its Fintech business development. In response to the Chinese government, PBC and regulatory authorities impose regulations over the Fintech business, intended to tackle potential risks from Fintech applications on the financial markets. It must be stressed that currently there is no single comprehensive law which regulates the Fintech business in China. Various solutions are applied to different parts of the market. All of the regulations are provided by different bodies, e.g., online payment by the PBC, peer-to-peer (P2P) lending by CBIRC, equity crowdfunding by CSRC, etc. (Pan and Yang 2019). Over the last decade, many efforts were implemented with the intention to strengthen the regulation of the Fintech activities. It is, however, one of the most important fields, where many challenges remain, and tasks must be addressed to provide the higher safety in this part of the financial market.

Apart from regulations related to the Chinese financial market, an important aspect is the international dimension of financial regulations. Is stems from the fact that the BRI triggers an international flow of capital between the member countries. According to the current regulations in Asia, each country is allowed to impose its own prudential regulation for financial institutions. The general problem is driven by the fact that the financial markets are not fully opened, and the degree varies between countries. Moreover, some of the countries have a poor financial market infrastructure and regulation. The differences involve not only the regulations but the whole institutional regimes and law systems. Some countries have a common law (e.g., Singapore, Malaysia, Hong Kong), others have a continental law (Central Asia), and others an Islamic law system (Middle East). It is a big obstacle for business, because it creates uncertainty and complexity for trade and cross-border investments. In such a situation, a successful implementation of the BRI requires harmonization of capital flow regulation while at the same time the process of financial liberalization in the region needs to be executed (Chen 2018, p. 8). Although China's banking sector is the major source of funding of the BRI, the Chinese banks are forced to strengthen their cooperation with foreign financial institutions along the 'Belt and Road' routes. While the financial liberalization process is taking place and will be intensified, the financial risks are not effectively controlled. It leads to the situation that the CBRC seeks for cooperation on cross-border supervisory cooperation with foreign regulatory bodies. It is working with regulators in the BRI countries to reduce the barriers and promote an open and fair regulatory environment for the international expansion of financial institutions. Additionally, the regulatory initiatives must exclude some negative practices, like destructive regulatory competition, etc. The aim is to create the most favorable environment for further investments. Regulators must provide systems of efficient communication of information, equal financial regulatory principles, investment opportunities, and risk restrictions. Another aspect related to the homogenization is connected with legal issues. Conflicting regulations and unclear investment procedures (e.g., procurement policies) are examples of the risks faced by private investors participating in the BRI. It is crucial to ensure partners that the internationally accepted good practices in awarding BRI projects are properly applied (Ghossein et al. 2018, p. 32).

In order to coordinate the regulatory initiatives, China has signed memoranda of understanding or agreements with financial regulatory authorities from many countries along the BRI (among them are European countries, like Italy and Switzerland). The aim was to improve the financial services in these countries and strengthen cooperation under the joint projects and to protect the participating countries.

In recent years, the so-called debt trap diplomacy that has occurred in some developing countries is seen as one of the main concerns of the BRI. In response, China pledges to improve the funding arrangements for projects along the BRI infrastructure network. The intention is to improve the conditions for the endangered developing countries and encourage them for further participation in the common projects.

Looking at the issue from a different angle, the BRI could serve as a catalyst for regulatory harmonization, especially regional harmonization in Southeast Asia. The opportunity to coordinate and improve the regulations is a big advantage for the whole region. There is, however, a risk that the participating countries have a different approach than China. It will be difficult to reconcile the adjustments they require to unique needs, regulatory objectives and risks arising from the BRI. Even for a country that has gone through an unprecedented economic recovery in the last four decades, the revision of the financial regulatory environment will still be a major challenge.

References

Balding, C. (2019, January 5). *China Has a Dangerous Dollar Debt Addiction*. BNN Bloomberg.

Bernanke, B. (2016, March 9). *A Fresh Approach to Fiscal Stimulus Is China's Only Solution to the Impossible Trinity Devaluations and Capital Controls Won't Work*. Bloomberg.

Binham, C. (2018, March 5). Shadow Banking Grows to More Than $45tn Assets Globally. *Financial Times*.

Bowman, J., Hack, M., & Waring, M. (2018, March). *Non-bank Financing in China*. Reserve Bank of Australia Bulletin.

Chen, J. L. (2018, January). The Cases Study of "One Belt and One Road" and "Made in China 2025" Impact on the Development of Taiwan's Machine Tool Industry. *International Business Research*.

Chiang, F. (2018, August 28). China's 'Belt and Road' Could Be a Debt Trap. *The Japan Times*.

Chorzempa, M. (2018, March 19). *China's Restructuring of Financial Regulation Is Good News for Reform*. Washington, DC: Peterson Institute for International Economics.

Choudbury, D. (2017, May 25). UN Warns About Financial Risks in China's One Belt One Road Project. *The Economic Times*.

Crabtree, J. (2019, April 25). China Needs to Make BRI More Transparent and Predictable. *Financial Times*.

DBS Group Research. (2016, April 7). *China: What Are Supply-Side Structural Reforms?*

DigFin. (2019, October 7). *Busting Six Myths About China's e-RMB*.

Djankov, S., & Miner, S. (2016, March). *China's Belt and Road Initiative: Motives, Scope and Challenges*. PIIE Briefing 16-2. Washington, DC: Peterson Institute for International Economics.

Duceux, A. J. (2018, December 20). *An Overview of Chinese Debt*. Liege: Committee for the Abolition of Illegitimate Debt.

Ehlers, T., Kong, S., & Zhu, F. (2018, February). *Mapping Shadow Banking in China: Structure and Dynamics* (BIS Working Paper No. 701).

Elliott, D. J., & Qiao, Y. (2015, May). *Reforming Shadow Banking in China*. Washington, DC: The Brookings Institution.

EY. (2019). Interpreting the BRRIC's Initiative to Expedite the Market Opening-Up for the Banking and Insurance Industries. In *China Further Opens Up Financial Sector*.

Farchy, J. (2016, May 9). New Silk Road Will Transport Laptops and Frozen Chicken. *Financial Times*.

Financial Stability Board. (2018, March 5). *Global Shadow Banking Monitoring Report 2017*.

FSB. (2018, March 5). *Global Shadow Banking Monitoring Report 2017.*

Gao, C. (2017, December 2). China, US Fight Over China's Market Economy Status. *The Diplomat.*

Ghossein, T., Hoekman, B., & Shingol, A. (2018). *Public Procurement in the Belt and Road Initiative* (MTI Discussion Paper No. 10). Washington, DC: International Bank for Reconstruction and Development/The World Bank.

Giuffrita, A. (2019, March 23). Italy and China in Plan for New Silk Road-Style Trade Network. *The Guardian.*

He, W. (2018). The Regulation of the Financial Sector in China: A Tale of Two Governments. *Journal of Corporate Law Studies, 18*(2), 339–380.

He, Q. (2019, May 24). The Debt Trap of One Belt, One Road: The Price of Following China. *The Epoch Times.*

Hongyuran, W., Yuzhe, Z., & Han, W. (2018, August 6). *Redrawing China's Financial Regulatory Landscape.* Caixin. www.caixinglobal.com. Accessed 21 June 2019.

Hornby, L., & Zhang, A. (2019, April 23). Belt and Road Debt Trap Accusations Hound China as It Hosts Forum. *Financial Times.*

Hsu, S. (2015, August). *One Belt One Road and the Roadmap to Financial Reform* (Binzagr Institute for Sustainable Prosperity, Policy Note No. 107).

Hsu, S. (2019, November 19). The Rise and Fall of Shadow Banking in China. How Shadow Banking Became the Catch-All for Riskier Finance. *The Diplomat.*

Jay-Pèrez, C., & Scissors, D. (2018, November). *Be Wary of Spending on the Belt and Road.* Washington, DC: American Enterprise Institute.

Kalish, I. (2016). *On the Horns of a Trilemma: Global Economic Outlook: 2nd Quarter, China* (pp. 4–7). Deloitte University Press.

Kwong, C. C. L., & Poon, T. S. C. (2019). On the Path to Liberalization: Emerging Issues of China's Banking Reform After Global Financial Crisis. *The Chinese Economy, 52*(2), 125–127.

Lan, P. (2018, January 4). *Regulatory Reshuffle in China's Financial Governance.* East Asia Forum.

Łasak, P. (2015). Regulatory Responses to the Chinese Shadow Banking Development. *Jagiellonian Journal of Management, 1*(4), 305–317.

Łasak, P., & van der Linden, R. W. H. (2019). The Effectiveness of the 'Belt and Road' Initiative in Tackling China's Economic Slowdown and Its Financial Implications Within a Policy Trilemma Context, Chapter 12. In E. Gualandri, V. Venturelli, & A. Sclip (Eds.), *Frontier Topics in Banking: Investigating New Trends and Recent Developments in the Financial Industry.* Cham: Palgrave Macmillan.

Lelyveld, M. (2017). *China Toughens Shadow Banking Controls.* http://www.rfa.org.

Li, Y. (2017, November). *China's Debt Problem and Rising Systemic Risks: Impact of the Global Financial Crisis and Structural Problems* (South Centre Research Paper No. 83).

Li, W., & Jin, D. (2018). On the Design of Financial Products Along OBOR. *The Journal of Finance and Data Science, 4*(2), 55–76.

Lo, C. (2015). *China's Impossible Trinity: The Structural Challenges to the "Chinese Dream"*. London: Palgrave Macmillan.

Moody's Analytics. (2018). *China Banking Insurance Regulatory Commission Replaces CBRC and CIRC.* www.modysanalytics.com. Accessed 21 June 2019.

Naughton, B. (2016, March 17–18). *Rebalancing, Restructuring and Reform: China 2016.* San Diego: School of Global Policy and Strategy, University of California.

Norton Rose Fulbright. (2018). *China Now – Regulatory Reform in the Financial Services Industry.* https://www.nortonrosefulbright.com/en/knowledge/publications/ec8bbc63/china-now---regulatory-reform-in-the-financial-services-industry.

Pan, D., & Yang, X. (2019). *The ICLG to: Fintech Laws and Regulations.* www.iclg.com. Accessed 21 June 2019.

Pei, M. (2019, February 15). Will China Let Belt and Road Die Quietly? *Nikkei Asian Review.*

Reeves, M., & Hu, D. (2015, December 7). What China's 13th Five-Year Plan Means for Business? *Harvard Business Review.*

Reuters. (2018, January 6). *China Tightens Regulations on Investment and Shadow Banking.*

Richter, W. (2019, April 26). *China Tries to Muscle in on Dollar as 'Payments Currency', but It's a Thankless Slog.* Wolf Street.

Sabine, P. (2016, November 1). One Belt, One Road's Digital Initiative Is Full of Potential, but Hong Kong Firms Need to Be Wary of Pitfalls. *South China Morning Post.*

Sheng, A., & Soon, N. C. (2016). *Shadow Banking in China: An Opportunity for Financial Reform* (pp. 98–99). Cornwall: Wiley.

Steil, B., & Smith, E. (2016, February 10). *Could China Have a Reserves Crisis?* https://www.cfr.org/blog/could-china-have-reserves-crisis.

Sun, G., & Payette, A. (2016). China and the Impossible Trinity: Economic Transition and the Internalisation of the Renminbi. *Contemporary Chinese Political Economy and Strategic Relations: An International Journal, 2*(3), 1049–1093.

The Economist. (2017, February 25). *In Fintech, China Shows the Way.*

van der Linden, R. W. H. (2008). Frontiers of Banks in a Global Economy, Chapter 8. In P. Molyneux & E. Vallelado (Eds.), *Palgrave Macmillan Studies in Banking and Financial Institutions.* London: Palgrave Macmillan.

Weinland, D. (2017, January 26). China Warned of Risk to Banks from One Belt One Road Initiative. *Financial Times.*

Weinland, D. (2018, January 8). China Shadow Bank Clampdown Eyes $2tn of Entrusted Loans. *Financial Times.*

Wells, P., & Weinland, D. (2017, January 26). Fitch Warns on Expected Returns from One Belt One Road. *Financial Times.*

Yi, G. (2018, December 17). *Deepen Reform and Opening Up Comprehensively: Create New Prospects for Financial Sector.* Beijing.

Zhang, L., & Tao, K. (2014, May). *The Benefits and Costs of Renminbi Internationalization* (ADBI Working Paper Series No. 481).

Zhou, X. (2018, November 8). China's Super Financial Regulator Headed by Vice-Premier More Powerful Than Ministries. *South China Morning Post.*

CHAPTER 6

Concluding Remarks and Recommendations

Abstract The aim of this chapter is to recap the nature of the 'new normal' growth of the Chinese economy and the constraints of the foregoing dynamism of the development processes. Among other factors, the following main obstacles for the further rapid economic growth can be enumerated: falling global and local demand, excessive debt and potential bubbles in the real estate and stock exchange markets, increasing shadow banking and its interconnectedness with the regular banking sector and the risk of capital flight. The main focus is directed at the verification of the impossible trinity theory in China's economic circumstances. During the last decade, the authorities tried to maintain the major aims of the theory at the same time, which means to circumvent the Mundell-Fleming model to some extent. In order to fulfill the aims of the 'new normal' economy, China needs to bend the rule and implement all three policy aims of the trinity in its own way. Due to the ineffectiveness of the demand-side monetary policy stimulus, implemented after the GFC, nowadays the Chinese authorities opt for a focus on a targeted fiscal policy and supply-side structural reforms. Such approach will support aggregate demand and growth, and at the same time will enable to reform and rebalance the economy in the longer term. To some extent, the BRI and its investments create an important stimulus in the route to a more sustainable economic growth path, however, at the same time it enforces more openness and a liberalized approach to the capital flows. Taking into account the growing impact of China's shadow banking on its financial

P. Łasak and R. W. H. van der Linden, *The Financial Implications of China's Belt and Road Initiative*,
https://doi.org/10.1007/978-3-030-30118-7_6

system, it is likely that the authorities have to give up the monetary autonomy for further strengthening the financial stability added as a fourth element of the impossible trinity theory after the GFC. As a result, the PBC might be focused more on currency stability than the monetary autonomy. In the near future and in combination with more capital liberalization this will cause the necessity to focus more on financial stability.

Keywords Mundell-Fleming model · 'New normal' growth of the Chinese economy · Rebalance the structure of the Chinese economy · Financial stability

After more than four decades of reforms to a market economy, China has undergone many socioeconomic transformations. From a closed to a more open and globalized economy; from a predominantly agricultural to more industrial and ultimately an increasing services economy; from mainly state-owned to more private-owned businesses; from a rural to a more urban society; from high to relatively low population growth; from low to an ever higher standard of living; from low-tech assembly to high-tech manufacturing; from controlled to more floating exchange rates and from mainly investment- and export-driven 'quantity' growth to more consumption- and innovation-led 'quality' growth.

Since 2010, China's GDP growth rates have gradually declining to the inevitably lower 'new normal' level of slightly above 6.0% at the end of 2019, the weakest in almost three decades, combined with a huge credit binge and resulting debt problem in the non-financial corporate sector in particular. As the current US–China trade dispute will have an adverse effect on exports, the Chinese economy will increasingly have to be driven by domestic demand. However, China's last major stimulus came in August 2015, when China abandoned its currency peg with the USD, and reduced the RMB's exchange rate three times in just one week. This was done to make the country more competitive, but it also caused shockwaves in markets worldwide and prompted cries of manipulation. Besides these factors, also the global slowdown, China's own falling local demands, the increasing shadow banking, the potential bubbles in the real estate sector and its corrupt political system have also contributed to the exhaustion of its growth potential. As a result, the government policy will now focus more on containing financial risks, entering a policy focused on deleveraging, and tackling quality-of-life issues.

During this decade, the Chinese policy makers have challenged the sustainability of the impossible trinity by adding financial stability as a fourth element into this theory. By extensively using its foreign reserves, China basically bowed to the trilemma under its recent 'new normal' growth model and ongoing liberalization strategy. The Chinese economy has accumulated such high levels of reserves that the authorities have tried to achieve a 'possible trinity' through a certain level of currency control and financial openness, while maintaining monetary autonomy. For more than a decade, China tries to maintain these three aims at the same time making use of the fact that the Mundell-Fleming model fails to consider the role of sterilization policy such as the sale of central bank bills. China has been able to circumvent the Mundell-Fleming model only when the RMB is subject to upward pressure. However, more recently the country has faced an increasing trilemma attempting to pursue monetary autonomy and limiting exchange rate flexibility, while at the same time facing large and growing international capital in- and outflows. Since the turn of the millennium, the authorities have mainly focused on the aim of a stable exchange rate combined with monetary autonomy (side C of the triangle). An increasingly open capital account, declining foreign reserves, and rising sterilization costs have made it impossible for the authorities to defy the 'unholy' trinity theory forever since they are forced to choose between monetary sovereignty and currency control. In contrast with a small and open economy like Singapore, China is a large economy with a high degree of internal orientation and is heavily indebted which will make monetary autonomy likely to be more effective in counteracting the effects of external shocks on its domestic economy. This will make it more appropriate to relinquish currency control in favour of control on interest rates as a tool for domestic economic management. The RMB internationalization has already deployed for many years, and China's decision to join the IMF's reserves currency basket list could be considered as a test case to loosen the currency control and hence to bend the impossible trinity theory. Liberalizing a currency regime from a fixed to a fully floating exchange rate needs to be managed amid volatility in global capital flows. Therefore, China's policy makers will have to reform their exchange rate system at a slow and steady pace since currency risks need to be managed when pursuing China's aim to fully participate in a globalized economy.

The pressure on the 'horns' of the trilemma or the three 'corners' of the triangle becomes even more magnified as there is also a desire for more financial liberalization including the interest rates which might threaten the monetary sovereignty and financial stability. This explains why the authorities prefer to balance 'several dishes at the same time' to move from an export- and investment-led economy to a consumption-led model without a 'hard landing,' to rein in speculation in property and equity markets without damaging vulnerable industries, to engage with free markets without being hit by volatility, and to expand its financial sector without suffering from the 'hot money' flows that destabilized South East Asia in the late 1990s. Based on experiences of these countries, there is a tendency to violate the trilemma in times of financial crisis and economic downturn. It is likely that China's capital account liberalization will need to go with loosening the grip on its currency. This also suggests that a possible solution for China's trilemma is to loosen capital controls in order to shift the RMB toward being a major trading and reserve currency and eventually a floating exchange rate combined with monetary autonomy so that the government can stimulate the economy. Since the GFC, the authorities have gradually moved from side C to side B of the triangle. However, in the case of the Chinese economy, there is still the possibility for many years to violate the trinity rule by using their huge accumulated stock of foreign reserves to stabilize the financial system which transforms the economy from trilemma into quadrilemma measured in terms of its official reserves. Since mid-2014 until present, when the RMB faced accelerating depreciation with a reverse movement in 2017, the PBC intervened to prevent a plunge, an effort that depleted China's foreign reserves by a massive USD 1 trillion and left the PBC with little choice but to tighten capital controls substantially.

The main benefits for China to bend the trinity rule is being listed in the IMF's reserve currency and being able to open its capital account without having too much currency fluctuation and losing its sovereignty in controlling interest rates. However, this actually comes with huge costs in terms of intensive use of monetary sterilization tools and especially the monetary reserves. Given the current state of the economy, it will be difficult to completely release the relatively stable exchange rate and sovereign monetary policy, which are needed as the tools to stimulate the economy. The authorities have made it clear that China will shift its economy from a focus on exports to a more consumption-based reliance. The RMB devaluations of August 2015, the largest in two decades, conflict with this policy aim as it will boost export activity and be counterproductive in China's attempts to increase its reliance on domestic consumption. Although a weaker currency can compensate for the higher current US trade barriers, a fall of the RMB can also feed the capital flight and undermine China's economic stability. Thus, to fulfill the aims of the 'new normal' economy, China needs to bend the rule and implement all three policy aims of the trinity in their own way.

There are several policy options to make the impossible trinity possible with their pros and cons. Based on experiences of the gradual economic reforms of the last decades, it is likely that in the near future the monetary and exchange rate policy including the use of capital controls will be implemented in a similar way whereby authorities sometimes tighten or loosen the reins depending on the degree of financial stability which has become even more important for an effective implementation of the BRI. The inconsistency of the Chinese approach to reform the currency regime reflects the delicate balancing act being attempted by the policy makers. On the one hand, they are pushing for reforms and liberalization in the currency markets and elsewhere in the economy. To some extent it is unavoidable in the increasingly open Chinese economy, growing shadow banking system and interconnectedness between traditional banking and non-bank financial institutions. On the other hand, they are mindful of the need to maintain stability on which its own political legitimacy is based. In other words, not only China's 'new normal' economy matters, but even more importantly its social stability is at stake. Since the demand-side policy stimulus with monetary means turned out to be rather ineffective after the GFC, the 13th FYP explicitly stresses another policy direction to address the 'new normal' economy with focus on a targeted fiscal policy and supply-side structural reforms. Although the government has marked the 70th anniversary of CPC rule on October 1, 2019 with the greatest display, the big question remains whether the CPC will be able to control their economy and continue to compensate for its slowdown to protect the social stability, given its dependency on the global demand.

Unlike China's monetary easing policy since 2012, a targeted fiscal policy can support aggregate demand and growth without creating an incentive for capital outflow. At the same time, a targeted fiscal approach would also serve the aims to reform and rebalance the economy in the longer term by making the social safety net stronger and promoting domestic consumption and services. Thus, in this way, China could effectively pursue both its short-term and longer-term objectives without placing downward pressure on the currency and without new restrictions on capital flows. In an interrelated combination with the targeted fiscal policy, an additional policy option is to implement supply-side structural reforms to pursue its 'new normal' direction and further unlock China's economic potential. The supply-side structural reforms consist of several elements, namely the key tasks to reduce overcapacity and inventories, to deleverage and lower costs and to shore up weak growth areas. These tasks are interconnected and mutually reinforcing and are aiming at a more sustainable development strategy to bypass the 'middle-income trap'. Furthermore, the supply-side structural reforms with 'Chinese characteristics' are also meant to contribute to a stable recovery of the global economy in the post-crisis era.

With the abolition of the term-limits to remain in power, president Xi Jinping has all the time to implement his grand OBOR project around six years after launching its initiative. In a way the BRI could be seen as Xi's answer to Donald Trump's #MAGA: 'Let's Make China Great Again.' In the short-term, it will become a balancing act to meet all the aims of the policy trilemma or quadrilemma. In case RMB internationalization and OBOR-driven investments and export take more time than expected, a gradual adjustment towards more monetary independence is likely. If RMB internationalization is more combined with excessive capital in- and outflow, it is likely that the authorities reinsert the reins via more capital controls. If the BRI export boost fails and at the same time the RMB's inclusion in IMF's reserves requires more capital mobility, it's probably more desirable to stabilize exchange rates more which will ultimately stimulate more trade and investment growth. This implies in the near future a gradual shift towards side A of the triangle.

In the short-term, it is advisable to restructure the Chinese 'new normal' economy first to a sustainable growth rate rather than ambitiously going to the next step without a strong foundation. There is not one single policy option, but only a choice among several painful measures which reflect the underlying structural problems in the Chinese economy, one that will take many years to rebalance. In the short-term, China will have to use its monetary reserves in an attempt to support its currency and guarantee financial stability without decreasing them too strongly. It is a dangerous gamble but one that is worth pursuing. If China succeeds, at least for a while, it can buy itself time to rebalance its domestic economy from slowing manufacturing to growing services and domestic consumption and claim to be the first country to solve a trilemma that has haunted economics for decades. The limited monetary autonomy, strongly managed exchange rate and partial capital liberalization as a mixture of central controls and market freedoms satisfy the conditions of a variation of the impossible trinity theory. However, deeper institutional financial reforms and an associated international financial regulatory framework are required to increase the role of markets, the private sector, competition and domestic consumption for driving productivity-led and greener growth in the future. This could make China's 'new normal' economy more stable and as soon as the sustainability has been embedded in the new development stage it would be the right time to fully liberalize the capital flows, the interest rates and thereafter the exchange rate system.

Since the turn of the millennium, China has used its monetary policy and its exchange rate as useful tools for its economic development. The authorities managed the RMB exchange rate and applied an independent monetary policy at the same time. However, after the GFC the government has implemented more managed floating than fixed exchange rates, but still focused their attention on monetary autonomy. At the same time, they enforced more openness and liberalized approach to the capital flows. The BRI and its investments enhanced this approach by intensifying the flow of capital (especially the FDI investments). The active fiscal stimulus and the excessive debt burden has led to a situation when further expansionary monetary policy will no longer be as efficient as it used to be. Taking into account the growing impact of China's shadow banking on its financial system, it is likely that the authorities have to give up the monetary autonomy for further strengthening the financial stability. As a result, the PBC might be focused more on currency stability than the monetary autonomy in the near future. Regarding the triangle representing the impossible trinity, it means that the policy goals will move from side B to side A of the triangle. Additionally, the accompanying further liberalization of the free flow of capital will cause the necessity to focus more on financial stability.

Bibliography

Aizenman, J. (2011, March 1). *The Impossible Trinity: From the Policy Trilemma to the Policy Quadrilemma*. Santa Cruz: University of California.

Aizenman, J., & Sengupta, R. (2012). *The Financial Trilemma in China and a Comparative Analysis with India*. UCSC and the NBER India: IFMR.

Aizenman, J., Chinn, M. D., & Ito, H. (2013). The "Impossible Trinity" Hypothesis in an Era of Global Imbalances: Measurement and Testing. *Review of International Economics, 3*(21), 447–458.

Ash, M. (2018, October 18). *China's Belt and Road Plan to Reshape the International Order.*

Balding, C. (2019, January 5). *China Has a Dangerous Dollar Debt Addiction.* BNN Bloomberg.

BBC Business. (2019, January 21). *China Economy: Annual Growth Slowest Since 1990.*

BDO. (2015, November). *One Belt One Road.* Singapore: BDO Advisory Pte Ltd. Retrieved from www.bdo.com.sg.

Beeson, M., & Li, F. (2016). China's Place in Regional and Global Governance: A New World Comes into View. *Global Policy, 7*(4), 491–499.

Bernanke, B. (2016, March 9). *A Fresh Approach to Fiscal Stimulus Is China's Only Solution to the Impossible Trinity Devaluations and Capital Controls Won't Work.* Bloomberg.

Binham, C. (2018, March 5). Shadow Banking Grows to More Than $45tn Assets Globally. *Financial Times.*

BIS. (2008). *Financial Globalisation and Emerging Market Capital Flows* (Vol. 44).

P. Łasak and R. W. H. van der Linden, *The Financial Implications of China's Belt and Road Initiative*,
https://doi.org/10.1007/978-3-030-30118-7

Bloomberg. (2019). *Xi's Leading China Toward Stagnation.*

Bowman, J., Hack, M., & Waring, M. (2018, March). *Non-bank Financing in China.* Reserve Bank of Australia Bulletin.

Cai, F., Garnaut, R., & Song, L. (2018). *China's 40 Years of Reform and Development: How Reform Captured China's Demographic Dividend.* Canberra: Australian National University Press.

Cai, P. (2017, March). *Understanding China's Belt and Road Initiative.* Sydney: Lowy Institute for International Policy.

Chatterjee, B., & Kumar, S. (2017, July 18). *Promises and Pitfalls of the Belt and Road Initiative.* Asia Pacific Bulletin, No. 388.

Chatzky, A., & McBride, J. (2019, May 21). *China's Massive Belt and Road Initiative.* Council on Foreign Relations (cfr.org).

Chen, C. C. H. (2018). *ASEAN Financial Integration and the Belt and Road Initiative: Legal Challenges and Opportunities for China in Southeast Asia.* In Z. Yun (Ed.), *International Governance and the Rule of Law in China Under the Belt and Road Initiative.* Cambridge: Cambridge University Press.

Chen, J. L. (2018, January). The Cases Study of "One Belt and One Road" and "Made in China 2025" Impact on the Development of Taiwan's Machine Tool Industry. *International Business Research.*

Chen, S., & Kang, J. S. (2018, January). *Credit Booms—Is China Different?* (IMF Working Paper, WP/18/2).

Chen, S., & Wu, N. (2015, October 7). *China Banking Sector.* DBS Group Research.

Chen, X., & He, Z. (2018, November). *16+1 Cooperation and China–EU Relationship.* Budapest: China-CEEC Institute.

Cheng, S. W. (2015, September 28). Overcapacity a Time Bomb for China's Economy. *South China Morning Post.*

Chiang, F. (2018, August 28). China's 'Belt and Road' Could Be a Debt Trap. *The Japan Times.*

Chien, J., & Randall, D. (2018). *Key Lessons for Policymakers form China's Financial Inclusion Experience.* The World Bank.

China Daily. (2017, April 26). *China Moves to Deleverage Without Destabilizing Growth.*

China Daily. (2018, March 18). *Europe on Path of Expanding Cooperation on BRI.*

China Daily. (2019, April 22). *Belt and Road Projects: Past, Present and Future.*

Chorzempa, M. (2018, March 19). *China's Restructuring of Financial Regulation Is Good News for Reform.* Washington, DC: Peterson Institute for International Economics.

Choudbury, D. (2017, May 25). UN Warns About Financial Risks in China's One Belt One Road Project. *The Economic Times.*

Chow, G. (2018). China's Economic Transformation. In F. Cai et al. (Eds.), *China's 40 Years of Reform and Development: 1978–2018.* Acton: ANU Press.

Cienski, J. (2011, June 15). Poland to China: you're fired. *Financial Times.*

CIMB Asean Research Institute. (2018, October). *China's Belt and Road Initiative (BRI) and Southeast Asia.* Kuala Lumpur.

Citi GPS. (2018, December). *China's Belt & Road at Five.* A Progress Report, Global Perspectives & Solutions.

Cookson, C. (2019, June 17). Africa to Propel World's Population Towards 10bn by 2050. *Financial Times.*

Cowen, T. (2017). *The Rise and Fall of the Chinese Economy.* YouTube.

Crabtree, J. (2019, April 25). China Needs to Make BRI More Transparent and Predictable. *Financial Times.*

Curran, E. (2018, September 17). *China's Debt Bomb.*

Dadabaev, T. (2018). "Silk Road" as Foreign Policy Discourse: The Construction of Chinese, Japanese and Korean Engagement Strategies in Central Asia. *Journal of Euroasian Studies, 9,* 30–41.

D'Amico, N. (2015, March). *Corruption and Economic Growth in China: An Empirical Analysis.*

Das, S. (2019). *China's Evolving Exchange Rate Regime* (IMF Working Paper, WP/19/50).

Davis, C. (2018, March 9). It Is Up to China to Save the Global Trading System. *Financial Times.*

DBS Group Research. (2016, April 7). *China: What Are Supply-Side Structural Reforms?*

Deloitte. (2019). *BRI Update 2019 - Recalibration and New Opportunities.*

Deloitte Insight. (2018). *Embracing the BRI Ecosystem in 2018: Navigating Pitfalls and Seizing Opportunities.*

Dieppe, A., Gilhooly, R., Han, J., Korhonen, I., & Lodge, D. (2018, January). *The Transition of China to Sustainable Growth—Implications for the Global Economy and the Euro Area* (ECB Occasional Paper Series No. 206).

DigFin (2019, October 7). *Busting Six Myths About China's e-RMB.*

Djankov, S., & Miner, S. (2016, March). *China's Belt and Road Initiative: Motives, Scope and Challenges.* PIIE Briefing 16-2. Washington, DC: Peterson Institute for International Economics.

Drysdale, P., & Hardwick, S. (2018). China and the Global Trading System: Then and Now. In L. Song & C. Feng (Eds.), *China's 40 Years of Reform and Development 1978–2018.* Canberra: Australian National University Press.

Du, Y., & Yang, C. (2015). Demographic Transition and Labour Market Changes: Implications for Economic Development in China. In I. Claus & L. Oxley (Eds.), *China's Economy: A Collection of Surveys.* Chichester, West Sussex: Wiley Blackwell.

Duceux, A. J. (2018, December 20). *An Overview of Chinese Debt.* Liege: Committee for the Abolition of Illegitimate Debt.

Eckert, J. (2016, June 23). *8 Things You Need to Know About China's Economy.* World Economic Forum.

Ehlers, T., Kong, S., & Zhu, F. (2018, February). *Mapping Shadow Banking in China: Structure and Dynamics* (BIS Working Paper No. 701).

Elliott, D. J., Kroeber A., & Qiao Y. (2015, March). *Shadow Banking in China: A Primer*. Washington, DC: The Brookings Institution.

Elliott, D. J., & Qiao, Y. (2015, May). *Reforming Shadow Banking in China*. Washington, DC: The Brookings Institution.

Ernst & Young. (2015, March). Riding the Silk Road: China Sees Outbound Investment Boom: Outlook for China's Outward Foreign Direct Investment.

EY. (2019). Interpreting the BRRIC's Initiative to Expedite the Market Opening-Up for the Banking and Insurance Industries. In *China Further Opens Up Financial Sector*.

Fan, D. (2016, October 18). Reflecting on Deng Xiaoping's 'Cat Theory' of Economic Reform. *The Epoch Times*.

Farchy, J. (2016, May 9). New Silk Road Will Transport Laptops and Frozen Chicken. *Financial Times*.

Feng, Y., Gabuev, A., Haenle, P., Bin, M., & Trenin, D. (2019, April 8). *The Belt and Road Initiative: Views from Washington, Moscow, and Beijing*. Beijing: Carnagie-Tsinghua.

Fidrmuc, J., & Huang, S. (2013). *Unemployment, Growth and Speed of Transition in China* (CESifo Working Paper Series No. 4410).

Financial Stability Board. (2018, March 5). *Global Shadow Banking Monitoring Report 2017*.

FSB. (2018, March 5). *Global Shadow Banking Monitoring Report 2017*.

Gao, C. (2017, December 2). China, US Fight Over China's Market Economy Status. *The Diplomat*.

Gao, S. (2017). Disequilibrium Between Regulation and Criminalization to Counter Financial Misconduct: The Case of Shadow Banking in China. *American Business Law Journal, 54*(2), 393–456.

García-Herrero, A. (2017, August). *China Cannot Finance the Belt and Road Alone*. HKUST IEMS No. 17.

Ghossein, T., Hoekman, B., & Shingol, A. (2018). *Public Procurement in the Belt and Road Initiative* (MTI Discussion Paper No. 10). Washington, DC: International Bank for Reconstruction and Development/The Wold Bank.

Giuffrita, A. (2019, March 23). Italy and China in Plan for New Silk Road-Style Trade Network. *The Guardian*.

Glawe, L., & Wagner, H. (2019). China in the Middle-Income Trap? *China Economic Review*. https://doi.org/10.1016/j.chieco.2019.01.003.

Gloria, E. (2014). *China's Exchange Rate Regimes and Their Policy Implications*. Asian Center.

Goldstein, M., & Lardy N. R. (2008). *China's Exchange Rate Policy: An Overview of Some Key Issues*. Washington, DC: Peterson Institute for International Economics.

Góralczyk, B. (2017). China's Interests in Central and Eastern Europe: Enter the Dragon. *European View, 16*(1), 153–162.

Green, F., & Stern, N. (2015, June). *China's "New Normal": Structural Change, Better Growth, and Peak Emissions.* Centre for Climate Change Economics and Policy, Policy Brief.

Griswold, D. (2019, April 2). Is China a Non-Market Economy? *The Bridge.* Mercatus Center George Mason University.

Guarino, A. (2017, July). *Shadow Banking in China: The Potential for Financial Domino Effect.* Global Risk Insight.

Gujon, M., & Guérineau, S. (2006, March–April). The Modification of the Chinese Exchange Rate Policy: Its Rationale, Extent and Recent Developments. *China Perspectives.* https://journals.openedition.org/chinaperspectives/607.

Gwiazda, A. (2017). The Sluggish Internationalization of the Renminbi. *Bank i Kredyt, 48*(5), 483–494.

He, Q. (2019, May 24). The Debt Trap of One Belt, One Road: The Price of Following China. *The Epoch Times.*

He, W. (2018). The Regulation of the Financial Sector in China: A Tale of Two Governments. *Journal of Corporate Law Studies, 18*(2), 339–380.

He, H. (2019, May 22). US-China trade war manufacturing exodus creating boom time for Chinese logistyce companies. *South China Morning Post.*

Ho, D. (2017, September 27). Cost of Funding 'Belt and Road Initiative' Is Daunting Task. *South China Morning Post.*

Hongyuran, W., Yuzhe, Z., & Han, W. (2018, August 6). *Redrawing China's Financial Regulatory Landscape.* Caixin. www.caixinglobal.com. Accessed 21 June 2019.

Hornby, L., & Zhang, A. (2017, December 4). China Hit by Gas Shortages as It Moves Away from Coal. *Financial Times.*

Hornby, L., & Zhang, A. (2019, April 23). Belt and Road Debt Trap Accusations Hound China as It Hosts Forum. *Financial Times.*

Hillman, J. (2018, January 25). *China's Belt and Road Initiative: Five Years Later.* Washington, DC: Center for Strategic & International Studies.

Hsu, S. (2015, August). *One Belt One Road and the Roadmap to Financial Reform* (Binzagr Institute for Sustainable Prosperity, Policy Note No. 107).

Hsu, S. (2019, November 19). The Rise and Fall of Shadow Banking in China. How Shadow Banking Became the Catch-All for Riskier Finance. *The Diplomat.*

Hu, X. (2010, July 26). *Exchange Rate Regime Reform and Monetary Policy Effectiveness.* Beijing: People's Bank of China.

Huang, P., & Liu, Z. (2017). *How the 16+1 Cooperation Promotes the Belt and Road Initiative.* China-CEEC Think Tank Series. London: Pathe International Ltd.

Huang, Y. (2017). *Cracking the Chinese Conundrum: Why Conventional Economic Wisdom Is Wrong.* Oxford: Oxford University Press.

Hurley, J., Morris, S., & Portelance G. (2018, March). *Examining the Debt Implications of the Belt and Road Initiative from Policy Perspective* (CGD Policy Paper No. 121), pp. 15–18.

Jay-Pèrez, C., & Scissors, D. (2018, November). *Be Wary of Spending on the Belt and Road*. Washington, DC: American Enterprise Institute.

Jin, J., Andersson, H., & Zhang, S. (2016). Air Pollution Control Policies in China: A Retrospective and Prospects. *International Journal of Environmental Research and Public Health, 13*(12), 1–22.

Johnson, K. (2018, February 2). Why Is China Buying Up Europe's Ports? *Foreign Policy*.

Kalish, I. (2016). *On the Horns of a Trilemma: Global Economic Outlook: 2nd Quarter, China* (pp. 4–7). Deloitte University Press.

Kavalski, E., & Mayer, M. (2019). *China Is Now a Power in Europe, but Fears of Interference in the EU Are Simplistic and Misguided*. The Conversation.

Khan, M. K., Sandero, I. A., Pratt, C. B., & Farid, T. (2018). China's Belt and Road Initiative: A Global Model for an Evolving Approach to Sustainable Regional Development. *Sustainability, 10*(11), 4234.

Kostecka-Tomaszewska, L. (2018). Economic Security of China: The Implications of the Belt and Road Initiative. *Optimum. Economic Studies, 4*(94), 166–182.

Králóvičová, M., & Žatko, M. (2016, August). *One Belt One Road Initiative in Central Asia: Implications for Competitiveness of Russian Economy* (Working Paper No. 2016/9). Maastricht School of Management.

Krukowska, M. (2016). China's 'One Belt, One Road' Strategy and Its Implications for the Global World Order. *International Business and Global Economy, 35*(1), 157–168.

Kwan, C. H. (2018). Issues Facing Renminbi Internationalization: Observations from Chinese, Regional and Global Perspectives. *Public Policy Review, 14*(5). Policy Research Institute, Ministry of Finance, Japan.

Kwong, C. C. L., & Poon, T. S. C. (2019). On the Path to Liberalization: Emerging Issues of China's Banking Reform After Global Financial Crisis. *The Chinese Economy, 52*(2), 125–127.

Lam, P. (2005). Energy in China: Development and Prospects. *China Perspectives, 59*, 14–25.

Lan, P. (2017, October 20). Scary Statistic: China's Debt to GDP Ratio Reached 257 Percent in 2017. *The National Interest*.

Lan, P. (2018, January 4). *Regulatory Reshuffle in China's Financial Governance*. East Asia Forum.

László, G. (2018, May 16). The Effects of the AIIB on the Multilateral Development banks' System. *GAGEO Geopolitikai Kutatóintézet*.

Lee, A. K. (2015). *China's Economy: The Hidden Truths—China's Economy Seen in the Undercurrent of Organized Unaccountability*. Global Era Public Interest Info Network.

Lee, I. H., Qingjun, X., & Syed, M. (2013, March). *China's Demography and Its Implications* (IMF Working Paper, WP/13/82).

Lelyveld, M. (2017). *China Toughens Shadow Banking Controls*. http://www.rfa.org.

Leonard, M. (2008). *What Does China Think?* London: Fourth Estate.

Li, L. (2018). *China's Manufacturing Locus in 2025: With a Comparison of "Made-in-China 2025" and "Industry 4.0"*. Technological Forecasting & Social Change No. 135.

Li, W., & Jin, D. (2018). On the Design of Financial Products Along OBOR. *The Journal of Finance and Data Science, 4*(2), 55–76.

Li, X. (2019). *Mapping China's 'One Belt One Road' Initiative*. International Political Economy Series. Aalborg: Palgrave Mcmillan.

Li, X., & Zeng, K. (2019, March). To Join or Not to Join? State Ownership, Commercial Interests, and China's Belt and Road Initiative. *Pacific Affairs, 92*(1), 5–26.

Li, Y. (2017, November). *China's Debt Problem and Rising Systemic Risks: Impact of the Global Financial Crisis and Structural Problems* (South Centre Research Paper No. 83).

Li, Y. (2018). The Greater Euroasian Partnership and the Belt and Road Initiative: Can the Two Be Limited? *Journal of Euroasian Studies, 9*(2), 94–99.

Liu, Z. (2016, October 23). China Ocean Strategic Industry Investment Fund to Promote 'Belt and Road' Initiative. *Global Times*.

Lo, C. (2015). *China's Impossible Trinity: The Structural Challenges to the "Chinese Dream"*. London: Palgrave Macmillan.

Lu. (2018, October). *Black Swans and Grey Rhinos: Demistyfiying China's Financial Risks and the Financial Regulatory Reform*. International Briefings.

Luo, B. (2015). China Will Get Rich Before It Grows Old: Beijing's Demographic Problems Are Overrated. *Foreign Affairs, 94*(3), 19–24.

Łasak, P. (2015). Regulatory Responses to the Chinese Shadow Banking Development. *Jagiellonian Journal of Management, 1*(4), 305–317.

Łasak, P., & van der Linden, R. W. H. (2019). The Effectiveness of the 'Belt and Road' Initiative in Tackling China's Economic Slowdown and Its Financial Implications Within a Policy Trilemma Context, Chapter 12. In E. Gualandri, V. Venturelli, & A. Sclip (Eds.), *Frontier Topics in Banking: Investigating New Trends and Recent Developments in the Financial Industry*. Cham: Palgrave Macmillan.

Manuel, A. (2017, October 17). China Is Quitely Reshaping the World. *The Atlantic*.

McBride, J., & Chatzky, A. (2019, May 3). *Is "Made in China 2025" a Threat to Global Trade?* Council on Foreign Relations.

McMahon, M., Schipke, A., & Li, X. (2018). *China's Monetary Policy Communication: Frameworks, Impact, and Recommendations* (IMF Working Paper No. WP/18/244).

Mehran, H., Quintyn, M., Nordman, T., & Laurens, B. (1996). *Monetary and Exchange System Reform in China: An Experiment in Gradualism* (International Monetary Fund Occasional Paper, 141, 2).

Misiągiewicz, J., & Misiągiewicz, M. (2016). China's "One Belt, One Road" Initiative—The Perspective of the European Union. *Annales Universitatis Mariae Curie-Skłodowska, XXIII*(1), 33.

Moody's Analytics. (2018). *China Banking Insurance Regulatory Commission Replaces CBRC and CIRC*. www.modysanalytics.com. Accessed 21 June 2019.

Morrison, W. M. (2018, February 5). *China's Economic Rise: History, Trends, Challenges, and Implications for the United States*. Congressional Research Service 7-5700. www.crs.gov. RL33534.

Mundell, R.A. (1960). The Monetary Dynamics of International Adjustment under Fixed and Flexible Exchange Rates. *Quarterly Journal of Economics, 74*(2), 227–257.

Nan, Z., & Shuiyu, J. (2019, March 11). Reforms to Put SOEs in Key Role for Initiative. *China Daily*.

National Development and Reform Commission. (2015, March 28). *Vision and Actions on Jointly Building Silk Road Economic Belt and 21-st-Century Maritime Silk Road, National Development and Reform Commission (NDRC)*, Ministry of Foreign Affairs and Ministry of Commerce of People's Republic of China, with State Council authorization.

Naughton, B. (2016, March 17–18). *Rebalancing, Restructuring and Reform: China 2016*. San Diego: School of Global Policy and Strategy, University of California.

Ndegwa, S. (2019, April 25). Belt and Road Initiative a Global Game-Changer. *Business Today*.

Ng, N. (2019). *The Possible Impact of China's Belt and Road Agreement with Italy*.https://p.dw.com/p/3F4S2.

Ning, Z. (2018, June 13). Is China's Growth Model a Threat to Free-Market Economics? *The Economist*.

Nomura. (2018 April 16), *Belt and Road: Globalisation, China Style*. Global Markets Research Anchor Report.

Northern Trust. (2017). *One Belt, One Road: A Global Overview*. NTAC: 3NS-20.

Norton Rose Fulbright (2018). *China Now – Regulatory Reform in the Financial Services Industry*. https://www.nortonrosefulbright.com/en/knowledge/publications/ec8bbc63/china-now---regulatory-reform-in-the-financial-services-industry.

O'Connor, S. (2018, May 24). *SOE Megamergers Signal New Direction in China's Economic Policy*. U.S.–China Economic and Security Review Commission, Staff Research Report.

Ohashi, H. (2018). The Belt and Road Initiative (BRI) in the Context of China's Opening-Up Policy. *Journal of Contemporary East Asia Studies, 7*(2), 85–103.

Pan, D., & Yang, X. (2019). *The ICLG to: Fintech Laws and Regulations.* www.iclg.com. Accessed 21 June 2019.

Parameswaran, P. (2019, May 15). Southeast Asia and China's Belt and Road Initiative. *The Diplomat.*

Pei, M. (2019, February 15). Will China Let Belt and Road Die Quietly? *Nikkei Asian Review.*

Pepermans, A. (2018). China's 16+1 and Belt and Road Initiative in Central and Eastern Europe: Economic and Political Influence at a Cheap Price. *Journal of Centemporary Central and Eastern Europe, 26*(2–3), 181–203.

Perkins, D. H. (2018). The Complex Task of Evaluating China's Economic Reforms, Chapter 8. In R. Garnaut, L. Song, & C. Fang (Eds.), *China's 40 Years of Reform and Development: 1978–2018.* Canberra: ANU Press, The Australian National University.

Poland to China: You're Fired. (2011, June 14). *Financial Times.*

Pradier, P. (2018, June 22). *The Chinese Hukou System Explained—What Is "Hukou" and How It Works.* New Horizons Global Partners.

PwC. (2016, February). *China's New Silk Route: The Long and Winding Road.* PwC's Growth Markets Centre.

PwC. (2017, February). *New Policy Direction for Establishing Regional Headquarters in Shanghai by Multinational Companies.* News Flash—China Tax and Business Advisory, Issue 5.

Quinglian, H. (2018, October 22). China's Growing Unemployment Crisis. *The Epoch Times.*

Rana, S. (2017, November 15). Pakistan Stops Bid to Include Diamer-Bhasha Dam in CPEC. *The Express Tribune.* tribune.com.pk.

Reeves, M., & Hu, D. (2015, December 7). What China's 13th Five-Year Plan Means for Business? *Harvard Business Review.*

Ren, B., & Chao, X. (2018). How Does the Urban–Rural Income Gap Affects the Quality of China's Economic Growth? *China Political Economy, 1*(1), 136–148.

Reuters. (2018, January 6). China Tightens Regulations on Investment and Shadow Banking.

Richet, X. (2016, May 9–10). The Belt & Road Initiative and EU–China Economic Relations: Trade, Finance, FDI. In *Presentation on the Turin Center on Emerging Economies Conference.*

Richter, W. (2019, April 26). *China Tries to Muscle in on Dollar as 'Payments Currency', but It's a Thankless Slog.* Wolf Street.

Ross, J. (2013, May 7). *The Truth About China, Statistically Speaking.* www.china.org.cn.

Sabine, P. (2016, November 1). One Belt, One Road's Digital Initiative Is Full of Potential, but Hong Kong Firms Need to Be Wary of Pitfalls. *South China Morning Post.*

Sabine, P. (2017, March 28). Belt and Road is 'Marshall Plan Without a War', Analysts Say, as Beijing and Banks Woo Private-Sector Investors. *South China Morning Post.*

Sajjanhar, A. (2017, November 28). *China's Belt and Road Initiative: Prospects and Pitfalls.* Institute for Defence Studies and Analyses.

Shek, C. (2019, May 23). Aiming for the Top: Can China Escape the Middle Income Trap? *CKGSB Knowledge Magazine.*

Shazada, R. (2019, March 7). Communism Is Returning to China. *Daily Times.*

Shen, S., & Chan, W. (2018, March 27). A Comparative Study of the Belt and Road Initiative and the Marshall Plan. *Palgrave Communications, 4*(1), 32.

Sheng, A., Edelmann, C., Sheng, C., & Hu, J. (2015). *Bringing Light upon the Shadow: A Review of the Chinese Shadow Banking Sector.* Hong Kong: Oliver Wyman and Fung Global Institute.

Sheng, A., & Soon, N. C. (2016). *Shadow Banking in China: An Opportunity for Financial Reform* (pp. 98–99). Cornwall: Wiley.

Shi, L. (2008). *Rural Migrant Workers in China: Scenario, Challenges and Public Policy* (Working Paper No. 89). Geneva: Policy Integration and Statistics Department, International Labor Office.

Shi, L. (2016). Recent Changes in Income Inequality in China. In *World Social Science Report: Challenging Inequalities, Pathways to a Just World.* Paris: UNESCO.

Shih, V. (2017, October 20). *Financial Instability in China: Possible Pathways and Their Likelihood.* Berlin: Mercator Institute for China Studies.

Song, L. (2018). *The Past, Present and Future of SOE Reform in China.* Canberra: Australian National University.

South China Morning Post. (2017, August 24). China Vows Big Winter Air Pollution Ban in Northern Cities.

Steil, B., & Smith, E. (2016, February 10). Could China Have a Reserves Crisis? https://www.cfr.org/blog/could-china-have-reserves-crisis.

Stuart-Haentjens, R. (2017, July 6). *China and the AIIB on the Belt and Road: Power Sans Control.* Global Risk Insights.

Sun, G., & Payette, A. (2016). China and the Impossible Trinity: Economic Transition and the Internalisation of the Renminbi. *Contemporary Chinese Political Economy and Strategic Relations: An International Journal, 2*(3), 1049–1093.

Szczudlik, J. (2017, November 30). China's 16+1 Poses Few Risks to Europe. https://reconnectingasia.csis.org/analysis/entries/china-poses-few-risks-to-europe/.

Taidong, Z., & Haibing, Z. (2018). China's Belt and Road Initiative: An Opportunity to Re-energize South-South Cooperation. *China Quarterly of International Strategic Studies, 4*(4), 559–576.

Tan, K. E. (2011, September 21). Production Efficiency Is Key to Maintaining China's Economic Growth. *Finance Asia.*

Tan, K. H., Ji, G., Chung, L., Wang, C.-H., Chiu, A., & Tseng, M. L. (2019). Riding the Wave of Belt and Road Initiative in Servitization: Lessons from China. *International Journal of Production Economics, 211,* 15–21.

Tan, Y. (2014). *Performance Risk and Competition in the Chinese Banking Industry* (p. 9). New York: Chandos Publishing.

Tang, X., McLellan, B., Snowden, S., Zhang, B., & Höök, M. (2015). Dilemmas for China: Energy, Economy and Environment. *Sustainability, 7,* 5508–5520. https://doi.org/10.3390/su7055508.

Taylor, T. (2019). http://conversableeconomist.blogspot.com/2019/02/chinas-high-savings-rate.html. Accessed 30 May 2019.

The Economist. (1999, April 1). *China and the WTO.*

The Economist. (2000, December 21). *Go West, Young Han.*

The Economist. (2011a, December 10). *All Change: China's Economy and the WTO.*

The Economist. (2011b, April 28). *Chinese Property and Investment: More on the Chinese Bubble Issue, by Buttonwood.*

The Economist. (2015, March 12). *A Tightening Grip.*

The Economist. (2016). *Our Bulldozers, Our Rules.*

The Economist. (2017a, May 13). *What Is China's Belt and Road Initiative? The Many Motivations Behind Xi Jinping's Key Foreign Policy.*

The Economist. (2017b, May 18). *Xi Jinping Is Enjoying a "Belt-and-Road" Glow: It Will Do Little to Strengthen His Hand at Home.*

The Economist. (2017c, February 25). *In Fintech, China Shows the Way.*

The Economist. (2018, July 26). *All Under Heaven: China's Belt-and-Road Plans Are to Be Welcomed—And Worried About.*

The Economist. (2019a, March 16). *China's Current-Account Surplus Has Vanished.*

The Economist. (2019b, April 20). *China's GDP: Growth in Train.*

The Five Main Projects of the Belt and Road Initiative: A Visual Explainer. (2019). *South China Morning Post.* https://multimedia.scmp.com/news/china/article/One-Belt-One-Road/index.html.

The Globalist. (2018, September 8). *China's Massive High-Speed Rail Network: From Zero to Leader in a Decade.*

The State Council Information Office of the People's Republic of China. (2018, June). *China and the World Trade Organization.*

Tiffany, N. G., & Chung, K. (2018, July 17). *Trade Conflict Between China and the United States and Its Impact on Hong Kong's Economy.* Research Office Information Services Division Legislative Council Secretariat.

Tracy, E. F., Shvarts, E., Simonov, E., & Babenko, M. (2017). China's New Eurasian Ambitions: The Environmental Risks of the Silk Road Economic Belt. *Eurasian Geography and Economics, 58*(1), 56–88.

Urban China. (2014). *Toward Efficient, Inclusive and Sustainable Urbanization*. Washington, DC: The World Bank Group.

van der Linden, R. W. H. (2008). Frontiers of Banks in a Global Economy, Chapter 8. In P. Molyneux & E. Vallelado (Eds.), *Palgrave Macmillan Studies in Banking and Financial Institutions*. London: Palgrave Macmillan.

van der Linden, R. W. H. (2010). Bank Strategy, Governance and Ratings, Chapter 12. In P. Molyneux (Ed.), *Palgrave Macmillan Studies in Banking and Financial Institutions*. London: Palgrave Macmillan.

van der Linden, R. W. H. (2013). Bank Performance, Risk and Securitisation, Chapter 11. In J. Falzon (Ed.), *Palgrave Macmillan Studies in Banking and Financial Institutions*. London: Palgrave Macmillan.

van der Linden, R. W. H. (2015). Lending, Investments and the Financial Crisis, Chapter 5. In E. Beccalli & F. Poli (Eds.), *Palgrave Macmillan Studies in Banking and Financial Institutions*. London: Palgrave Macmillan.

Vinels, P. (2018, December 15). *Advancing ASEAN's Digital Economy* "East Asia Forum".

Vörös, Z. (2010). EU–China Relations: "Race" for Raw Materials. In Á. Tuka & I. Tarrósy (Eds.), *Borderless Europe: Challenges–Opportunities* (pp. 91–101). Pecs: Publikon Kiado.

Wang, J., Zhao, J., Ning, Y., & Yu, P. (2009). Transformation of Chinese State-Owned Enterprises: Challenges and Responses. *Multinational Business Review, 17*(4), 99–122.

Wang, L. (2019, March 23). *China–Africa Cooperation Under the Belt and Road Initiative (BRI): Africa Sees the Way Forward*. Global Research.

Wang, Y., & You, J. (2012). Corruption and Firm Growth: Evidence from China. *China Economic Review, 232*(2), 415–433.

Wei, Z., Song, X., & Wang, D. (2017). Manufacturing Flexibility, Business Model Design, and Firm Performance. *International Journal of Production Economics, 193*, 87–97.

Weidou, N. (2007). China's Energy—Challenges and Strategies. *Frontiers of Energy Power Engineering in China, 1*(1), 1–8.

Weinland, D. (2017, January 26). China Warned of Risk to Banks from One Belt One Road Initiative. *Financial Times*.

Weinland, D. (2018, January 8). China Shadow Bank Clampdown Eyes $2tn of Entrusted Loans. *Financial Times*.

Weinland, D. (2019, January 23). China Bad Debt Disposals Hit Levels Not Seen for 20 Years. *Financial Times*.

Wells, P., & Weinland, D. (2017, January 26). Fitch Warns on Expected Returns from One Belt One Road. *Financial Times*.

Wildeau, G. (2017, October 26). China Backs Away from Long-Term GDP Targets. *Financial Times.*

Wilson, J. (2018). *Connecting the Asia-Pacific: Australian Participation in China's Regional Infrastructure Initiatives.* Ultimo: Australia–China Relations Institute (ACRI).

Windsor, C., & Halperin, D. (2018, September). *RMB Internationalisation: Where to Next?* Reserve Bank of Australia Bulletin.

Wong, D., & Koty, A. C. (2018, December 14). The US–China Trade War: A Timeline. *China Briefing.*

Wood, A. J. (2017, August 25). *China-Thailand Rail Connection: A Silk Road Tourism Legacy.* https://www.eturbonews.com/162675/china-thailand-rail-connection-silk-road-tourism-legacy.

WTO. (2018). *World Trade Statistical Review 2018.*

Wu, J., & Ma, G. (2016, May). *Whither China? Restarting the Reform Agenda.* University Oxford Scholarship Online.

Wuthnow, J. (2017). *Chinese Perspectives on the Belt Road Initiative: Strategic Rationales, Risks, and Implications.* Center for the Study of Chinese Military Affairs, Institute for National Strategic Studies, "China Strategic Perspectives", No. 12.

Xing, C., Yang, P., & Li, Z. (2018, October). The Medium-Run Effect of China's Higher Education Expansion on the Unemployment of College Graduates. *China Economic Review, 51,* 181–193.

Xu, S., & Chen, L. (2019, August 15). *China's Belt and Road Initiative: Recalibration and New Opportunities.* Deloitte Insights.

Yi, G. (2018, December 17). *Deepen Reform and Opening Up Comprehensively: Create New Prospects for Financial Sector.* Beijing.

Yongquan, L. (2018). The Greater Eurasian Partnership and the Belt and Road Initiative: Can the two be linked? *Journal of Eurasian Studies, 9 (2)*, 94–99.

Yu, J. (2018). *The Belt and Road Initiative: Domestic Interests, Bureaucratic Politics and the EU–China Relations.* LSE Research Online. http://eprints.lse.ac.uk. Accessed 14 Apr 2019.

Zakić, K., & Tešić, K. (2018). Managing Regional Development in CEE Countries—The Example of Initiative 16+1. *Progress in Economic Sciences, 5,* 95–109.

Zhang, L., & Tao, K. (2014, May). *The Benefits and Costs of Renminbi Internationalization* (ADBI Working Paper Series No. 481).

Zhang, Y. (2019, April 7). Ice Silk Road Framework Welcomed by Countries, Sets New Direction for Arctic Cooperation. *Global Times.*

Zhao, M. (2006, May). *External Liberalization and the Evolution of China's Exchange System: an Empirical Approach* (World Bank China Office Research Working Paper No. 4).

Zheng, Y., Yi, J., & Chen M. (2007). *Revaluation of the Chinese Currency and Its Impacts on China* (China Policy Institute and Centre for Global Finance, Discussion Paper, 24). University of Nottingham.

Zhou, X. (2018, November 8). China's Super Financial Regulator Headed by Vice-Premier More Powerful Than Ministries. *South China Morning Post.*

https://www.ipe.com/infrastructure/chinas-belt-and-road-initiative-new-routes-to-profit/realassets.ipe.com/infrastructure/chinas-belt-and-road-initiative.

Index

P. Łasak and R. W. H. van der Linden, *The Financial Implications of China's Belt and Road Initiative*,
https://doi.org/10.1007/978-3-030-30118-7

The manufacturer's authorised representative in the EU is Springer Nature Customer Service Centre GmbH, Europaplatz 3, 69115 Heidelberg, Germany. If you have any concerns regarding our products, please contact ProductSafety@springernature.com

Printed and bound by CPI Group (UK) Ltd, Croydon, CR0 4YY
30/09/2026
02225656-0003